THE EUROPEAN UNION SERIES

General Editors: Neill Nugent, William E. Paterson, Vincent Wright

The European Union series is designed to provide an authoritative library on the European Union, ranging from general introductory texts to definitive assessments of key institutions and actors, policies and policy processes, and the role of member states.

Books in the series are written by leading scholars in their fields and reflect the most up-to-date research and debate. Particular attention is paid to accessibility and clear presentation for a wide audience of students, practitioners and interested general readers.

The series consists of four major strands:

- General textbooks
- The major institutions and actors
- The main areas of policy
- The member states and the Union

The series editors are **Neill Nugent**, Professor of Politics and Jean Monnet Professor of European Integration, Manchester Metropolitan University, and **William E. Paterson**, Director of the Institute of German Studies, University of Birmingham.

Their co-editor until his death in July 1999, **Vincent Wright**, was a Fellow of Nuffield College, Oxford University. He played an immensely valuable role in the founding and development of *The European Union Series* and is greatly missed.

Feedback on the series and book proposals are always welcome and should be sent to Steven Kennedy, Palgrave, Houndmills, Basingstoke, Hampshire RG21 6XS, UK, or by e-mail to s.kennedy@palgrave.com

General textbooks

Published

Desmond Dinan **Ever Closer Union: An Introduction to European Integration** (2nd edn)
[Rights World excluding North and South America, Philippines & Japan]

Desmond Dinan **Encyclopedia of the European Union**
[Rights: Europe only]

Simon Hix **The Political System of the European Union**

John McCormick **Understanding the European Union: A Concise Introduction**

Neill Nugent **The Government and Politics of the European Union** (4th edn)
[Rights: World excluding USA and dependencies and Canada]

John Peterson and Elizabeth Bomberg **Decision-Making in the European Union**

Ben Rosamond **Theories of European Integration**

Forthcoming

Simon Bulmer and Andrew Scott **European Union: Economics, Policy and Politics**

Andrew Scott **The Political Economy of the European Union**

Richard Sinnott **Understanding European Integration**

Also planned

The History of the European Union

The European Union Source Book

The European Union Reader

Series Standing Order (*outside North America only*)

ISBN 0–333–71695–7 hardcover
ISBN 0–333–69352–3 paperback

Full details from www.palgrave.com

Environmental Policy in the European Union

John McCormick

palgrave

First published 2001 by
PALGRAVE
Houndmills, Basingstoke, Hampshire RG21 6XS and
175 Fifth Avenue, New York, N.Y. 10010
Companies and representatives throughout the world

PALGRAVE is the new global academic imprint of
St. Martin's Press LLC Scholarly and Reference Division and
Palgrave Publishers Ltd (formerly Macmillan Press Ltd).

ISBN 0–333–77203–2 hardback
ISBN 0–333–77204–0 paperback

This book is printed on paper suitable for recycling and
made from fully managed and sustained forest sources.

A catalogue record for this book is available
from the British Library.

Library of Congress Cataloging-in-Publication Data

McCormick, John, 1954–
    Environmental policy in the European Union / John McCormick.
      p. cm. – (European Union series)
    Includes bibliographical references and index.
    ISBN 0–333–77203–2 – ISBN 0–333–77204–0 (pbk.)
      1. Environmental policy – European Union countries.   I. Title.
  II. Series.

GE190.E85 M33 2000
363.7′056′094 – dc21   00-067097

10   9   8   7   6   5   4   3   2   1
10 09 08 07 06 05 04 03 02 01

Printed in China

Contents

List of Tables and Figures

Tables

Figures

Preface

When most Europeans think about the European Union, the kinds of issues that come most readily to mind include the single market, agricultural policy, the euro, controversies involving the European Commission, and – more recently – attempts to build a common European foreign and security policy. These are the matters most often covered by European media, which devote much less time and space to the other policy areas affected by integration, such as transport, regional policy, development, consumer issues and – most notably – the environment. The unfortunate effect of all this has been to give the impression that the EU devotes most of its time to a select group of often controversial policy problems. In fact, its interests are much broader, and the implications of its work are much deeper.

In few places has the impact of European integration been more telling than in the field of environmental policy, where the European Union has helped encourage government, industry and citizens in the member states to develop a response to problems that are often better dealt with at the regional rather than the national level. The result has been an expanding body of law dealing with issues as varied as air and water quality, waste management, the control of chemicals, the use of pesticides, noise pollution, acid rain, fisheries management, energy efficiency and climate change. Reaching agreement on a joint response to such matters has not always been easy, and the effects of EU policy have been mixed, but there is now a broad consensus that the efforts made at the European level to develop policies on the environment have helped make the EU a cleaner, quieter and healthier place in which to live.

This book is designed to provide a broad-ranging overview and assessment of the environmental policy of the European Union. I wrote it for three main reasons. First, while EU environmental policy has been the subject of a growing body of research, most of it is very specialized. There are many excellent studies of particular environmental problems, of the character of EU environmental law, and of the effects of EU law on the member states, but they all assume a high level of prior knowledge on the part of their readers regarding the EU policy process in general, and the EU record on the environment in particular. This book is designed to be a stepping stone between the general and the particular, to help clarify the parameters of EU policy, to explain and analyse its underlying motives and principles, and to help readers better understand the implications of that policy.

Second, it comes as a recognition of the growing maturity of the EU record on the environment, and is an attempt to draw more attention to that record. The literature on European integration is unbalanced in terms of the attention paid to economic and foreign policy issues, and it is time that the studies in these areas are joined on the bookshelves by more studies of the other policy areas in which the EU is active. Hopefully this will help add more balance to the debate about Europe, and draw more attention to the less controversial issues in which the EU has been involved.

Third, national governments on every continent are involving themselves in regional integration programmes. Many have developed cooperative policies on the environment because they have found that environmental problems go beyond national borders, and are inextricably linked to the development of regional and global markets. The European Union is the most advanced of the experiments in regional integration, and it is critical that we understand the strengths and weaknesses of that experiment if we are to understand the potential for regional integration as a means of addressing environmental problems more generally.

The book is not based on any particular theory or philosophy, nor does it attempt to justify existing models of the EU policy process, nor to construct new models. I tend to agree with the views of Helen Wallace in her introduction to the third edition of *Policy-Making in the European Union* (Oxford University Press, 1996, pp. 9, 11–12). Noting the existence of a 'bewildering range of analytical approaches to European integration', she expresses her preference for what she calls the seamless web approach: 'Modern governance, at least in western Europe, involves efforts to construct policy responses at a multiplicity of levels, from the global to the local. The European arena constitutes points of intense interface and competition between levels of government and between public and private actors. What interests us is what clusters of factors generate an agreement that on specific issues the EU level should predominate as the preferred policy arena'. This is what interests me also.

The resulting book has two personalities: it is both a study of European environmental policy in particular, and of the EU policy process in general. When I began my research in 1995, there were very few published studies of the EU policy process, and it struck me during subsequent interviews in Brussels that much of what I was learning about the intricacies of that process had never been committed to print. Given my interest in the policy process generally and in environmental policy specifically, it seemed logical to combine the two. Hence this book can be approached either as a study of EU environmental policy that makes some broader comments about the EU policy process, or as a study of the EU policy process that uses the environment as a case study.

I have had a professional interest in environmental issues since the early 1980s, when I was living in London and working first for the World Wide Fund for Nature, and then for the International Institute for Environment and Development. That interest carried over into my academic research, where it combined with my research on the European Union to carry me naturally into a focus on the environmental policy of the EU. I am now a faculty member at Indiana University in Indianapolis, about as far away from the political struggles in Brussels as it is possible to be. The distance has its advantages though – I can watch developments in the EU without being sidetracked by the often very narrow coverage of EU affairs in the European media, and I can compare European approaches to environmental issues with those of the federal and state governments in the United States.

The key component in the research for this book was a six-week secondment to DGXI in Brussels in May and June of 1996. As well as taking part in meetings within the Commission, the Council of Ministers and Parliament, I also had the opportunity of talking with many of the officials of all three institutions, and of having access to documents relating to the development of policy and law within DGXI. Those six weeks turned out to be an invigorating research experience, and the book would have been much poorer without the opportunities it provided.

I would like to begin by thanking Jonathan Davidson at the European Commission office in Washington DC for putting me in touch with Tom Garvey, deputy director-general of what was then DGXI, who in turn was responsible for getting me past the front door and for opening many other doors within the corridors of DGXI. I owe a particular debt of gratitude to Pat Murphy, my mentor for the six weeks, who introduced me to all the right people, pointed me in the right directions and made sure that I had access to the information I needed. He was a busy man and didn't need me periodically putting my head around his door, but he always found the time to talk to me (even over Sunday breakfasts), giving me many valuable insights into the workings of DGXI and the Commission more generally.

Also in DGXI I would like to thank Ute Koch for taking care of all the administrative details and showing me how things worked, Dawn Adie and Gian-Luigi Ruzzante for guiding me around the goldmine that is the library at DGXI, and Reinhilde Lambert and Marika Paukkunen for arranging my visits to the Council and Parliament. For taking time to talk with me and providing many valuable insights, I would like to thank Henning Arp, Nicholas Banfield, Jean-Guy Bartaire, Margaret Brusasco-MacKenzie, Goffredo Del Bino, Rob Donkers, Bertil Heerink, Jorgen Henningsen, Volker Irmer, Ludwig Krämer, Grant Lawrence and – outside the EU institutions – Tony Long at the World Wildlife Fund, and Regina Schneider and Karola Taschner at the European Environmental Bureau. I'm also very grateful to Suzette O'Brien, Cynthia Whitehead and Jerome Woodford for arranging accommodation in Brussels, and to John Balch for lending me his laptop.

The Office of Faculty Development at Indiana University in Indianapolis provided generous funding support for this project, and the Office of International Programs at Indiana University in Bloomington covered the costs of travel through a President's Council on International Programs research award. Marian Shabaan at the University Library at Indiana University in Bloomington did a great job of digging out material for me, and saved me hours of searching.

I spent the spring of 1999 on a sabbatical at the Centre for

European Studies at the University of Exeter, where I was able to teach a graduate seminar on EU environmental policy. I would like to thank Bogdan Szajkowski, Bob Lewis and Alan Davidson for setting up the sabbatical, the students – Michael Darvell, Barbara Frysztacka, Jeanette Loje, Martine Roussel and Dimitris Saharides – for providing a valuable and unwitting sounding board for my ideas, and Iain Hampsher-Monk, Andrea Hibbert and Keith Zimmerman for taking care of administrative matters in the Department of Politics. My thanks also to the staff of the Greenpeace office in Exeter for giving me access to their resources.

Steven Kennedy continued to be a paragon among publishers, displaying his usual efficiency, enthusiasm and professionalism, and the series editors and anonymous reviewers provided very helpful comments on earlier drafts of the book. Finally, my love and thanks to my wife Leanne for being as steady as a rock.

Links to Web sites relating to European Union environmental policy can be accessed via the author's 'The EU on the Web' links page at the EU Resource Area of the publisher's Web site at http://www.palgrave.com/politics/eu/euontheweb.htm or by going directly to the relevant page on the author's Web site at http://php.iupui.edu/~jmccormi/enviropolicy.htm

JOHN MCCORMICK

List of Abbreviations

ACE	Actions by the Community Relating to the Environment
ACEA	European Automobile Manufacturer's Association
ACNAT	Actions by the Community for Nature
ACP	Africa, Caribbean, Pacific countries
ALTENER	Programme for the Promotion of Renewable Energy Sources in the Community
BAT	best available technology/techniques
BATNEEC	best available technology not entailing excessive cost
CAP	Common Agricultural Policy
CEECs	Central and Eastern European Countries
CEGB	Central Electricity Generating Board (UK)
CFP	Common Fisheries Policy
CITES	Convention on International Trade in Endangered Species
COE	Community Operations Concerning the Environment
COREPER	Committee of Permanent Representatives
CORINE	Coordination Information Environment
DG	directorate-general
EAP	Environmental Action Programme
ECPS	Environment and Consumer Protection Service
EDG	Environment directorate-general
EEA	European Environment Agency
EEB	European Environmental Bureau
EFTA	European Free Trade Association
EINECS	European Inventory of Existing Chemical Substances
EIONET	European Environment Information and Observation Network
ELV	emission limit value, *or* end-of-life vehicle
EMAS	eco-management and audit scheme
EMEP	Co-operative Programme for Monitoring and Evaluation of the Long-range Transmission of Air Pollutants in Europe

ENDS	Environmental Data Services
EP	European Parliament
EWC	European Waste Catalogue
GMO	genetically-modified organism
IIASA	International Institute for Applied Systems Analysis
IMPEL	EU Network for the Implementation and Enforcement of Environmental Law
IPCC	UN Intergovernmental Panel on Climate Change
IPPC	integrated pollution prevention and control
LCP	large combustion plant
LIFE	Financial Instrument for the Environment
LRTAP	long-range transboundary (or transport of) air pollution
MEP	Member of the European Parliament
NCB	National Coal Board (UK)
NGO	non-governmental organization
NIMBY	not in my back yard
ODS	ozone-depleting substances
OECD	Organization for Economic Cooperation and Development
PHARE	Poland and Hungary Assistance for Economic Restructuring
PIC	prior informed consent
QMV	qualified majority voting
SAVE	Specific Actions for Vigorous Energy Efficiency
SEA	Single European Act
SST	supersonic transport
TAC	total allowable catch
UNECE	UN Economic Commission for Europe
UNEP	UN Environment Programme
WEEE	waste electrical and electronic equipment
WQO	water quality objective
WWF	World Wide Fund for Nature
CFC	chlorofluorocarbon
CO	carbon monoxide
CO_2	carbon dioxide
HCFC	hydrochlorofluorocarbon
NH_3	ammonia
NO_2	nitrogen dioxide

NOx	nitrogen oxides
O_3	ozone
PCB	polychlorinated biphenyl
PCT	polychlorinated terphenyl
SO_2	sulphur dioxide
SPM	suspended particulate matter
UV-B	ultraviolet B
VOC	volatile organic compound

Three Explanatory Notes

European Union law

EU law comes in three main forms: regulations, directives and decisions. When a piece of law is adopted, it is given a number which consists of the year of adoption and the sequential number of the law in that year. For regulations, the sequential number comes first and the year comes second, hence the 1991 regulation on the ozone layer is 594/91. With directives and decisions, the opposite is true, so that the 1996 directive on air quality is 96/62 and the 1999 decision on packaging waste is 99/177.

Every piece of law consists of five main sections: the title (which has several elements, including the number and the type of law), the powers on which the law is based (such as Article 175), a series of recitals which explain the background, the aims and the objectives (which always begin with the word 'Whereas'), the key provisions (which are divided into articles), and the date by which the law must be transposed or implemented.

A complete listing of EU environmental legislation including year, number, title and brief description compiled by the author is available at the EU Resource Area of the publisher's Web site at http://www.palgrave.com/politics/eu/

Terminology

I have used the term European Union throughout except where referring exclusively to a period or an issue which applies directly to the European Economic Community or the European Community.

Article numbers

The Treaty of Amsterdam introduced a new numbering system for the Articles of the EC and EU treaties. Throughout the book

I use this new system except where referring in a time-specific sense to the numbers used prior to Amsterdam. Listed below are the pre- and post-Amsterdam equivalents of articles referred to in the book:

Old	New		Old	New
2	2		130r	174
3b	5		130s	175
3c	6		130t	176
30	28		155	211
36	30		169	226
100	94		171	228
100a	95		235	307\

The key treaty provisions relating to environmental policy are summarized in the Appendix on page 300.

Introduction

Environmental policy is one of the most rapidly expanding areas of European Union (EU) policy activity. A substantial body of European environmental law has found its way into the statute books, environmental problems are high on the agenda of the Council of Ministers, disputes over environmental issues have been the subject of many of the key decisions of the European Court of Justice, and the performance of the EU in this area has been the focus of a growing body of scholarly research. It is strange, then, that so little is yet understood about the motives underlying EU environmental activities, about the way in which the EU defines the term 'environment', about the relationship between the economic and environmental priorities of the EU, about the relative merits of supranational and national responses to environmental management needs, or about the effects of EU policy.

Most of the uncertainties stem from the relative novelty of the EU record in this field. The first Community law on the environment was adopted in 1959, and the first Community Environmental Action Programme was adopted in 1973, but it was not until the signature of the Single European Act in 1987 that environmental protection was formally recognized as part of the legal competence of the European Community. The years since then have seen a flurry of legislative and policy activity, with EU institutions addressing a broadening base of environmental issues. From a time when most legal activity was focused on matters such as air and water quality, waste management and the control of chemicals, the EU has become involved in problems as varied as the protection of wildlife, the conservation of energy, the control of genetically modified organisms, the promotion of organic agriculture, the management of fisheries, the control of acid pollution, and international attempts to address the problem of global warming.

Where the European Community once saw environmental protection as subsidiary to the greater interest of building the

1

single market, the last few years have seen the environment emerging as a European policy interest in its own right. There has been a new maturity in the principles pursued by the EU, a greater understanding of the causes and the nature of transboundary and shared problems, and a greater level of certainty and confidence in the responses and methods adopted by the EU institutions.

The implications, costs and benefits of regional rather than national approaches to dealing with environmental problems are still not yet fully understood, but as the EU record in this field both broadens and deepens, so a greater appreciation is developing among those active in the environmental policy field about the merits of the regional approach: it addresses problems which do not respect national frontiers; joint action and burden-sharing encourage national governments to take action where otherwise they may have been reluctant; progressive governments can increase the pressure for a more ambitious overall set of objectives; the forces of regional economic integration provide a compelling motive force for countries to agree to joint action; wealthier states can provide resources that can help offset the economic burden of environmental regulation in poorer states; and the regional approach encourages the generation and better use of data on the causes of environmental problems and the efficacy of responses.

It is now safe to say that environmental policies in the European Union are made more as a result of the requirements of EU law than as an consequence of domestic needs and pressures. There are no longer 15 sets of national environmental policies, but – in most areas – a single set of regional policies. The member states still often have their own priorities, to be sure, which are a function of a combination of local economic, social and political factors, but the most important environmental decisions now taken by the governments of the member states come in response to the obligations inherent in their membership of the European Union.

Environmental policy in context

All policy areas interact with one another. The positions and the actions of policymakers in one area inevitably have an impact on those in other areas, driving decisions about how to allocate and share finite resources such as funds, staff and time, and generating consequences as decisions and actions in one area limit or prompt actions in another. Perhaps more than any other area of public policy, the environment both impacts and is impacted by activities in almost every other area of public policy. The links are most obvious with policies relating to industry, the economy, agriculture, energy, transport, water supply, sanitation, urban and rural development and health care, but the argument can also be made that environmental quality has implications for policy areas as varied as education, poverty, overseas development aid and housing.

European integration was initially concerned mainly with quantitative issues, notably reducing the barriers to trade with a view to promoting cooperation and helping Europe exploit its natural and human resources in order to maximize profits and opportunities, and to stop Europeans going to war with one another. As the European experiment proceeded, however, it became increasingly clear that integration had qualitative dimensions as well. There were early concerns that differences in environmental standards could be a barrier to free trade, but integration also showed clearly the contrast between the benefits of progressive policies on the environment and the costs of ignoring or overlooking the impact of industrial and agricultural activity on environmental quality.

The pressure for European policies on the environment has grown as the implications of regional integration have been more widely understood. Not only has the growing wealth of Europeans encouraged them to care more about qualitative issues such as the provision of good education, improvements in health care and efforts to ensure clean air and water, but regional integration has had a number of effects which have helped draw more public attention to environmental matters than might otherwise have been the case:

- In their rush to capitalize on the Common Agricultural Policy, European farmers have used more chemical fertilizers and herbicides, have adopted more intensified farming techniques, and have converted more woodland to farmland.
- The opening of borders among the EU member states has combined with the development of new transport networks

and cheaper travel brought by airline deregulation to contribute to a growth in the tourist trade, to a greater volume
of traffic on European roads, and to new pressures being
exerted on areas of natural and historical value.

- The increased consumption of the expanding European
  middle class, whose size has grown in part in response to the
  new economic opportunities offered by the single European
  market, has led to an increase in waste generation, prompting the need for pan-European policies designed to manage
  the disposal of that waste. The demands of the European consumer have also led to an increase in the number of vehicles
  on the road and to growing energy consumption, both of
  which have had a negative impact on the state of the European environment.
- The opening of borders has encouraged the governments of
  EU member states to work cooperatively on transboundary
  issues. Where independent national governments might have
  been inclined to ignore entreaties from their neighbours that
  could not be backed up with significant economic threats,
  regional integration has seen the member states of the EU
  work more creatively towards the solution of problems such
  as acid pollution, where the biggest producers have not always
  been the biggest victims.

While policymakers of the 1950s and 1960s understood little
if anything of the environmental implications of domestic policy,
or of their plans for the European Economic Community, by the
mid-1980s they had begun to develop a wider appreciation of
what they were doing. Hence the agreement of the 1985 European Council that environmental policy should be 'an essential
component of the economic, industrial, agricultural and social
policies implemented by the Community and by its Member
States', and its acknowledgment that 'coherent action' was
needed to protect the environment 'where isolated action is
unlikely to prove effective and may even be harmful'.

Since the passage of the Single European Act in 1987, environmental protection has been recognized as part of the legal
competence of the European Union, and it is now one of only
four policy areas (the others being consumer protection, culture
and health) that are formally recognized as a component of
all other EU policy activity. With the passage of Maastricht in

1993, it was understood that the economic activities of the EU should be sustainable, meaning that they should not undermine or compromise the opportunity or potential for future exploitation. From a time in the 1960s and 1970s when the priorities of European integration were largely economic, by the 1980s and 1990s there was more of a balance between economic efficiency and environmental sustainability, and an understanding that successful policies in one area were heavily dependent on successful policies in the other.

The role of theory

Attempts to theorize the process of European integration and to develop explanatory models for the European policy process are handicapped by the unprecedented nature of the European Union as an institution or process, and by its constantly changing character. Multiple terms have been used in an attempt to pin down its identity – from de Gaulle's 'concert of states' to Thatcher's 'family of nations' – and scholars have variously labelled it a proto-federation, an organization with supranational tendencies, a partnership, a consociational democracy, and an experiment in 'cooperative federalism' or 'collective sovereignty'. It has even been argued that it is not really an institution, but is better approached as an ideal or a process.

Although realism is usually associated with cooperation on security and military issues, it has something to offer attempts to understand the evolution of European Community environmental policy in the sense that powers over environmental policy were initially given to the Community institutions only to the extent to which it suited the member states. In an anarchic situation (one lacking an authority capable of addressing transboundary environmental problems), it might be argued that the member states were rational actors that cooperated in order to address a shared problem; in this case, environmental degradation. Realists argue that the quest for security by one state may leave other states insecure; applied to environmental policy, the attempt by a progressive state such as Germany, Denmark or the Netherlands to tighten its environmental standards has caused concerns in other member states about the implications for free trade.

While competition and conflict are at the heart of realist analyses, functionalist theory is more directly applicable to the environmental case, and particularly to any attempts to understand why the Community became involved in environmental issues. Functionalism is based on the argument that integration has its own internal dynamic, and that if states co-operate in selected limited policy areas and create new bodies to oversee that cooperation, then they will find themselves co-operating in other policy areas through an 'invisible hand' of integration. In other words, integration has its own internal logic, contracts have an almost irresistible authority, and while the European Economic Community began life with a limited number of goals – such as building a common market, developing a customs union and applying a common agricultural policy – it ineluctably found itself drawn into cooperation on other, supporting policy areas such as environmental management.

Neofunctionalism builds on these arguments by suggesting that prerequisites are needed before integration can proceed, including favourable public opinion, a desire by elites to promote integration for pragmatic rather than altruistic reasons, and the delegation of powers to a new supranational authority. In the case of the environment, the first of these came with the rising awareness in Western societies in the 1960s about the impact of industry and consumerism on the environment; the second came in the early 1970s when the leaders of the member states agreed to cooperate on environmental matters; and the third came following the Single European Act when the environment was made a formal policy concern of the European Community. Neofunctionalism suggests that when these pre-requisites have been met, joint action in one policy area will create pressures that will cause spillover into other, related areas. In particular, technical spillover became a motive force as disparities in environmental standards led the member states to work towards common standards in order to remove barriers to the single market, and led them increasingly to institutionalize the European response to environmental policy needs. In most cases, the new pressures led to an overall tightening of standards, and in some cases it led to compromises by which poorer states were given more time to meet selected environmental objectives of the EU.

What of the role of theory in terms of understanding how decisions are now made on environmental issues? The first theory of interest is federalism, which is controversial because it involves the surrender of sovereignty by the member states. The EU is not a federal entity, that is, one with different levels of government enjoying independent powers. The key to decision-making among the EU institutions still rests very much with the European Council and the Council of Ministers, which are both intergovernmental bodies (in which decisions are reached as a result of discussions among largely self-interested national government leaders or their ministers) rather than supranational bodies (which would have powers over the member states, and be driven by the interests of the group rather than by those of the individual member states).

To some extent, the concept of subsidiarity – which charges that the EU institutions should deal only with those policy matters best dealt with at the European level, leaving the rest to national or local government – has pushed the EU closer to the point of becoming a federal entity, but the balance of power over decision-making varies from one policy area to another. While issues such as education, policing and tax policy are still very much the preserve of the member states, the environment has been 'federalized' as a policy issue in the sense that the balance of power has shifted more towards the EU. In other words, environmental policy in the member states is now arguably driven more by decisions reached through negotiation within the EU institutions than it is by decisions reached independently by the governments of the member states.

The limited explanatory value of the intergovernmental and supranational approaches is addressed to a large extent by the notion of multi-level governance. This is based on the idea of different and overlapping sets of competence among multiple levels of government, and suggests that authority is dispersed among these different levels, and involves multiple policy actors with multiple powers and interests. In the case of environment policy, we have national ministers making decisions in the Council of Ministers, but we also have decisions being influenced by information being generated by the European Environment Agency, policy development being driven by technical experts in the European Commission, pressure being brought to bear on the policy process by increasingly well-organized interest groups, policies being implemented by national and local authorities (whose cooperation is thus critical), and a significant body of law and policy being generated by agreements reached in international organizations which are themselves being heavily influenced by the economic power of the European Union. In some respects, the idea of multi-level governance is simply an acknowledgement that the EU is both a remarkably complex polity, that it is changing, and that it will eventually evolve into a different kind of political entity about whose features we can only make educated guesses.

Implications for the member states

The most significant effect of the expansion of European activities on environmental matters has been the changes wrought on policy in the member states as national and local governments have addressed these matters. Prior to the advent of European integration, national governments – or, at least, those which had addressed environmental problems – saw those problems purely in terms of national interests. The needs of environmental management were defined nationally, and where there was international pressure to address shared problems, negotiations were carried out in a spirit of competition rather than of cooperation. In the case of the poorer European states, such as Greece, Portugal and Spain, there was little or nothing in the way of domestic environmental laws or policies, and their governments saw economic development as more urgent than the environmental impact of such development.

The member states continue to have different policy styles, which are a reflection of their different environments and of their political, economic and social traditions. In demographic terms, they vary from the densely populated and highly urbanized core focused on the Benelux countries and northern Italy, to the sparsely populated Arctic regions of northern Sweden and Finland. In economic terms, they vary from the wealthy and service-oriented golden triangle between London, Hamburg and Paris, to the older industrial regions of northern Britain and eastern Germany, to the poorer agricultural regions of Greece, Portugal, Spain and Ireland. In climatic terms they vary from the balmy temperatures of the Mediterranean to the damp and windswept northwestern coasts to the permafrost found north of the Arctic Circle. In geographical terms they vary from the islands of Greece and Scandinavia to the highlands of the Alpine regions, the mountains of Spain, and the plains of northern Europe.

The member states all have their own administrative and legislative traditions as well. For example, the British have taken a devolved and decentralized approach to environmental regulation and have preferred to reach voluntary agreements with industry, and to persuade rather than to command and control. Policy in Germany is heavily influenced by its federal administrative structure, by the different priorities of the *länder*, and by the role of the Greens in both national and local government. A combination of late industrialization and rapid and unregulated urban growth in recent years has meant that policy in Greece, Spain and Portugal is still in a reactive phase; a combination of weak administrative structures and relatively low levels of public awareness have kept the environment low on the policy agenda in all three countries. In Italy, the economic division between the wealthy north and the relatively poor south has undermined attempts to build national policies and institutions (for more details on the environmental priorities and policy styles of the member states, see Hanf and Jansen, 1998).

The effect of European integration has been to reduce the differences in the approaches taken by the member states, and to compel them to move more towards a common definition of environmental problems and of the best ways of addressing them. It has had at least four key effects on the domestic policies of the member states:

- They have had to think much more about such issues in supranational terms, with the common European interest replacing multiple sets of national interests as the key driving force in their considerations. The need to build the single market has compelled them to work cooperatively both on defining problems and on agreeing responses to such problems.

- They have had to adopt the same institutional, legal and procedural responses to these problems. There are still 15 sets of national institutions, and the items on national environmental agendas are occasionally still different; for example, the British have their concerns with nature and wildlife, the Germans have their concerns with forests, the older industrial regions have their concerns with urban renewal, the southern states have their concerns with the condition of the Mediterranean, and so on. However, where universal problems have been identified, universal responses have been adopted under the guidance of EU law, thereby bringing the policies of the member states much more closely into alignment with one another.

- They have had to become used to multi-level governance in the formulation and implementation of environmental policies. Not only have they had to reach agreement among themselves, but they have also had to reach common agreement in the face of demands made by extra-European actors in negotiations on such issues as global warming and trade in endangered species of wildlife.

- They have become subject to far greater external pressures, their policies now being driven by the compromises reached as a result of discussion among the member states, rather than as a result of domestic debates among interested parties, notably industrial and agricultural interests. Policies are driven by differences in the economic priorities of richer and poorer states, by the need to build the infrastructure needed to promote the single European market, and by the cumulative interests of national and pan-European interest groups.

Arguments and organization of the book

The chapters that follow are based around four fundamental arguments about the nature of EU environmental policy. These are as follows:

- The European Union does not have an environmental policy. Instead, it has a series of policies relating to specific environmental issues such as air and water quality, waste management, chemicals and so on, some of which are better developed than others. A recent tendency by the Commission to develop strategies, framework directives and programmes rather than laws suggests that the balance is changing. Where the Community in the 1970s and early 1980s was dabbling with tools such as the setting of quality objectives and emission limits, and in some senses trying to micromanage the problems of the environment, it has more recently taken a more holistic approach to these problems, and thus is moving closer to the development of an environmental policy.

- The definition of 'environmental' policy conventionally used both by the EU institutions and by commentators on EU environmental policy is limited, idiosyncratic and still tied too much to the early history of EU activities in this area. This book adopts a much broader definition, and thus makes the case that the EU has been involved in a much broader set of policy issues than is conventionally understood.

- The European Commission has been a creative and productive policy entrepreneur, the often technical nature of many environmental laws giving policy specialists within the Commission and the Council of Ministers much latitude over the formulation of policy. At the same time, the Commission has developed a close working relationship with industry, which has been able to use its strengths to exert influence over the development of EU environmental policy.

- The effect of EU environmental policy has been to replace the individual approaches and interests of the member states with a broader, supranational attitude towards environmental problems, which are now seen much less as local issues and much more as regional issues. At the same time, regional cooperation has made the EU a key player in international negotiations on environmental policy, thus EU values and approaches have had an impact far beyond the borders of the member states.

The chapters that follow set out to answer two questions: how and by whom is environmental policy made in the EU, and with what effects? The first question is addressed in Part I, which examines the policy process. Chapter 1 attempts to define the parameters of environmental policy, arguing that it has been strangely defined both by EU institutions and by commentators, and provides a general survey of the environmental issues on which the EU has been most active; these include water quality, waste control, air quality, fisheries conservation, protection from radiation, the control of chemicals, energy conservation, the protection of biodiversity, and reduction of pollution from noise.

Chapter 2 describes and assesses the manner in which the EU approach to environmental matters has evolved since the 1950s, noting the reactive nature of much early policy, and the more proactive nature of policy following the Single European Act which made environmental management one of the formal policy responsibilities of European integration. It ends with a summary of the manner in which the EU approaches to environmental issues have matured in recent years.

Chapter 3 surveys the key principles underlying EU environmental policy, and discusses the manner in which the policy agenda is developed. It argues that a number of the principles are contradictory, and that they are not always reflected in the goals and the underlying rationale of EU environmental laws. It also concludes that much of what the EU has done in the environmental field has been opportunistic and improvizational rather than deliberately planned, a reflection in part of the manner in which the EU itself has evolved and changed.

Chapter 4 explains the process by which environmental laws and policies are proposed and developed, focusing in particular on the role of the Commission, the European Parliament and key external forces. It concludes that the most influential actors in environmental policy formulation are the technical units within the Commission, and the national and industrial sector experts consulted by the Commission. Relatively speaking, Parliament, the environmental lobby and national enforcement agencies have a much lesser role in the process.

Chapter 5 examines the process of policy adoption and implementation, focusing on the roles in this process of the Council of Ministers, the European Court of Justice and the Commission. It reviews the preconditions for successful implementation, argues that implementation is the weakest stage in the EU environmental policy process, and analyzes the reasons behind the mixed record in this area in regard to environmental laws.

The effects of EU environmental policy are addressed in Part II of the book, which offers case studies of the EU record in several key areas. Chapter 6 looks at the broad-ranging problem of chemicals in the environment, the EU response to which dates back to 1967 and which has since expanded to include laws directed at controlling the use of dangerous substances, controlling the import and export of chemicals, protecting consumer health and safety, and promoting research on the toxicity of chemical compounds. The chapter also looks at EU policy on waste management, an issue which has taken on new dimensions as member states produce more waste but run out of sites for safe disposal.

Chapter 7 examines the EU record on dealing with air and water quality issues, both of which have been the subject of an extensive body of laws; the former deal with emissions into the air from road vehicles, fossil fuels and industrial plants, while the latter promote the protection of freshwater, marine water, surface water and groundwater. Recent years have seen a move towards strategic responses both to air and water quality issues.

Chapter 8 takes a particular element of the air quality problem – acidification – which stands as one of the true success stories of EU environmental policy; the European Union has been a key player in encouraging the governments of member states to work together on the resolution of this most obviously regional of all environmental problems. National governments tried their best to achieve agreement among themselves in the 1970s and 1980s, and while they made considerable headway, it was only with the agreements reached under the auspices of the Community in the 1980s that the two major laggards – West Germany and Britain – were finally brought into the fold.

Chapter 9 assesses the EU record on nature and natural resources. As well as assessing policies on biodiversity and genetically modified organisms, which are conventionally defined as part of the environmental remit of the EU, it also looks at activities in key areas of natural resource management, including fisheries, agriculture, forestry and energy conservation. These are issues that are normally defined as 'environmental' at the national level, but are commonly left out of discussions about EU environmental policy.

Chapter 10 offers an analysis of the role of the EU as an actor in international negotiations on environmental issues. Contrasting the record on the ozone layer (where agreement was reached very quickly) and climate change (where it was not), it argues not only that many of the most important initiatives taken by the member states have come in response to EU law, but that the EU has become a powerful player in international negotiations on environmental problems.

PART I

THE POLICY PROCESS

Chapter 1

Policy Parameters

Until the late 1980s, the process of European integration was associated most often in the public mind with economic and agricultural matters. The issues that drew the attention of policymakers and the media – even if the public was often less than thrilled – included subsidies to farmers, the promotion of free trade, competition policy, battles over the budget, harmonization of standards and the role of the European Community in international trade. For no particularly logical reason, a number of social scientists described these as matters of 'high' or 'hard' policy.

Since the early 1990s, the balance has shifted. The debate over European integration has expanded to incorporate a broader set of so-called 'soft' or 'low' policy areas such as consumer affairs, regional policy, development aid, social policy, technology and the environment. The change in focus came partly out of a new awareness that economic integration demands cooperation in a broader variety of policy areas than those originally envisioned by the authors of the Treaty of Rome. It was also prompted by a new realization that a multinational approach to many of these policy problems is often more effective than independent national approaches. Furthermore, cooperation in these areas has proved less controversial than it has been in matters of 'hard' policy.

The altered dimensions of the debate drew new levels of attention to Community activities on the environment, where it became clear that different standards were a significant barrier to the single market. The response has been remarkable: by the end of 1999, the EU had published five environmental action programmes, adopted nearly 850 pieces of environmental law, published numerous green and white papers, created a European Environment Agency to improve the quality of data-gathering, established a Green Forum to promote non-governmental input into policy-making, run several programmes designed to finance environmental protection, and developed strategic approaches to problems in several key policy areas, including air and water quality.

Impressive though they are, however, these achievements should be treated with caution. Much of what the EU has done in the environmental field has been spillover from its primary concern of building the single market, its policies have often been opportunistic rather than deliberate, it has occasionally had an idiosyncratic notion of what constitutes an environmental issue, and the record on policy implementation has been mixed at best. It was only with the adoption of the Single European Act in 1987 that environmental policy became formally part of the European agenda, and that the Community began to address environmental problems for their own sake. The focus of its activities still does not always coincide with 'the environment' as it is conventionally understood by most national policymakers, there are substantial gaps in its range of activities, and its policy goals are sometimes long on broad principles and short on specific programmes.

This opening chapter is an attempt to clarify the nature of environmental policy as it is understood by EU policymakers. It begins with a discussion of the parameters of the environment as a policy arena, tries to pin down the underlying principles of EU environmental policy, and provides an overview of the activities of the EU in 14 key policy areas, several of which are considered in more depth in later chapters. It argues that the parameters of EU environmental policy are badly defined, and that the EU has been more productive – and involved in a greater variety of policy areas – than is conventionally acknowledged either by the EU itself or by commentators on EU environmental policy.

What is environmental policy?

The institutions of the European Union have an odd notion of the meaning of the word 'environment'. Take, for example, the way in which responsibilities have been divided up among the directorates-general of the European Commission; while the Environment DG (EDG) is responsible for most of the issues conventionally defined by national policymakers as 'environmental' (such as air and water pollution, and waste management), fisheries conservation is part of the remit of the Fisheries DG, forestry and the control of pesticides are the responsibility of the Agriculture DG, and organic farming comes under Health and Consumer Protection. At the same time, EDG is responsible for a number of issues which are not 'environmental' as the term is conventionally understood at the national level, including noise pollution and civil protection.

A search through EU documents for a definition of 'environmental policy' raises as many questions as it answers. For example, the annual *Directory of Environmental Legislation in Force* (published by the European Commission) is restricted mainly to legislation generated by the EDG. Because the EDG has been responsible in the past for consumer issues and public health protection, the list includes laws on consumer credit, cancer prevention and the control of narcotics. At the same time, the directory *excludes* laws on fisheries management, energy conservation and organic agriculture, apparently because these are matters which come under the aegis of other DGs. A search through the EUR-Lex directory of EU legislation adds to the confusion. The pages relating to environmental policy list the EU's activities in such areas as waste management, air quality and biodiversity, but exclude its work on fisheries conservation, forestry and the control of pesticides.

These idiosyncrasies are reflected in studies of European environmental policy, most of which selectively focus on the issues dealt with by the EDG, while largely ignoring those dealt with by other DGs. The advice they provide is sometimes contradictory, often incomplete, and occasionally eccentric. For example, John Salter's guide to EU environmental law includes secondary 'environmental' laws dealing with such matters as the control of animal and vegetable diseases, the acidity of wine, and even television broadcasting (1995, chapter 7). Ludwig Krämer argues that environmental issues include the protection of archaeological heritage (1995, p. 41). Richard Macrory suggests that while the regulation of pollution and the protection of wildlife would be described by many environmental lawyers as their 'core concerns', it is also clear that many other areas of law – such as health and safety at work, land-use planning and consumer protection – have 'substantial environmental impli-

cations', and that 'the principles upon which apparently unconnected areas of law, such as competition or trade law, operate
may be far from neutral in their potential impacts on the environment' (1996, p. 3).

The problem of definition is a consequence mainly of the
manner in which the European response to environmental issues
has evolved: as discussed in Chapter 2, that response was long
driven less by a rational attempt to understand and resolve
environmental problems, and more by the often reactive and
improvisational manner in which the interests and priorities of
European integration developed. Because Community activity
on the environment was initially driven by a desire to remove
barriers to free trade and to protect human health, the Community was active on issues such as air and water pollution, the
control of chemicals and pesticides, and the conservation of fisheries, but was less active on issues such as forestry, land and soil
management, or energy conservation, none of which were raised
in the early debates over free trade. In some cases, policy priorities were determined by institutional accident: for example,
the high level of EU activity on chemicals policy is explained in
part by the fact that European environmental laws were initially
developed in the directorate-general of the European Commission responsible for industrial affairs, thus chemicals were very
much a part of the programme to develop common policies on
industry from the outset.

In a sense, trying to define the parameters of the environment
is an exercise in futility, because almost every activity in which
humans take part and governments take an interest – particularly agriculture, industry, transport, energy, rural development
and urban development – has an environmental element. As the
European Green Forum puts it,

> there is no such thing as an 'environmental sector'. Pollution
> and other types of damage to the natural environment and
> human health take place in the real sectors of society such
> as agriculture, industry and transport. Successful policies
> leading to sustainable development will have the potential
> to benefit the whole of society. This will require the full par-
> ticipation of stakeholders in all sectors. (Statement on envi-
> ronmental integration to the 1998 Cardiff summit of the
> European Council, DGXI Web page, 1998)

However, it is important to be clear about the meaning of 'the environment', for three main reasons:

- Since the Single European Act (SEA), 'environmental protection requirements' have had to be integrated into all the other activities of the EU. This cannot be done effectively unless it is understood just when and where the environment needs protecting, what kinds of activities have or do not have an environmental component, and where the responsibilities of the EDG begin and end.
- The EU institutions must work with national and local administrative agencies that have their own understanding of the term; if the three levels have different ideas about the parameters of environmental policy, effective coordination and cooperation will be difficult to achieve.
- No analysis of EU environmental policy can be complete unless the parameters of that policy are fully understood, and unless the activities of the EU in all the areas conventionally defined as being part of 'environmental policy' are fully assessed.

For the purposes of the chapters that follow, then, 'the environment' is defined as the natural surroundings in which humans exist and the natural resources on which they depend, 'environmental issues' as matters relating to the impact of human activities on those surroundings, those resources and on humans themselves, and 'environmental policy' as any actions deliberately taken – or not taken – by government that are aimed at managing human activities with a view to preventing harmful effects on nature and natural resources, and ensuring that man-made changes to the environment do not have a harmful effect on humans. Some of the issues that are typically defined as 'environmental' are listed in Table 1.1.

The priorities of European policy

Before discussing the specific actions taken by the EU in the field of environmental policy, it is important to be clear about the underlying policy priorities of the Union. There is no European Union environmental policy as such, and responses to environmental issues have developed incrementally rather than as a

TABLE 1.1   *Key environmental issues*

Air quality	Ozone layer depletion
	Global warming
	Pollution: acidification, tropospheric ozone, vehicle and industrial emissions
Water quality	Pollution: acidification, sewage, industrial emissions, urban runoff, agricultural runoff, oil spills
	Algal growth (eutrophication)
	Siltation
	Overextraction
Waste	Production, disposal and shipment
Renewable natural resources	Water (pollution, overuse, siltation)
	Air (pollution)
	Forests (deforestation, pollution)
	Soils (erosion, loss of fertility, contamination)
	Fisheries (overfishing, pollution)
	Crops and arable land (loss to urban spread, desertification, and soil erosion; contamination by chemical fertilizers, pesticides and herbicides)
	Recreational (pollution, loss to urban spread)
Energy	Pollution from fossil fuels
	Nuclear power
	Promotion of energy efficiency
	Promotion of clean and renewable energy
	Overuse of fuelwood and biomass
Biodiversity	Endangered/threatened species (trade, protection)
	Natural habitats (wetlands, forests, marshes, mangroves, coral reefs)
	Wild genetic resources

result of a blueprint of any kind. Thus there is no EU environmental 'mission statement', and the priorities of the EU must instead be sought in a combination of (1) the objectives listed in the Fifth Environmental Action Programme (EAP); (2) the mission statement of the Environment DG (EDG); and (3)

Article 174 of the treaties. A study of these three sources produces a list of six major objectives:

*Preserving, protecting and improving the quality of the envi-
ronment* (Article 174). Noble though this goal may be, it uses
adjectives which have very specific meanings, but which may
not be the meanings intended by their authors, and which are
contradictory. The term 'preservation' has conventionally been
taken to mean leaving a species or a habitat in its natural
state, and has implied the absence of exploitation involving
change. Yet the EU has also adopted the notion of sustainable
development (see below), which implies managed exploitation,
or the efficient use of natural resources. Furthermore, while
'preservation' and 'protection' imply a lack of change, 'improving' implies the acceptance of man-made change, and thus the
three terms would appear to be incompatible. Even if we accept
the notion of 'improvement' as a goal of environmental policy,
does this imply the restoration of the environment to a pre-
industrial state, or to some idealistic human notion of what it
should be like?

Protecting human health (Article 174). This is an objective
which goes substantially beyond the bounds of environmental
policy, because not all activities aimed at protecting human
health have an environmental dimension, and vice versa.
Nowhere in the body of EU law and policy is it explained where
the interests of public health end and concern for the quality of
the environment begins, and yet the two goals have often been
used to justify EU activity. A study of EU water quality legislation, for example, reveals that the rationale behind many early
laws was the protection of public health – ensuring that water
was clean enough to drink and to swim in. By the late 1980s,
however, the public health and environmental arguments were
being quoted together, and in some cases the protection of the
aquatic environment was the sole concern.

*Prudent and rational (or equitable (EDG)) utilization of
resources* (Article 174), *or the maintenance of continued access
to natural resources* (Fifth EAP), *and the preservation of the
rights of future generations to a viable environment* (EDG). This
notion is emphasized in the addition to Article 2 of the treaties

of the goal of 'sustainable and non-inflationary growth respecting the environment', a concept otherwise known as 'sustainable development' or 'conservation'. It is commonly interpreted as having an economic motivation, or as being a management principle, but there is a problem with the terms 'prudent' and 'rational', which are subjective and can be defined to have very different meanings. For an ecologist, for example, the 'rational' use of forests might mean their management as habitats or ecosystems, while the timber industry might define the term as meaning the removal and replanting of trees in the interests of providing a steady source of wood, pulp and paper.

Promoting measures at the international level to deal with regional or worldwide environmental problems (Article 174). Introduced by Maastricht, this is the least troublesome of the key objectives. As noted in Chapter 10, the EU has adopted numerous laws implementing the terms of international environmental treaties, and has become increasingly active in international negotiations on global, regional and transboundary problems such as climate change, acid pollution, and the management of shared rivers and fisheries. The European Environment Agency, meanwhile, has been active in improving the quality of the data gathered on the quality of the European environment, thereby providing stronger foundations to the underlying rationale and goals of policy.

Improvement (or maintenance (Fifth EAP)) *of the quality of life* (EDG). This is a concept that is so broad and general as to be impossible to measure or define, so it is largely meaningless as a policy objective. How can we know when we have succeeded in maintaining or improving the overall quality of life? Who would be in favour of a *reduction* in the quality of life? What factors should be included and excluded from the measurement of the quality of life?

Increased environmental efficiency (EDG). The environmental debate in recent years has seen more attention paid to the idea of eco-efficiency, meaning improvements in the efficiency with which resources are used so that consumption can be reduced. While this has been discussed within industry and think-tanks, leading to the concepts of Factor Four and Factor Ten (respectively, reducing resource use by a factor of four, and reducing resource use to the extent needed to achieve sustainable development – see *ENDS Report* 271, September 1997, pp. 20–4), it has not yet found its way into the core of EU policy, beyond the attempts made to reduce waste and to promote energy efficiency. As with much national policy within the member states, European environmental policy is still heavily driven by reacting to problems rather than preventing the problems from being created, despite the centrality of the prevention principle to that policy (see Chapter 3).

The formal goals of EU environmental policy may provide some clarity to the EU definition of 'the environment', but they are no more than broad principles. The true measure of the definition of EU policy lies in the specific actions agreed and taken. Many of the specific policy interests and priorities can be gleaned from the content of action programmes, white papers green papers and specialist reports, but the most telling indicators of those interests can be found in the environmental *acquis*, or the body of laws developed by the EU which reflects the specific obligations agreed by policymakers.

Bypassing the EU's own limited definition of the environmental *acquis* – which is heavily based on the output of the EDG – and applying a definition of environmental policy that is more in keeping with the definition employed at the national level, it transpires that the EC/EU by the end of 1999 had adopted 845 pieces of environmental law. Using the adoption of these laws as a measure, and ranking them according to the adoption of new laws (see Figure 1.1), EU environmental policy has so far focused on 14 key areas:

1 *Water quality.* The EU's programme of water pollution control is one of the oldest segments of EU environmental policy, and the focus of the biggest body of EU environmental legislation to date: more than 16 per cent of new laws, and more than 10 per cent of all laws. The underlying logic of European cooperation in this sector is clear given that many of the longest rivers in Europe (such as the Danube, the Elbe and the Rhine) cross national borders, that the welfare of coastal waters affects multiple jurisdictions, that water is put to many different uses, and that every consumer is reliant on water in several ways.

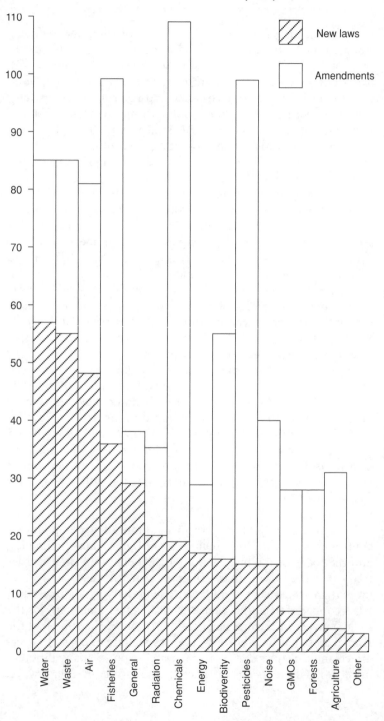

FIGURE 1.1　EU environmental laws by subject, 1958–99

The earliest EU legislation on water was motivated mainly by concerns for public health, and was based on the setting of water quality objectives for drinking and bathing water, aimed at ensuring no damage to human health. The first EU law on water pollution was adopted in 1973 and dealt with the biodegradability of detergents. It was followed in 1975 and 1976 with two broader-ranging pieces of legislation: the surface water directive, which was designed to establish common standards for surface water abstracted for use as drinking water, and the bathing water directive, which was designed to improve the quality of water used for swimming and bathing. The 1975 directive was motivated mainly by public health concerns, but it had the effect of controlling pollution by setting mandatory values (required of all states) and guide values (ideal goals) for nearly 50 parameters, including colour, odour and quantities of chemicals and heavy metals.

The first law aimed at protecting the aquatic environment as such, rather than human health, was the 1976 directive on the discharge of dangerous substances into inland, coastal and territorial waters. This combined the water quality objective approach with the setting of emission limit values, included lists of controlled substances, and paved the way for a series of directives on pollutants such as mercury and cadmium. A supplementary 1980 directive set binding quality targets for drinking water throughout the Community, and was followed by several more laws dealing with the quality of water as it affected freshwater fish and shellfish, and placing limits on emissions from the paper pulp and titanium dioxide industries, and on nitrates from agriculture.

Except for the protection of shellfish, the management of marine pollution has been a relatively small part of the EU water quality programme, and most activities in this area have been driven by the requirements of international treaties to which the EU is party. The 1977 accident at the Bravo-Ekofisk drilling rig in the North Sea and the 1978 grounding of the oil tanker *Amoco-Cadiz* off the coast of Brittany heightened public and political awareness about the threats faced by coastal waters in particular, but the Commission did little more than agree an action programme, create a consultative committee and set up data-exchange systems.

Following a ministerial review of water policy in 1988, there was agreement that several important gaps existed on water policy, the most important need being a programme to deal with urban waste water treatment. In 1991, Directive 91/271 was adopted, giving urban areas deadlines of between four and 14 years to set up collection and biological treatment systems for domestic waste water, and creating a permit system for discharges from 11 industries in the food processing sector.

At the same time, the Commission, the Council of Ministers and Parliament had all begun thinking about a more global and strategic approach to water policy, an approach that was confirmed by the conclusions of a Water Conference held in Brussels in 1996 – delegates agreed that EU water policy was fragmented, and that there was a need for a new water framework directive that would bring together all the requirements for water quality management into a single system, and coordinate all the different objectives for which water was protected. It was decided to base the system around river basins instead of political boundaries, and it was agreed that the four basic objectives of EU water policy were the protection of aquatic ecology, the protection of habitats, the maintenance of clean drinking water and the protection of bathing water.

2   *Waste control.* The growth in the production of waste from agriculture, mining, industry and domestic households prompted the Community in the second half of the 1970s to begin developing a series of measures on waste management, aimed at reducing the amount of waste produced, encouraging the recycling or reuse of waste, improving controls on waste disposal, and controlling the transport of wastes across national borders.

The first major piece of legislation was the 1975 framework directive on waste, which was designed to harmonize national waste measures, encourage member states to draw up national waste management plans, prevent waste generation and encourage waste recovery. The energy crisis of 1973 emphasized the importance of reducing waste generation and prompted renewed interest in recycling, so the new waste directive proved less politically contentious in the Council than did the directives on air and water quality that were then under discussion (Johnson and Corcelle, 1995, p. 184).

Several other directives were also agreed on radioactive waste, waste oils and sewage sludge, but it was not until the Seveso scandal in 1982–83, when barrels of hazardous waste collected after an accident at a chemical plant in Italy disappeared and were later found in France, that waste became a prominent political issue. A committee of inquiry set up by the European Parliament highlighted the problem of the transport of toxic and hazardous wastes, particularly across borders, leading to a 1984 directive on shipments of hazardous waste. Progress on the issue was hampered by a debate over the definition of the term 'waste', and another over whether or not wastes were goods that could be traded as freely as any other commodity.

Subsequent directives focused on the disposal of specific wastes such as packaging, batteries and accumulators. Several directives have also been adopted to deal more generally with hazardous wastes and pollution from waste incinerators, and an Eco-label scheme has been developed to reward manufacturers for making products that are environmentally friendly. More recently, the EU has turned its attention to the development of an integrated product policy designed to minimize resource use, avoid the use of hazardous substances, prolong product life, and make reuse and recycling easier. At the same time, it has been considering proposals aimed at reducing the amount of electrical and electronic waste being produced by consumers, and at dealing with the disposal of end-of-life vehicles.

3   *Air quality*. Given that air is a common pool resource that does not respect national boundaries, and that different air quality standards could act as a technical barrier to the single market, it is not surprising that the EU has been active in promoting the harmonization of the air pollution control strategies of the member states. Although the first piece of EU law on air pollution was a 1970 directive on carbon monoxide and hydrocarbon emissions from road vehicles, the bulk of the key pieces of law date from the late 1980s, and most are based either on setting uniform air quality standards for specified pollutants or on controlling emissions from particular sources, such as vehicles or industrial plants.

EU policy on air quality has used multiple different control methods – including air quality standards, emission limit values, and reductions by manufacturers in the production of pollutants – and has focused on six main areas: limits on emissions from road vehicles, controls on the content of fuels, emissions from industrial plants, the reduction of acidification, rules on specific air pollutants, and contributions to international attempts to limit the use of chemicals that deplete the ozone layer and to address the causes of climate change. Directives have been adopted on the sulphur and lead content of fuels, limits have been set for sulphur dioxide, particulates and nitrogen dioxide, controls have been placed on the production of chlorofluoro-carbons and other ozone-depleting substances, and the EU has been active in international negotiations on the reduction of greenhouse gases. An extensive body of legislation has been developed to reduce pollution from road vehicles, including carbon monoxide, hydrocarbons, nitrogen oxide and lead. Finally, several key pieces of legislation have been adopted aimed at reducing pollution from industrial plants, mainly with a view to dealing with acid pollution.

Just as discussions had led to the conclusion in the early 1990s that there was a need for a more global approach to water policy, so there was a concern that the EU lacked an overall policy on air pollution. The response was the 1996 framework directive on ambient air quality, which was designed to harmonize air quality assessment and management and to generate new laws dealing with 12 specific pollutants. From this, 'daughter' directives (laws dealing with more specific elements of a problem) were subsequently developed on sulphur dioxide, lead, fine particles, nitrogen dioxide, benzene, carbon monoxide, polyaromatic hydrocarbons and heavy metals. Also in 1996, the EU adopted a pollution prevention and control directive designed to encourage an integrated approach to air, water and soil pollution.

A proposal to develop a carbon tax to be placed on all the users of fossil fuels proved too controversial to win the necessary political support (see section on energy conservation below), so the European Commission instead focused in the late 1990s on an Auto-Oil programme aimed at bringing together the Commission and the oil and motor industries to investigate ways of reducing vehicle emissions and promoting cleaner fuels in the most cost-effective manner. The programme spawned proposals for directives on vehicle emissions and fuel quality, and resulted in agreements on the phasing out of leaded fuels, and the cutting of emissions of key pollutants such as nitrogen oxides and carbon monoxide. The Auto-Oil programme was also reflective of growing agreement on the need for an overall EU air quality strategy based around a five-year cycle of reviews of the threats posed to air quality, and of the progress being made in improving it.

4 *Fisheries conservation.* This is an issue that is rarely described as 'environmental' either by the EU – which normally considers it a part of fisheries policy – or by commentators on EU policy. However, the EU's activities in regard to the conservation of fisheries are very much a part of the idea of managing natural resources (see Coffey, 1996), and a substantial body of law has been agreed aimed at managing and conserving European fisheries. It is time that these were seen as a central element of EU environmental policy.

The need to balance the demands of the fishing industry with diminishing fish stocks is at the core of the Common Fisheries Policy (CFP), finally fully developed in 1983 after several years of discussion. The first two regulations on fisheries were passed in 1983, setting up a Community system for the management of fishery resources, and establishing the necessary technical measures. A directive was also passed establishing the rules for recording information on fish catches. Conservation is now promoted through a permit system, the establishment of protected areas where fishing is restricted or banned, and the use of technical measures such as controls on the mesh size of nets and minimum sizes or weights for fish that are landed. Total allowable catches are fixed annually on the basis of studies of fish populations, and agreements have also been reached with third countries and international organizations on catches outside EU territorial waters.

The EU has also approved the terms of several international treaties on fisheries, such as the 1982 Reykjavik convention on north Atlantic salmon and the 1986 protocol to the Atlantic tuna convention. Furthermore, it has become a member of the Northwest Atlantic Fisheries Organization (a Canadian-based body set up in 1979 to promote the conservation of fisheries resources in the northwest Atlantic), and has developed plans for fisheries conservation in the Baltic, the Mediterranean and the Antarctic. In 1999, the Commission suggested to the Council of Ministers and Parliament that interactions between fisheries and marine ecosystems should be integrated into the

CFP, suggesting a trend towards closer identification of fisheries policy with environmental management policies.

5   *General provisions*. Not all EU environmental laws are focused on particular issues or problems; instead, nearly 30 have been passed to deal with broader organizational matters, including the following:

- projects to improve the quality of information, statistics, financial monitoring and reporting;
- the eco-management and audit scheme (EMAS), a voluntary programme aimed at promoting the use of environmental management systems and auditing by industry, and providing information on environmental performance to the public;
- institutional developments, such as the creation of the European Foundation for the improvement of living and working conditions in 1975, of the European Environment Agency in 1990, and of the European Green Forum in 1993;
- a 1985 directive on environmental impact assessment, aimed at encouraging evaluation of the environmental impact of public and private projects;
- programmes of action on the environment in the Mediterranean (MEDSPA) and the coastal waters of northern Europe (NORSPA);
- environmental funding projects, such as Actions by the Community Relating to the Environment (ACE), Actions by the Community for Nature (ACNAT), the financial instrument for the environment (LIFE), and the Cohesion Fund.

6   *Radiation*. Often ignored in most studies of EU environmental policy have been its activities – mainly under the aegis of the European Atomic Energy Community, or Euratom – in the field of protection from radiation and radioactivity. The first law passed by the Community on an environmental problem was a 1959 directive on ionizing radiation, which obliged Euratom to lay down standards for protecting the health of workers and the public from ionizing radiation, monitoring radioactivity in the air, water and soil, and keeping the Commission informed about plans for the disposal of radioactive waste. A 1975 directive launched a programme on the management and storage of radioactive waste, and the Community subsequently addressed issues such as the reprocessing of irradiated nuclear fuels, established conditions on imports from

third countries following the Chernobyl disaster, decided actions to be taken in the event of radiological emergencies or nuclear accidents, and set up procedures to be followed with shipments of radioactive wastes.

7   *Chemicals.* The control of dangerous chemicals and other substances has been at the heart of the single biggest body of EU environmental law – by the end of 1999, 109 laws (more than one in eight of all EU environmental laws) had the control of chemicals as their focus. Only 19 of these were new laws, however; the focus of Commission efforts has been on developing and amending about half a dozen key pieces of early legislation. EU chemicals policy has so far focused on four main areas of activity: the handling of new chemicals, accidents at chemical plants, the use of pesticides, and trade in dangerous chemicals.

Directive 67/548 on the classification, packaging and labelling of dangerous chemicals is often described (wrongly) as the first piece of Community environmental law, even though it was passed in order to clear the way for trade in chemicals rather than to protect the environment. Since amended nearly 40 times, the original directive was based on Article 100 of the Treaty of Rome (now Article 94), and was driven by concerns about barriers to free trade and by threats to human health, particularly the health of workers. There was no mention of environmental concerns in the early chemicals legislation, and the word 'environment' was only added to 67/548 with the sixth amendment in 1979 (79/831). This amendment also introduced a preventive element by requiring that producers or importers of more than one tonne per year of a new substance register the substance with the competent national authority, and that the registration must be recognized by all other member states. The list of substances covered by 67/548 has grown, and additional directives have been adopted dealing with specific substances, such as solvents, paints, varnishes and pesticides.

Restrictions have also been placed on the marketing and use of dangerous substances, such as PCBs, PCTs, benzene in toys and asbestos, and on pollution caused by asbestos and cadmium. Prompted by a number of headline-making industrial accidents in the 1970s – notably those at Flixborough in England and at Seveso in Italy – the Community adopted a 1982 directive on industries in fields related to chemicals or energy, obliging them to take every possible measure to prevent accidents, and requiring them to notify competent authorities if their activities involve dangerous substances. In the late 1980s and early 1990s a number of regulations were adopted aimed at controlling the import and export of dangerous chemicals.

In 1998, the Commission launched a thorough review of EU chemicals policy, prompted in part by pressure from several member states for a more proactive approach to controlling the risks and phasing out the use of hazardous chemicals, and in part by dissatisfaction among member states regarding the lack of progress in various areas of chemicals policy, such as the programme for assessing and managing the risks posed by existing chemicals (*ENDS Report* 279, April 1998, p. 39)

8   *Energy conservation.* EU energy policy is concerned mainly with managing sources and supplies, but since the late 1980s it has also included attention to the environmental consequences of energy exploitation and use. Measures to limit emissions from vehicles and industrial plants and to reduce the sulphur content of fuel have been driven by concerns over air quality, but can also be seen as early attempts to integrate environmental factors into energy policy. The Community began dabbling in 1978–80 with measures to reduce the energy consumption of household appliances and road vehicles, adopted a 1985 directive on reductions in oil consumption, and launched a programme in 1989 to promote efficient electricity use. However, it was only in the 1990s that more work was done on measures to promote energy conservation, partly under the SAVE and SAVE II programmes. The Commission and Parliament also began making calls in 1997–98 for increased use of renewable energy, to meet as much as 12–15 per cent of EU primary energy needs by 2010 (up from just under 7 per cent then), but the idea met with lukewarm responses from energy ministers and energy producers.

Undoubtedly the most controversial policy suggestion in the field of energy policy has been the carbon tax, which has first mooted in 1990. The idea was to impose a penalty on energy use, with the amount of tax varying according to the thermal content of the fuel; the income would then be used to promote the use of environmentally friendly energy sources. The tax was accepted in principle by energy and environment ministers in 1991, but there was strong opposition from the coal and oil industries, concerns that it would undermine competitiveness, and a veto from Britain which was opposed in principle to the idea of the EU being able to levy taxes (Matláry, 1997, pp. 68–70). The proposal had still not been formally withdrawn by the Commission as of mid-1999, but there were few prospects of it going through without – at a minimum – the Americans and the Japanese adopting the idea as well.

9   *Biodiversity.* The protection of biodiversity (wildlife and natural habitats) is one of the core issues of environmental policy at the national level, but has been a relatively recent addition to the EU agenda. Its late arrival was due in part to the early focus of the Community on problems related to industry, and in part to questions raised in the Council of Ministers about the legal basis of Community action given that it was moving away from the economic activities that were at the foundation of the Treaty of Rome. There was almost no mention of the issue in the First Environmental Action programme (EAP), and – according to Johnson and Corcelle (1995, p. 298) – it appeared in the Second EAP in large part because of pressure from the European Parliament. It is now regarded as a permanent part of the EU environmental agenda, but most of the laws adopted by the EU on the protection of wildlife and natural habitats have come in response to the terms of international treaties.

At the core of EU policy on biodiversity are two pieces of law: the 1979 directive on the conservation of wild birds, and the 1992 habitats directive. Using Article 235 (now 307) of the treaties as its legal justification, the former was based on the argument that many species of Europe's wild birds were declining, and that since most of them were migratory species, they were part of the common heritage of the Community, and an effective response demanded transboundary co-operation. Stretching a point, the directive also argued that the conservation of wild birds was a necessary part of the Community objectives of improving living conditions, and ensuring harmonious development of economic activities and a continuous and balanced expansion. The directive places a general duty on member states to maintain the populations of wild birds by creating protected areas, managing habitats, and prohibiting the killing or capture of vulnerable species, or damage to nests and eggs.

For its part, the 1992 habitats directive is aimed at encouraging the development of a comprehensive network of protected areas under the label Natura 2000, designed to promote the maintenance of threatened species and habitat types. Member states were asked to carry out an assessment of the listed types within their borders, then to submit a list to be considered as Sites of Community Importance.

Rather than being EU initiatives, most of the remaining laws and amendments dealing with biodiversity approve the terms of selected international treaties, notably the 1973 Convention on Trade in Endangered Species (3626/82 and multiple amendments), the 1979 Berne Convention on European Wildlife and Habitats (82/72), the 1979 Bonn Convention on Migratory Species (82/461), and the 1980 Canberra Convention on Antarctic Marine Living Resources (81/691).

10   *Pesticides*. Although they arguably come under chemicals policy, an entire sub-family of laws has been adopted on pesticides and their residues in foodstuffs. The first came in 1974, with a directive establishing maximum levels of pesticide residues in animal feed, and a second in 1976 did the same for fruit and vegetables. A 1978 directive introduced the same kinds of requirements on the classification, packaging and labelling of pesticides as were contained in directive 67/548 on dangerous chemicals, but the Community went a step further in 1979 by banning the use of certain pesticides and related products, including DDT and compounds of mercury (79/117). Human health was again at the heart of the directive, but environmental damage – particularly harm to birds and wildlife – was quoted as another motivation.

Relatively few pesticides were covered by the 1978 directive, and member states were allowed to ban other pesticides in their own territories and to establish maximum levels for pesticide residues in food, creating a messy situation in which inconsistent national laws and limits were allowed to coexist (Lister, 1996, p. 245). The result was the adoption of directive 91/414, which imposed standardized scientific reviews on all pesticides and their ingredients marketed in the Community, the goal being to create an EU-wide list of permitted products by 2003. The review process moved very slowly, however, prompting suggestions for a review of pesticides policy.

11 *Noise pollution.* It is debatable whether or not noise is really an environmental issue. It is only in exceptional circumstances that noise can cause any harm to humans or nature, thus it is arguably more a matter of public nuisance, in the same vein as offensive sights and smells. However, it is always described as an environmental issue by the Commission, and the EDG has a substantial number of staff working on making the EU a quieter place in which to live. The laws so far adopted have focused mainly on reducing the noise produced by motor vehicles, construction plant, aircraft and domestic appliances. In several cases, these laws were prompted by standards developed by international organizations such as the International Labour Organization (ILO) and the International Civil Aviation Organization (ICAO).

The first directive on noise came in 1970 and was aimed at motor vehicle exhausts. Its benefits were quickly cancelled out by the increase in the volume of urban road traffic, so later amendments – beginning in 1976 – imposed tighter controls. The target noise levels remained optional until 1992, when directive 92/97 made them mandatory. Meanwhile, directives were also adopted aimed at motorcycles and tractors, and a 1984 directive on construction plant led to a string of daughter directives on compressors, tower cranes, welding generators, power generators and concrete breakers. Encouraged by standards developed by the ICAO in the early 1970s, the Commission developed a directive on noise from subsonic aircraft (80/51), but failed to win agreement on limiting noise from helicopters or trains (Johnson and Corcelle, 1995, pp. 293–5). Following the adoption of a 1992 directive on aircraft, noise policy entered something of a state of limbo; in an attempt to give it new life, a draft directive on 55 types of outdoor equipment was published by the Commission in early 1998, and a framework directive on environmental noise measurement, mapping and control in late 1998.

12 *Genetically modified organisms* (GMOs). Like noise, there is some question whether or not genetic modification is an environmental issue. It can be when modifications made to one species are transferred by accident to another, but most of the public debate about GMOs in the member states has so far focused on public health, and most European consumers have been more worried about GMOs in the food they eat than

about their ecological impact. Furthermore, the Commission has made GMO policy the responsibility of the Health and Consumer Protection DG rather than the Environment DG. Nonetheless, it is still defined by the Commission as one of its environmental priorities.

The genetic modification of plants – for example to improve their productivity and their resistance to disease – only became a mainstream public issue in the mid-1990s, but the EU institutions had already been addressing the matter for several years. The Commission announced plans to develop proposals for the management of GMOs in 1986, and the first two pieces of law were adopted in 1990: a directive on the contained use of GMOs in laboratories and similar situations, and a directive on their deliberate release, both of which have since been amended several times. The first directive focuses on controlling routine releases to the outside environment in wastes, for example, and accidental releases which might affect the health of workers, nearby populations or the environment, while the second covers experimental release and the use of GMOs in products. The second directive in particular has caused delays in the marketing of GMOs, drawing complaints from the European biotechnology industry which argues that it is being placed at a disadvantage to North American and Japanese competitors.

13   *Forestry*. The EU has not been significantly involved in forestry management, limiting itself to the development of programmes to protect forests from pollution and fire. The former began in 1987 and is based on the development of a forest observation network designed to produce inventories of damage and to improve understanding of the effects of pollution and of methods of restoring damaged forests. The latter began in 1992 and is aimed at promoting fire prevention and forest monitoring measures. The EU has also been working since 1989 to set up a European Forestry Information and Communication System to collect data on the forestry industry.

While forestry management is still seen as very much a domestic matter for the member states, except where transboundary pollution has caused forest dieback and the death of trees, this may be about to change. In November 1998 the Commission adopted a communication (Com(98)649) on a forestry strategy for the EU. Based primarily on Agenda 2000 proposals for Eastern European enlargement, it suggested protecting and restoring the ecological quality of forests and extending the present area of exploitable forest. It also noted the potential of forests as a source of biomass for energy generation. While agriculture ministers endorsed the proposal, however, they emphasized that forestry policy was still the preserve of the member states (*European Policy Analyst*, 1st quarter 1999, pp. 54–5).

14   *Organic agriculture.* The Common Agricultural Policy (CAP) was initially concerned almost exclusively with protecting the economic interests of farmers, and with providing them with a guaranteed minimum income for their produce. Because this also tended to encourage factory farming and the use of chemical fertilizers and pesticides, the CAP was long the focus of criticism from environmental groups, but little was done other than to respond to the impact of intensive agriculture. For example, a 1985 regulation (797/85) introduced the concept of environmentally sensitive farming into the CAP, and a 1991 directive (91/676) imposed controls on nitrates.

By the 1990s, organic agriculture had begun to appear on the EU policy agenda, the core of its programme being regulation 2092/91 which came as a response to the growing consumer demand for organic produce and to the argument by the Commission that rules were needed on production, labelling and inspection in order to promote fair competition. Given the new emphasis on integrating environmental considerations into all the other activities of the EU, issues such as organic farming are likely to continue to move up the policy agenda.

This brief survey of EU environmental policy shows that European activity on environmental issues has been far broader than EU institutions themselves admit, and than most commentators appreciate. While the literature on EU environmental policy has been mainly restricted to issues such as air and water quality, waste management, chemicals and pesticides, the EU has been active in the conservation of fisheries, reducing the impact of radiation on human health, conserving energy, protecting wildlife and promoting organic agriculture. While the EU lacks a comprehensive environmental policy, it has developed an increasingly coherent set of policies in a growing variety of areas that come under the general rubric of the 'environment'.

At the same time, its activities in this area have drawn increased political and public attention. The next chapter will show that the restricted definition of 'environmental' used by the Community – and then by the EU – was a result of the initial focus on developing environmental policies because of concerns about the effect of different environmental standards on the internal market, and as a means to protecting human health. More recently, environmental policies have been driven more by concerns about the state of the environment, and by the argument that many environmental problems are better dealt with by the member states working in concert rather than separately. The result has been a switch in the focus of law and policy towards environmental management in its own right.

Chapter 2

Policy Evolution

The environment was a latecomer to the policy agenda of European integration. Just as most national governments in the 1950s and 1960s paid little attention to the environmental implications of economic development, so the construction of the EEC was driven primarily by the quantitative dimensions of building the common market, with relatively little attention paid to its qualitative aspects. Such action as the Community took on environmental matters before 1972 was incidental to the central goal of removing the barriers to trade, and focused on harmonizing national environmental laws with a view to removing obstacles to that goal. During this period, the EEC lacked a sense that it was building an environmental 'policy', if a policy is defined as an inclusive and rational set of management objectives.

However, just as many national governments began turning their attention to the environment in the 1970s, so too did the EEC. The institutional structure of the European Commission was changed so as to give greater definition to the development and implementation of environmental law and policy, decisions by the Court of Justice helped provide more focus to the legal basis of that policy, action programmes on the environment were published which outlined the general goals and principles of Community policy, the body of environmental law grew, and a number of landmark laws were passed dealing with such issues as air and water quality and waste production. In 1987, the Single European Act confirmed that environmental management was one of the formal policy goals of European integration, finally giving the Community a legal base from which to proceed. Thereafter, environmental management was promoted more often as a goal in its own right rather than as an activity that was incidental to the single market.

Since 1987, EU environmental policy has matured, and has moved steadily up the agenda of European integration. There is little question any longer that this is a policy area in which the EU should be involved, and that the EU has often encouraged a higher level of environmental protection within the member states than might otherwise have been the case. By the late 1990s, the Commission was beginning to take a broader strategic approach to environmental issues, and was developing new instruments for environmental protection more suited to the nature of regional problems. It had begun to propose fewer new laws, instead focusing more attention on improving the record on the implementation of existing laws, and it was becoming a more active participant in its own right in negotiations on international and global problems. Finally, data gathered by the European Environment Agency was providing a better idea of the extent of environmental problems and of the progress (or lack of progress) on the part of the member states in addressing those problems.

The environment is now one of the primary policy interests of the EU, and is not only the subject of a substantial body of law, but is also one of the only four policy areas that must be considered in the development of all EU policy (the others being consumer protection, culture and health). From a time when the Commission responded in a piecemeal fashion to a limited set of environmental problems – and mainly in the interests of removing barriers to free trade and the common market – it is now involved in developing a more strategic approach to environmental issues, and in building something that comes much closer to a true environmental policy.

Phase I: focus on the common market (1957–72)

The three European Communities began life as experiments in economic integration, with relatively narrow and specific objectives. The work of the six founding member states was mainly quantitative in the sense that European integration was driven primarily by a desire to promote economic cooperation and development. While 'an accelerated standard of living' was one of the fundamental goals of the Treaty of Rome, priority was given during the 1960s to the development of a common market, common external tariffs, and common policies on such issues as transport, agriculture and investment. Qualitative issues such as the improvement of working conditions and education were lower on the list of priorities.

There was no reference to the environment in any of the writings or speeches of Jean Monnet, Robert Schuman or Paul-Henri Spaak, nor in the conclusions of the Messina Conference or the Spaak Committee which preceded the Treaties of Rome, nor in the 1951 Treaty of Paris or the 1957 Treaties of Rome. As far as national governments in Europe in the 1950s were concerned, the environment was a policy issue whose significance varied from marginal to non-existent. Article 36 of the EEC treaty even seemed to set the scene for the eventual treatment of environmental protection as a national matter. It made the reactive argument that Articles 30–34 (prohibiting restrictions on trade) should not preclude restrictions on imports and exports on grounds of 'the protection of health and life of humans, animals or plants', a clause which is interpreted by Rehbinder and Stewart (1988, p. 16) as an implication that 'the basic competence for environmental protection is vested in the member states'.

The earliest initiatives on the environment arose out of the Euratom treaty which, while it was concerned mainly with research, investment and supplies, makes reference in Article 2(b) to the need to 'establish uniform safety standards to protect the health of workers *and of the general public*' (emphasis added). More specifically, Article 30 of the Euratom treaty mentions the need to lay down basic standards 'for the protection of the health of workers *and the general public* against the dangers arising from ionising radiation'. In 1959, this was used as the basis for the first piece of European environmental law, Directive 59/221, which established the basic standards for the protection of the health of workers and the public against the dangers arising from ionizing radiation.

Most of the earliest pieces of Community environmental law came out of creative interpretations of the Preamble to the EEC treaty, and combinations of Articles 2, 100 and/or 235. While the treaty gave the Communities 'competence' (legal powers or responsibility) over very few specific policy areas, and economic integration was clearly the first order of business, the Preamble did include reference to the importance of 'the constant improvement of the living and working conditions' of the peoples of the member states. Article 2 included among the tasks of the Community the promotion of 'a harmonious development of economic activities, a continuous and balanced expansion, an increase in stability, [and] an accelerated raising of the standard of living'.

For its part, Article 100 authorized the Council of Ministers, acting unanimously on a proposal from the European Commission, to 'issue directives for the approximation of such provisions laid down by law, regulation or administrative action in Member States as directly affect the establishment or functioning of the common market'. In other words, it might be argued that differences in environmental standards constituted a barrier to free trade, and should be addressed by harmonization. Initially, the Commission took the Article to mean that it could only react to an action by a member state that affected the common market, but legal writers subsequently argued that the Commission could use it proactively to propose measures even in areas where no legislation already existed in the member states (see Rehbinder and Stewart, 1985).

Finally, Article 235 allowed the Council of Ministers – in consultation with the Commission and Parliament – to take appropriate measures 'if action by the Community should prove necessary to attain, in the course of the operation of the common market, one of the objectives of the Community and this Treaty has not provided the necessary powers'. This was clearly a back door into the treaty that was looser in its requirements than Article 100 (which, for example, limited the Community to the adoption of directives), and has been described as a 'juristic artifice' (Freestone, 1991). Among its strangest results was the claim in the recitals to directive 79/409 (concerning the hunting, capture and killing of wild birds) that conserving wild birds was necessary 'to attain, within the operation of the common market, the Community's objectives regarding the improvement of living conditions, a harmonious development of economic activities throughout the Community, and a continuous and balanced expansion'.

The few specific environmental initiatives taken in this first phase consisted of the following:

- One directive and two amendments (59/221, 62/1633 and 66/45) developed by Euratom on the basis of Article 30 of the Euratom treaty, establishing standards to protect workers and the public from ionizing radiation;
- Laws driven by controversial and debatable readings of Article 100 (for more details, see Rehbinder and Stewart, 1988, pp. 21–6), and resulting in two directives on vehicle emissions (70/220 and 72/306), one on noise from vehicle exhausts (70/157), and the directive that is most often (but wrongly) described as the Community's first piece of environmental legislation – directive 67/548 on the classification, packaging and labelling of dangerous chemicals (together with one amendment). Illustrating the motives behind this early legislation, directive 70/220 on carbon monoxide and hydrocarbon emissions from road vehicles was agreed in response to legislative proposals in West Germany and France that would have tightened their national vehicle emission controls, thereby threatening uniform European standards (Rehbinder and Stewart, 1988, p. 17).

A glance at these initiatives, combined with a reading of the Treaties of Paris and Rome, shows quite clearly that – in this first phase – such environmental measures as were agreed were unconnected elements in the general drive to harmonize the national laws of the member states, and that they were incidental to the primary goal of building a common market. The preamble to most of the earliest pieces of EU environmental law noted the dangers of creating 'unequal conditions of competition . . . [which might] affect the functioning of the common market'. By the end of the 1960s, however, it was becoming clear to many in western Europe and North America that hopes for an improved standard of living were being compromised by environmental deterioration, making it difficult for the Community to ignore the problem, and ultimately compelling it to approach the environment as a policy issue in its own right.

Phase II: the environmental revolution (1973–86)

One of the consequences of the political, economic and social changes that took place in industrialized states in the late 1960s was that environmental issues moved further up the agendas of international organizations and national governments alike. Western publics began to criticize the postwar focus on material growth and affluence, were made aware of the limits to that growth, and began raising questions about the quality of their lives. The change of emphasis was symbolized by the widespread rejection among the younger generation of the values (as they understood them) of older generations, and of popular support for issues such as the civil rights movement in the United States, and opposition to the war in Vietnam and all that it represented. The work of the Club of Rome – published as *The Limits to Growth* (Meadows *et al.*, 1972) – concluded that the roots of the environmental crisis lay in exponential growth, and that the exhaustion of resources would lead to catastrophe, a point that was briefly underlined by the economic and energy crises of 1973–74.

With this new focus on qualitative policy issues, it was not surprising that there should be public concern about environmental deterioration. The extent to which human activities had caused systemic problems with potentially harmful consequences for almost everyone in industrialized societies had already been illustrated in 1962 with the publication of *Silent Spring* by Rachel Carson, which drew public attention to the harmful effects of chemical pesticides and insecticides. Subsequently, a series of newsworthy disasters graphically underlined the negative impact of human activity on the environment: the pit-heap collapse in the town of Aberfan in Wales in 1966, the wreck of the oil tanker *Torrey Canyon* off southwest England in 1967, the blowout of an oil well off the coast near Santa Barbara, California, in 1969, and emerging news during the 1960s of the effects on human health of the contamination of fish by mercury and other chemicals in the sea near the town of Minamata in Japan.

A political focus for the new interest in the environment was provided by the 1972 United Nations Conference on the Human Environment, held in Stockholm. For the first time, representatives of a substantial number of national governments (113 in all) met to discuss the problems of the environment, and agreed that the scale of such problems was worsening, and that the need for international cooperation in formulating a response was growing (for details, see McCormick, 1995, chapter 3).

This led to a strengthening of domestic laws in EEC member states, notably Germany and the Netherlands, which led in turn to a growing realization among Community leaders that the strengthening of national environmental law was accelerating the creation of actual or potential trade distortions that posed a threat to the construction of the common market. The issue was first formally raised in a July 1971 communication from the Commission to the Council of Ministers.

Lodge argues that the new interest in a Community environmental policy was 'spurred not so much by an upsurge of post-industrial values ... or to give the EC a "human face" as by the realisation that widely differing national rules on industrial pollution could distort competition' (1989, p. 320). However, the words and actions of European leaders suggest that at least some of them were looking at the bigger picture. Meeting at a summit conference in Paris in October 1972, the heads of government of the six founding EEC member states and the three 'adherent' states (Britain, Denmark and Ireland) agreed that economic expansion was not an end in itself, and that Community activities on the environment should be accelerated. The conclusions of the summit gave a little more focus to Article 2 of the Treaty of Rome by noting that economic expansion 'should result in an improvement in the quality of life as well as in standards of living ... [and] particular attention will be given to intangible values and to protecting the environment'.

As was the case with much of the content of the concluding statements of Community summits (institutionalized as the European Council in 1975), this was a very general sentiment that could be interpreted in any number of ways. In retrospect, however, it can be seen as marking the beginning of a more structured EEC approach to the environment, which was given more substance in 1973 by three initiatives: the creation of a small Environment and Consumer Protection Service (ECPS) within DGIII (the directorate-general of the Commission responsible for industrial policy), the creation of a Committee on the Environment in the European Parliament, and the request from its members that Community institutions draw up an environmental action programme.

The latter was duly drafted, and adopted in November 1973 as the Programme of Action of the European Communities on the Environment (now known as the First Environmental Action Programme (EAP)). Designed to run until 1976, the EAP was not a comprehensive policy statement, nor was it legally binding. However, it outlined principles and set objectives, and thus was the first step in the construction of a Community policy. Economic motives were still to the fore; the Programme noted that the task of the EEC was

> to promote throughout the Community a harmonious development of economic activities and a continuous and balanced expansion, which cannot now be imagined in the absence of an effective campaign to combat pollution and nuisances or of an improvement in the quality of life and the protection of the environment . . . [It] is therefore necessary to implement a Community environment policy.

The Second EAP was adopted in 1977 to cover the period 1977–81, and built on the general policy directions outlined in its predecessor. While neither Action Programme gave the EEC legal competence in the area of environmental policy, they established several principles that are still at the core of EU environmental policy, including the following:

- Because prevention is better than cure (a statement that marked a shift in Community priorities away from remediation), environmental impacts should be considered at the earliest possible stage in decision-making.
- Because the standard of scientific and technological knowledge should be improved with a view to taking effective action, research should be encouraged.
- With some exceptions, the polluter should pay.
- Activities in one member state should not cause deterioration in the environment of another, member states should coordinate their national programmes rather than developing them in isolation, and national policies should be harmonized within the Community.
- The Community and the member states should be active in international organizations dealing with the environment, and a common point of view would give them greater authority and effectiveness.
- In the spirit of the principle of subsidiarity, pollution control should be carried out at the appropriate level.

These developments might have given the Community more direction and power, and helped produce a growing volume of legislative output from the Commission, but – as Krämer observes (1996, p. 298) – there was little legal or political foundation on which to build, so the 'methods, tools and instruments for policy design and implementation had first to be invented and tested'.

The primary legal justification continued to be sought in creative interpretations of Articles 100 and 235 of the EEC Treaty, sometimes alone and sometimes together. The validity of using Article 100 was upheld by the Court of Justice in a March 1980 decision (*Commission* v. *Italy*, Case 91/79) concerning a 1973 directive (73/404) on the biodegradability of detergents. The Italian government argued that it did not have to meet the deadline provided by the directive because it dealt with the protection of the environment, which was not part of the Community's competence, and therefore was less a directive than a special form of international convention. In responding, the Court argued that 'provisions which are made necessary by considerations relating to the environment and health may be a burden upon the undertakings to which they apply and if there is no harmonisation of national provisions on the matter, competition may be appreciably distorted'.

The Court reached another important decision in February 1985 (*Procureur de la République* v. *Association de Défense des Bruleurs d'Huiles Usagées (ADBHU)*, Case 240/83). Under directive 75/439 on waste oils, which was based on Articles 100 and 235, member states were required to set up a safe system for their disposal, which meant establishing zones within which licensed companies could collect and/or dispose of the oil 'where appropriate in the zone assigned to them by the competent authorities'. This notion was challenged by the French association of oil burners (ADBHU) on the grounds that the imposition of a system of permits and zones was incompatible with the principle of the free movement of goods. This was overruled by the Court, which argued that the principle of freedom of trade was not absolute but was subject to certain limits, and that those limits had not been exceeded. It went a step further by stating that the directive 'must be seen in the perspective of environmental

TABLE 2.1   *The evolution of EU environmental activity*

Phase I (1957–72)

1959   Passage of first Euratom environmental law (Directive 59/221)
1967   Passage of first EEC environmental law (Directive 67/548)
1972   (June) United Nations Conference on the Human Environment, Stockholm; (October) EEC heads of government agree that Community environmental activities should be accelerated

Phase II (1973–86)

1973   Creation of Environment and Consumer Protection Service in DGIII; creation of Committee on the Environment in European Parliament; adoption of First Environmental Action Programme (1973–76)
1974   Creation of the European Environmental Bureau
1977   Adoption of Second Environmental Action Programme (1977–81)
1980   Court of Justice decision *Commission* v. *Italy* (91/79) upholds validity of using Article 100 of Treaty of Rome as justification for Community environmental law
1981   Creation of DGXI
1983   Adoption of Third Environmental Action Programme (1982–86); (April) barrels of waste from Seveso accident found
1984   Creation of COE, first Community environment fund
1985   Court of Justice decision *Procureur de la République* v. *ADBHU* (240/83) confirms that environmental protection is one of 'essential objectives' of the Community; European Council confirms importance of Community environmental policy; Creation of CORINE

Phase III (1987–92)

1987   Single European Act adds Title VII (Environment) to Treaty of Rome, and extends qualified majority voting to environmental proposals; adoption of Fourth Environmental Action Programme (1987–92); European Year of the Environment

TABLE 2.1 *Continued*

1988	Creation of ACE, second Community environment fund
1989	Creation of separate portfolio for the environment in the European Commission; creation of PHARE programme
1990	Creation of ACNAT, third Community environment fund; decision taken to create European Environment Agency
1992	Creation of LIFE, fourth Community environment fund; United Nations Conference on Environment and Development, Rio de Janeiro; creation of IMPEL

Phase IV (1993–)

1993	Maastricht treaty lists the environment as a policy goal of the EU; adoption of Fifth Environmental Action Programme (1993–2000); European Environment Agency begins work; creation of General Consultative Forum on the Environment
1994	Creation of Cohesion Fund
1995	Publication of the first triennial report on state of the environment (Dobris Assessment)
1997	Creation of European Consultative Forum on Environment and Development (European Green Forum)
1998	Publication of the second triennial report on state of the environment; Creation of AC-IMPEL
1999	Amsterdam treaty makes sustainable development a goal of the EU; as part of the Prodi reforms, DGXI renamed Environment DG

protection, *which is one of the Community's essential objectives*' (emphasis added). The Court thereby established that environmental protection was a core concern of the Community, and confirmed that Article 235 could not only be used as a supplementary legal basis to Article 100, but as the legal basis for Community environmental policy (Jans, 1996, p. 274).

As the legal basis for EC action changed, so did the institutional arrangements. Veteran bureaucrats in the Commission remember the late 1970s as being a good time for moving legislative proposals through the decision-making system to adoption – there were still only nine member states, and the political and economic stakes were not as high as they were subsequently to become. One veteran recalls that he and his colleagues felt like pioneers, that there were substantial funds available to carry out studies prior to making legislative proposals, and that the Commission process was 'much less bureaucratic' than it was to become. Circumstances began to change with Greek accession to the Community in 1981, which was instrumental in a decision to reorganize the Commission so that every member state could have a directorship-general; the ECPS was upgraded to become a directorate-general in its own right (DGXI), and its workload began to increase. A reorganization of the College of Commissioners led to the creation of a new portfolio for transport and the environment, which went to Stanley Clinton Davis of Britain in 1985–89. In 1989, a separate environment portfolio was created for the first time, and was given to Carlo Ripa de Meana of Italy.

The new interest of the Community in environmental matters became evident in the relative flood of new legislation emanating from the Commission; in the period 1973–82, more than 110 regulations, directives and decisions were adopted, covering issues as varied as water quality, air quality and the disposal of hazardous wastes, and including what remain to this day some of the most important pieces of European environmental law:

- Directive 75/440, establishing the principles and standards necessary to improve drinking water quality (which was later defined by Directive 80/778).
- Directives 75/442 and 78/319 on waste production, disposal and recovery.
- Directive 76/464, regulating discharges of dangerous substances into surface water (and introducing the concept of best available technology, or BAT), and Directive 80/68, which did the same for groundwater.
- Directive 79/409 on the protection of wild birds and their eggs, nests and habitats.
- Directive 79/831, the sixth amendment to Directive 67/548 on the classification, packaging and labelling of dangerous substances. This amendment introduced requirements for pre-marketing notification of new substances.

- Directive 80/779 on sulphur dioxide and suspended particulates, the first piece of Community-wide legislation to establish mandatory air quality standards.
- Directive 82/884, setting Community-wide limits on lead concentrations in the air.

Three events in 1983 prompted a quickening of the pace by which Community environmental policy was institutionalized. The first was the adoption of the Third Environmental Action Programme to cover the period 1982–86. While it built on its predecessors, it also introduced new concepts, the most significant of which was that environmental policy should be integrated into the other sectoral policies of the Community. The Programme also listed priorities for the first time; these included the use of environmental impact assessments, the reduction of pollution at source with a view to preventing air, freshwater, marine and soil pollution in particular, the reduction of noise pollution, control of transfrontier pollution and chemicals, control of waste (especially toxic and dangerous waste), the development of clean technologies, the protection of environmentally sensitive areas, and cooperation with developing countries on environmental matters.

The second event was an incident in 1983 which not only drew renewed public attention to the threats posed to the European environment, but also led to a change in awareness within the Commission. Drums of hazardous waste thought to contain dioxin and originating from Seveso in northern Italy (the site of an industrial accident in 1976) went missing in 1982, and later surfaced in northern France (see Chapter 6). The European Parliament set up a committee of inquiry into the incident (the Pruvot Committee), which censured the Commission for having failed to live up to its responsibilities in overseeing the implementation of Community law, specifically a 1978 directive on the harmonization of arrangements for the disposal of toxic and dangerous waste (78/319). Implementation now became of much more concern to the Commission, and the legal unit of DGXI was expanded, subsequently becoming considerably more active in pursuing the implementation of EU law (Haigh and Lanigan, 1995).

The third event was the conclusion of the European Council summit in Stuttgart in June 1983. Germany had the presidency at the time, and Community leaders were meeting against a background of rising concern about news regarding the effects of air pollution on German forests, and of rising support for the Greens, who had won their first seats in the Bundestag in March. With West German prompting, the Council adopted a declaration recognizing 'the urgent necessity of accelerating and reinforcing action at national, Community and international level aimed at combating the pollution of the environment. It underlines in particular the acute danger threatening the European forest areas, which calls for immediate action'.

The impetus for change was maintained at the March 1985 European Council in Brussels (during the Italian presidency). While its decision to complete the single market by 1992 stole the headlines, the Council, 'having acknowledged that [environmental] policy can contribute to improved economic growth and job creation . . . affirms its determination to give this policy the dimension of an essential component of the economic, industrial, agricultural and social policies implemented by the Community and by its Member States'. It also acknowledged the need for member states 'to take coherent action in the Community framework to protect the air, the sea and the soil, where isolated action is unlikely to prove effective and may even be harmful'. Finally, it decided to declare 1987 the European Year of the Environment in an attempt to draw more public attention to the European dimensions of environmental protection.

Environmental policy was given a further boost with changes in the balance of political power arising out of the expansion of Community membership in the 1980s. During the era of the Nine, there had been a tension created by the environmental activism of Germany, the Netherlands and Denmark, the reticence of the UK and Ireland, and the 'neutrality' of the remaining members (Johnson and Corcelle, 1995, p. 8). The accession of Greece in 1981, and of Spain and Portugal in 1986, combined with the back-door accession of East Germany in 1990, changed the balance of economic and political interests towards countries for which economic development was a priority, where records on environmental protection were poor, and where bodies of national environmental law were weak. Financial assistance programmes were created to help the poorer states, and derogations from the requirements of Community law became more common – for example, Greece, Ireland and

Portugal were allowed to increase emissions of sulphur dioxide and nitrogen oxides under the 1988 large combustion plant directive, while all other member states had to make large reductions (see Chapter 8).

The production of legislative proposals by the Commission meanwhile continued to accelerate, and their focus began to change. While those in the 1970s had been aimed largely at limiting pollution and 'nuisances', and taking a curative or 'command and control' approach, by the mid-1980s the EC had moved more towards a preventive approach (Johnson and Corcelle, 1995, pp. 4–5). Prevention, for example, was behind the environmental assessment directive (85/337), and behind laws on the provision of financial aid for the development of clean technologies (1872/84). In the period 1983–86, nearly 100 new regulations, directives and decisions were adopted, once again including substantial pieces of legislation:

- Directive 84/360 limiting emissions from large industrial plants.
- Directive 84/631 on the transfrontier shipment of hazardous waste.
- Directive 85/203 on air quality standards for nitrogen dioxide.
- Directive 85/210 on the lead content of petrol.
- Directive 85/337 on environmental impact assessments.
- Directive 85/338 creating CORINE (Coordination Information Environment), a programme for gathering and co-ordinating information on the state of environment.
- Regulation 797/85 introducing the concept of environmentally sensitive farming into the Common Agricultural Policy.

Phase III: the EU establishes legal competence (1987–92)

Lacking either a legal basis or any truly structured sense of direction, the Commission approach to environmental issues until the mid-1980s was piecemeal and reactive, with a tendency to address problems on an *ad hoc* basis that depended largely on a combination of opportunism and the personal preferences of DGXI officials or incumbent environment Commissioners. The turning point came in 1987 when environmental protection was finally recognized as part of the legal competence of the Community with the passage of the Single European Act (SEA). Although the key objective of the SEA was the accelerated completion of the single market and the final removal of all remaining barriers to the free movement of people, money, goods and services by the end of 1992, the SEA also had four important effects on how environmental policy was made.

First, it responded to the lack of a clear legal base for Community environmental policy by introducing a new Title VII (Environment) to the Treaty of Rome, the consequence of which was to move environmental policy from being a *de facto* element of Community policy to a *de jure* element. Community goals were defined in Article 130r as preserving, protecting and improving the quality of the environment, helping protect human health, and ensuring rational use of natural resources. These were very broad objectives, but they allowed the Commission to start making legislative proposals in areas where they had not yet been active, such as the protection of natural habitats, and freedom of access to environmental information (Haigh and Baldock, 1989, p. 20). There was a reiteration of the principles of taking preventive action, rectifying environmental damage at source, and ensuring that polluters paid, but – more significantly in policy terms – the SEA also confirmed that 'environmental protection requirements shall be a component of the Community's other policies' (Article 130r(2)). In no other area of Community policy at that time was there such a sweeping proviso, and it greatly increased the powers of DGXI both in proposing new laws and in checking on the environmental impact of laws and policies being developed in other parts of the Commission.

Second, the SEA *appeared* to extend qualified majority voting (QMV) in the Council of Ministers to environmental proposals. Because most pieces of environmental legislation before 1987 were based on Articles 100 and 235 and required unanimity, not only could one member state block legislation, but more time had to be invested in developing proposals acceptable to all the member states, and there was always the danger that legislation might have to be watered down to the level of the lowest common denominator. In other words, the final content of the law would impose only minimal requirements on member states, leaving it to individual countries to decide if they wanted to adopt tighter domestic measures so long as these were not a barrier to the creation of the single market. With QMV, it would be impossible for any one member state to block a proposal, so reluctant member states would be obliged to work harder to reach agreement.

Unfortunately, the relevant section of the SEA (Article 100a) was ambiguous on where QMV or unanimity should apply, and the Commission and the Council of Ministers applied different interpretations. It took a Court of Justice decision to clarify the matter. In *Commission* v. *Council* (Case 300/89), the Court ruled in June 1991 that directive 89/428 (establishing procedures for harmonizing the reduction and elimination of pollution by waste from the titanium oxide industry) was void, on the grounds that because its main purpose was the improvement of conditions of competition in the titanium dioxide industry, and because it therefore concerned the establishment and functioning of the single market, it should have been based on Article 100a (which could be approved by a QMV) rather than Article 130s (one of the environmental provisions added by the SEA). Directive 89/428 was subsequently replaced by 92/112.

Third, with the environmental interests of the Community now much more firmly expressed, the Commission no longer had to rely for its legal justification on the twilight world between Articles 100 and 235, and the role of DGXI – until then a relatively minor actor in the Commission bureaucracy – was fundamentally altered. It now became more involved in tracking the progress of legislative proposals as they moved from one institution to another, and in liaising with those institutions to ensure that they considered the environmental impact of their deliberations. It was able to build on the already extensive body of EU legislation to exert its powers more effectively, and other DGs began to appreciate that DGXI was not as weak and peripheral as it had been, but was taking decisions that had an impact on the work of many other parts of the Commission (Haigh and Lanigan, 1995).

Finally, as the competence of the Community in environmental policy was more tightly defined, a new emphasis began to be placed on the importance of objective and reliable information as a foundation for effective policy. The importance of the preventive and precautionary approach to environmental management emphasized the need for more and better scientific and technical information, including more reliable assessments of current conditions and improved methods for monitoring change. Arguments along these lines were made at the December 1988 European Council meeting in Rhodes, and were supported by the Environment Committee in Parliament. In a speech before Parliament in early 1989, Commission president Jacques Delors promised to set up 'a European measurement and control network . . . responsible for measurement, verification, information and sounding the alert' (European Commission, 1989, p. 14). A regulation was developed by the Commission, and adopted as 1210/90 in 1990, making a commitment to establish a European Environment Agency (EEA).

The launch of the Agency was delayed because of a tussle involving France's refusal to agree a site for the headquarters of the Agency pending a decision that the plenary meeting chamber of the European Parliament would be based permanently in Strasbourg. The EEA finally began work in 1993 from offices in Copenhagen, with Domingo Jiménez-Beltrán as its first executive director. Its work is not restricted to the EU, but covers the whole of Europe. Its job is to collect, process and provide the Commission in particular with the information needed to identify and develop new legislative and policy proposals, and to take up the work of CORINE. One of its specific obligations is to produce triennial reports on the state of the European environment. Earlier reports had been published in 1986 and 1992, but the EEA reports were more thorough and authoritative. The first was published in 1995 as *Europe's Environment: The Dobris Assessment* (Stanners and Bourdeau, 1995), which drew on a series of pan-European ministerial conferences in Dublin (1990), Dobris Castle in the Czech Republic (1991) and Lucerne (1993). The second was published in 1998 (EEA, 1998).

The impact of the SEA on Community environmental policy was strengthened by the publication of the Fourth Environmental Action Programme (1987–92) (*Official Journal*, C.238, 7.12.87). This emphasized the need to set environmental quality standards, and the importance of implementing Community law. It built on principles that had appeared in early EAPs, and added a number of new goals including the management of natural resources, notably soil, and coastal and mountain zones.

Another important development since the late 1980s has been the emergence of the European Commission as an actor on the international environmental stage. Several Community decisions and regulations dating back to the mid-1970s had been agreed as a means of implementing the terms of international treaties of which the Community was a signatory; these included 75/437 on marine pollution from land-based sources, 81/462 on transboundary air pollution, and 86/238 on Atlantic tuna. The process of working to develop agreements among the member states led the Commission to appreciate more fully the central role it had to play in international negotiations, and the Commission moved from trying to reconcile the needs of the member states to actively helping negotiate and draft international agreements. The change was summarized by the proclamation at the 1990 Dublin summit of the European Council that the Community, 'as one of the leading collaborations of the world . . . has a special responsibility to protect and enhance the natural environment not just of the Community itself but of the world of which it is a part'. The treaties exhort the EU to ensure the consistency of its external activities only in fields such as security and economic and development policies, but the Commission has nonetheless played a leading role in discussions at fora such as the 1990 World Climate Conference, the 1992 UN Conference on Environment and Development in Rio de Janeiro (the Earth Summit), and the meetings among parties to the Climate Change Convention (see Chapter 10).

Another important development in Phase III was the strengthening of the Community's ability to finance environmental management projects. The first Community environment fund – Community Operations Concerning the Environment (COE) – had been established by regulation 1872/84 in 1984, and provided support for projects aimed at developing new technologies and protecting sensitive areas. It was superceded in 1988 by Actions by the Community Relating to the Environment (ACE), which set aside 24 million ecu over four years for environmental projects, but which was curtailed prematurely in 1990 to make way for an even bigger project – Actions by the Community for Nature (ACNAT) – focused on maintaining or reestablishing threatened habitats and endangered species.

Meanwhile, more focused projects made funds available for

the Mediterranean (MEDSPA) and the North Sea (NORSPA). These were all replaced in 1992 by LIFE (*L'Instrument Financier pour l'Environnement*), which allocated 400 million ecu over three years for projects that included the promotion of sustainable development, new clean technologies, waste storage and disposal, and habitat protection. Until the establishment of the Cohesion Fund (see below), LIFE was the closest the Community had come to the creation of a structural fund for the environment (Salter, 1995, p. 5/91).

The growing importance of EU institutions in the generation of environmental laws and policies has been reflected in the growth of activities by interest groups working at the European level. The environmental lobby in Brussels is still modest in size – less than a dozen groups have opened offices there – but most of the growth has taken place since the passage of the Single European Act. The oldest environmental group is the European Environmental Bureau (EEB), founded in 1974 to act as an umbrella for local, national and regional groups. It worked in a vacuum until 1986, when it was joined by Friends of the Earth, which was followed in 1988 by Greenpeace, in 1989 by the World Wide Fund for Nature and Climate Network Europe, in 1992 by the Transport and Environment Federation, and in 1993 by Birdlife International (Long, 1998, p. 107). At the same time, an expanding community of groups representing the interests of industry has become active in Brussels, including such bodies as CEFIC (the European Chemical Industry Council), CONCAWE (representing the oil industry), the European Federation of Waste Management, and EUREAU (representing water suppliers) (see Chapter 4).

The Commission has long been a champion of the role of non-governmental organizations (NGOs) in the policy-making process, and has provided them with considerable assistance. For example, it has funded the EEB since its creation and prompted the foundation in 1993 of the General Consultative Forum on the Environment, designed to provide representatives of NGOs, industry, business, local authorities, trade unions and academia with a channel through which they could advise the Commission on policy development. Now known more commonly as the European Green Forum, its membership has been expanded to non-EU states, and it has been given increased independence. Also in 1997, an EU decision (97/872) set aside nearly three million ecus in annual funding for European-level environmental NGOs.

Meanwhile, public opinion has been supportive of the role of the EU in environmental policy. While debates have continued to rage about the merits of the expanding powers of the EU and its activities – for example, in the social sphere – relatively few doubts apparently remain in the minds of Europeans about the value of EU activity in the field of the environment. Recent Eurobarometer polls have consistently found that about 80 per cent of Europeans consider environmental protection an 'immediate and urgent problem' and that about 63–68 per cent believe that decisions on the environment should be taken at the EU level rather than at the national level. The strength of public opinion has also been reflected in the growth of green political parties, which by January 1999 had nearly 150 members in 11 of the 15 national legislatures of the EU member states (the exceptions being Greece, Portugal, Spain and the UK), and following the June 1999 elections had 37 members in the European Parliament from 11 member states.

Phase IV: consolidation (1993–)

In many respects, the environmental policy of the EU has begun to come of age since 1993, helped by a combination of a change of leadership in the Commission, changes in the membership of the EU and the need to prepare for eastward expansion. Furthermore, progress on the completion of the single market has combined with the controversies over Maastricht and the single currency to encourage the EU to shift to a focus on 'soft issues' with which European voters can identify. *The Economist* was even prompted to suggest in 1998 that soft issues such as humanitarian aid, consumer affairs, civil rights and the environment 'are likely to dominate the Union's business in the decade or two to come' (12 September, p. 60).

The passage of the Treaty on European Union in 1993 had a number of evolutionary effects on European environmental policy. Most importantly, the environment was finally listed as a policy goal of the EU in the all-important opening articles.

Article 2 confirmed that one of the objectives of European integration was 'to promote throughout the Community a harmonious and balanced development of economic activities, [and] sustainable and non-inflationary growth respecting the environment', while Article 3 listed 'a policy in the sphere of the environment' as one of the 20 'activities' of the Community. The goal of 'promoting measures at [the] international level to deal with regional or worldwide environmental problems' was added to Article 130r, and changes to Article 130s allowed qualified majority voting to become the rule on most environmental matters, the exceptions including decisions on environmental taxes, town and country planning, water resource management, and issues relating to energy supply.

With Community competence over environmental policy greatly strengthened after 1987 by the Single European Act, the director-general of DGXI, Laurens Brinkhorst, determined on the need to develop a fifth EAP aimed at giving the Commission a more structured and strategic approach to environmental policy development. In developing the new programme, which was significantly different in content and philosophy from its four predecessors, the Commission attempted to look ahead ten years and to project the development of a true environmental policy. The Fifth Environmental Action Programme (1993–2000) also moved beyond environmental protection and placed a new stress on sustainable development, which it defined as 'continued economic and social development without detriment to the environment and natural resources, on the quality of which continued human activity and further development depend' (*Official Journal*, C138, 17.05.93). (Sustainable development was subsequently moved to the Preamble of the treaties by the Treaty of Amsterdam.) The Fifth EAP noted the need for reuse and recycling, for the rationalization of the production and consumption of energy, and for the alteration of consumption and behaviour patterns. It focused on problems with trans-European dimensions (climate change, acidification, threats to biodiversity, water pollution, deterioration of the urban environment, deterioration of coastal zones, and waste) and targeted five sectors for special attention: industry, energy, transport, agriculture and tourism.

The Treaty of Amsterdam – which came into force in May 1999 – had fewer constitutional implications for environmental policy than either the SEA or Maastricht, but was not without significance. Decisions on new environmental laws under Article 130s had been subject until then to the cooperation procedure, but those on the approximation of laws concerning the internal market under Article 100a had been subject to the codecision procedure, leading to the risk of conflict over which Article should be the legal basis for action on the environment. Amsterdam all but eliminated the cooperation procedure, reducing the risk of disagreements on the legal base.

More importantly, Amsterdam pushed the principle of sustainable development into the heart of the treaties. Sustainable development and environmental protection were added to the recitals for the first time, and where Maastricht had made mention of 'sustainable and non-inflationary growth respecting the environment', Article 2 in the Preamble was now rewritten to make one of the Community's goals 'a harmonious, balanced *and sustainable* development of economic activities' (emphasis added). At the same time, a new Article 3c (Article 6 in the renumbering introduced under the treaty) was created which charged that 'environmental protection requirements must be integrated into the definition and implementation' of all the Community policies and activities listed in Article 3.

More significant than these 'constitutional' changes, however, have been the normative changes that have taken place on the ground, particularly in the way that the Commission has approached environmental policy. Six changes have been especially notable.

First, the Santer Commission (1995–99) placed a new emphasis on consolidating existing activities rather than launching new initiatives. The change was due partly to the legal force given by Maastricht to subsidiarity, which led to the tabling of fewer new proposals and the withdrawal of some. Figure 2.1 shows clearly that the relative volume of new legislation and amendments has changed significantly in recent years. While as many as 80–90 per cent of environmental laws adopted by the Council of Ministers in the late 1970s were new, the proportion was down to 40–50 per cent by the early 1990s, even falling as low as 20 per cent in 1995 and 1997. Of the 306 pieces of legislation adopted in 1995–99, 72 per cent were amendments of existing laws. At the same time, there was a growth in the number of green papers and white papers, the former designed to stimulate discussion on environmental issues, and the latter to outline policy positions. This was in part a response to complaints that the Commission consulted too little and too late in the development of legislative proposals (see Chapter 4).

The trend was clearly reflected in the Commission's annual work programmes; while they routinely outlined dozens of proposals for new laws in the run-up to the completion of the single

FIGURE 2.1　EU environmental laws by year, 1958–99

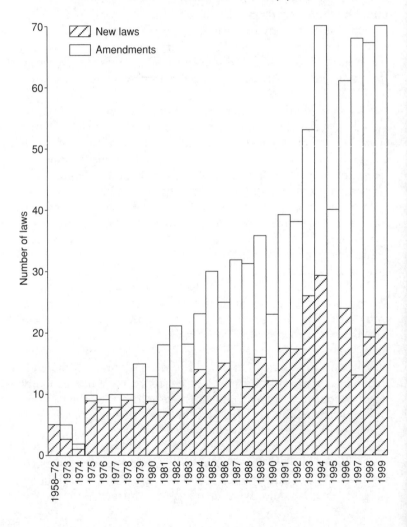

market at the end of 1992, the programme for 1995 proposed just 19 new laws, and the programme for 1996 was notable for its emphasis on discussion rather than legislation. Driven by the theme of 'stimulating more and legislating less', the Commission promised nearly 50 action plans and 35 measures aimed at stimulating public debate. In the environmental field, only two new legislative initiatives were proposed, while the Commission proposed stimulating public debate on reaching voluntary agreements with industry, the use of green levies and charges, the need to improve implementation, and future directions on noise, waste and recycling (European Commission, 1996). The 1997 and 1998 programmes focused on the need to look at the environmental implications of other policies, the latter placing a particular emphasis on the problems of enforcement. The 1999 programme was dominated by an evaluation of the Fifth EAP.

The second normative change has been the greater awareness within the Commission of the need to ensure coordination among the DGs with an interest in environmental issues. The effect of the principle of integrating environmental protection requirements with other policies (introduced by the SEA and strengthened by Amsterdam) has been to oblige the Commission to ensure that legislative proposals are widely distributed and discussed before being sent to the Council and Parliament. This has meant often lengthy interactions involving the Environment DG, the *cabinets* of interested Commissioners, officials from other interested DGs, the Committee of Permanent Representatives (COREPER), representatives of the member states in Council working groups, Parliament and its committees, the Economic and Social Committee, the Committee of the Regions, national bureaucrats, representatives of non-EU governments where necessary, the European Green Forum, and representatives of industry and environmental NGOs. In an attempt to improve policy integration, DGXI in 1996 launched a reorganization aimed at improving internal coordination and at helping it keep up with developments in other units of the Commission.

Third, the Commission has been concerned about the problem of implementation. As discussed in Chapter 5, cases of non-implementation, non-compliance, partial compliance and incorrect application have persisted. Prompted by its lack of powers of enforcement, and its need to rely on the member states and watchdogs (such as NGOs and private citizens) to report problems, the Commission supported the creation in 1992 of the EU Network for the Implementation and Enforcement of Environmental Law (IMPEL). This brings national enforcement authorities together informally at biannual meetings chaired jointly by the Environment DG and the member state holding the presidency of the EU. Its goal is to improve implementation by encouraging the exchange of information and experience and improving communication among the Commission and the member states. However, until the Commission has more power to oblige national governments to transpose EU law into national law, to closely monitor the application of EU law, and to compel relevant national and local authorities to apply the law and report on its application, problems with implementation will remain.

Fourth, disparities in environmental quality and in national legislative responses to environmental problems have been emphasized by the expansion of EU membership. There has always been a multispeed approach to environmental protection in the EU, with some member states being in favour of tighter regulation and others not. The balance shifted in favour of a more aggressive approach in 1995 when Austria, Finland and Sweden, all countries with strong national records in environmental policy, joined the EU. The balance will likely shift in favour of a less aggressive approach when poorer Central and Eastern European states (CEECs) join the EU. It is already clear that countries such as Poland, Hungary and the Czech Republic have much to do to meet the environmental policy conditions required for entry; for example, they lack national strategies and have a poor record on monitoring and enforcing national law (*Environmental Liability Report*, January 1996, pp. 7–8).

The process of adjustment has been anticipated to some extent in cooperative programmes aimed at helping poorer EU member states and CEECs make the transition. For example, the PHARE programme was created in 1989 to provide economic assistance to Poland and Hungary, but has since expanded to almost all CEECs. Its environmental element was initially reactive in the sense that it focused on providing equipment, studying specific problems, and helping establish standards and regulations, but it now supports activities linked to national environmental policy implementation. In its first five years of operation (1990–95) it spent about 430 million ecus on environmental and nuclear safety projects. Meanwhile, the Cohesion Fund – set up in 1994

– has helped compensate Greece, Portugal, Spain and Ireland for the costs of tightening environmental regulations, and by 1998 its budget had grown to nearly 2.9 billion ecus.

The environment is a key element in the Agenda 2000 programme. Proposed by the Commission in 1997, this is aimed at promoting growth and competition while strengthening and reforming EU policies to deal with enlargement, and emphasizes the need to help aspirant members adopt key pieces of EU environmental law. The environment has been slipping down the policy agenda in eastern Europe as governments have put more effort into economic growth, and there are concerns that approximating the environmental laws of the CEECs to those of the EU will be expensive – current plans are to spend at least one billion euros per year for the period 2000–06. In May 1998, an informal network called AC-IMPEL was created to bring together officials from CEEC governments and those from EU member states to discuss implementation issues in the period leading up to accession.

The fifth normative change in the EU approach to environment policy has involved a fundamental reappraisal of the instruments the EU uses in its approach to environmental management. Following the model of the member states, EU policy has so far focused mainly on a 'command and control' approach that sets uniform standards, mandates the methods required to meet such standards, and tries to assure compliance through monitoring the activities of member states (Golub, 1998a, p. 2). Thus, the EU has limited emissions from road vehicles and combustion plants, set limit values for discharges of dangerous substances into water, and placed limits on noise levels from machinery.

In recent years, there has been a shift away from this approach at the level both of the EU and of the member states. Inherent problems with command and control – such as the economic inefficiencies that tend to arise from the imposition of uniform standards and targets – have combined with concerns about worsening economic problems such as unemployment, and the need for the EU to become more competitive in the global market, to encourage a new focus on more flexible, cost-effective and market-based solutions to environmental problems, tailored to different environmental needs and conditions.

Among the more notable examples has been a reconsideration of the EU approach to acidification (see Chapter 8). Until

1996–97, the EU had focused on limiting motor vehicle emissions, reducing the sulphur content of fuel, and encouraging a sliding scale of percentage reductions in emissions of sulphur dioxide and nitrogen oxides. While these measures contributed to a halving of SO_2 emissions in the EU, some of the progress was being undone by the growth in road traffic, and there were concerns about the ability of CEECs to reduce their emissions without compromising their economic development goals. The result was an inclination to move away from imposing reduction targets on member states and industry (the source-based approach) and towards basing those targets instead on differences in the sensitivity of different environments to acidifying pollutants (the effect-based approach); this was the focus of an EU acidification strategy under development in 1996–99.

Finally, the mid-1990s saw the Commission moving increasingly towards a strategic approach to environmental problems. Rather than trying to deal with particular problems, the Commission has been developing more global responses to interrelated problems. This has been reflected in the passage of laws such as the 1996 directive on integrated pollution prevention and control (96/61) and the 1996 framework directive on air quality (96/62), the proposal for a framework water directive that was published in 1997, the development of the Auto-Oil programme aimed at eliciting the support of the oil and motor industries in reducing vehicle emissions, the work begun in 1996 on an acidification strategy, the review of chemicals policy that was begun in 1998, and the publication in 1998 of discussion papers on strategies for biodiversity, forestry, energy efficiency and eastward expansion of membership. These initiatives suggest that EU policy is steadily moving towards an integrated and broad-ranging approach to environmental managent, and is perhaps building the foundations for a common environmental policy.

Chapter 3

Policy Principles and Agenda-Setting

The most heated debates about the nature and significance of European integration have so far focused on three issues: the relative powers of the EU institutions and of the member states, the gap between the powers of the EU institutions and the abilities of European citizens to influence those powers, and questions about which policy areas are better dealt with by the member states and which by the EU.

The debates are complicated by the misunderstandings that surround the powers of the European Union. Most Europeans have an opinion about the EU and its activities, but most have only a patchy grasp of how it actually works. In Eurobarometer polls in 1997 and 1998, for example, 75 per cent of respondents gave themselves a failing score when asked how much they felt they knew about the EU. The misunderstandings have multiple sources, not least of which has been the failure of political scientists to reach agreement on the character of the EU. It is more than a conventional international organization, but it is less than a state. Establishing its character has been made more difficult by the rearguard actions fought by European governments in the name of national sovereignty, which have combined with the pioneering nature of the EU experiment to produce a system of policy-making that is segmented, complex, often unpredictable and constantly changing. Unlike the founders of the United States or the French Fifth Republic, the founders of the European Union did not draw up a constitution to serve as the blueprint for a new system of government, but instead reached some general agreements about some policy goals, and have spent the last 50 years editing those agreements in order to redefine the nature of integration. The treaties are thus something of a 'rolling constitution'.

The misunderstandings have been compounded by questions regarding the principles upon which the goals of European inte-

69

gration have been based. Concerns about 'creeping federalism' seem very real to those who fear that cooperation has gone beyond the core objectives of the treaties, and that the EU has become involved in policy areas that cannot always be justified as being part of the single market experiment. Even where such policy areas have been integrated into the treaties, it is not always clear what objectives have driven the subsequent formulation of policy. This is certainly true of the environment, on which – as argued in Chapter 1 – even the EU institutions are not always agreed when it comes to explaining parameters and objectives.

As a prelude to the discussion in Chapters 4–5 about the EU environmental policy process, this chapter begins with an examination of the principles that underlie that process. Several are clearly outlined in the treaties, but others must be teased out of the treaties, out of the general as well as the specific objectives of European integration, and out of the actions of EU institutions. Unfortunately, while they should clarify the goals of EU environmental policy, several introduce additional ambiguities into those goals. The chapter continues with a discussion of the impulses which have driven the EU environmental agenda, guidance for which cannot always be found in the treaties. As with all policy-making systems, there are formal procedures under which laws and policies are developed, but much of what the EU has done in the environmental field has been opportunistic and improvisational rather than deliberately planned. Much else has grown out of the unexpected ramifications of integration and harmonization in apparently unrelated policy areas.

The legal basis for EU policy

Most democracies base their system of government on a constitution, a codified set of goals and principles outlining the powers, obligations and responsibilities of government, the limits on the actions of government institutions and elected officials, and the rights of citizens. Assuming they are respected, constitutions provide a point of departure for understanding how a system of government functions, but they usually do no more than outline the boundaries of legitimate action. Within those boundaries, the routine processes of politics and government are driven as often as not by informal sets of rules and traditions. This is especially so with the EU, which lacks a formal constitution in the sense that there is a single document that lays out its powers and the limits on those powers, and the central content of which is changed only by formal amendments, by the passage of new laws, by court decisions, or by custom.

The key sources of formal EU authority can be found at three different levels (for more details, see Baldwin, 1995, chapter 8):

1 *Primary rules*. The foundation of the EU legal order consists of the founding treaties (Paris 1951 and the two Treaties of Rome of 1957) together with the changes made to them by the Merger Treaty of 1965, the Single European Act of 1986, the Treaty on European Union of 1992, the Treaty of Amsterdam of 1997, and the forthcoming Treaty of Nice. These contain the basic outline of the goals and organization of the European Union, offering a framework whose details are often provided by the laws developed by EU institutions and implemented by the member states. The SEA, Maastricht and Amsterdam amended many of the elements of the treaties of Paris and Rome, and significantly extended the competence of the EU and the powers and reach of EU institutions. Out of all the treaties – which between them amount to something like a constitution for the EU – have come many changes and developments in the policy directions taken by the EU. They have also spawned a large body of laws and judicial interpretations that, to varying degrees, are binding on the member states.

2 *Secondary rules*. Using the general principles outlined in the treaties, EU institutions have agreed a substantial body of laws that contain the details on how the broad goals are to be achieved. These laws take three main forms:

● *Regulations* are the most powerful and play a central role in developing a uniform body of law. Usually fairly narrow in their intent, they are often designed to lay down rules of procedure or technical standards, or to amend or adjust an existing law. Regulations are binding in their entirety on all member states, are directly applicable in the sense that they do not need to be turned into national law, and go into immediate force on a specified date. They must be based on particular provisions of the treaties, and they are subject to judgements by the European Court of Justice.

Of the 845 environmental laws that had been adopted by the EU by the end of 1999, 256 (or just over 30 per cent) were regulations. The common use of regulations is a consequence in part of the technical nature of many environmental problems, and of the use of standard-setting in responding to those problems. For example, regulation 259/93 sets up a common system for monitoring, supervizing and controlling the shipment of wastes, while regulation 2847/93 and a series of amendments establish a system to ensure compliance with rules on the Common Fisheries Policy, notably those related to monitoring the conservation of fisheries. Other regulations establish – or add to – lists of controlled substances or protected species. For example, regulation 3626/82 approves the terms of the Convention on International Trade in Endangered Species, and numerous amendments have added more species to the protected list.

- *Directives* are binding on member states in terms of their goals and objectives, but the member states are free to decide how best to achieve those goals. Most focus on outlining general policy objectives, while some are aimed at harmonization (bringing different national laws into line with one another). Implementation requires changes in national laws which must be made by a specified date, normally within two to three years of adoption. The governments of the member states must tell the European Commission what they plan to do to achieve the goals of a directive.

To muddy the waters a little, it has been established through the case law of the European Court of Justice that certain directives can have 'direct effect' on member states even when they have not been transposed into national law. This can happen only where a law imposes clear, unambiguous and unconditional obligations on the member states, and where the obligations are not dependent upon further implementing measures. Sunkin *et al.* (1998, pp. 14–17) identify three kinds of environmental directives that are capable of having direct effect: those which specify limits or values for discharges which are precise, unconditional and not dependent upon further action by member states (such as 76/464 on water pollution); those prohibiting the use of substances or their discharge into the environment (such as the 1980 groundwater directive); and those which impose a clear obligation on member states to take action (such as the 1985 environmental impact assessment directive).

By the end of 1999, 353 of the environmental laws adopted by the EU (just under 42 per cent of the total) were directives. Examples include the directives on waste (75/442), dangerous substances (76/464), pollution from industrial plants (84/360), surface water quality (75/440), bathing water (76/160), drinking water quality (80/778), pollution from large combustion plants (88/609) and urban waste water treatment (91/271).

- *Decisions* are also binding and can be aimed at one or more member states, at institutions, or even at individuals. However, they are usually fairly specific in their intent, have administrative rather than legislative goals, and in some cases are non-binding.

  By the end of 1999, the EU had adopted 236 decisions on the environment (or 28 per cent of all environmental laws adopted). Almost all the international conventions signed by the Community have had their terms approved in the form of decisions, which have also been used to set up programmes (such as those on energy efficiency, monitoring CO_2 emissions, environmental statistics and environmental consultative committees), and to address administrative issues such as standardized questionnaires relating to water directives (92/446) and guidelines on costs and fees relating to the eco-label scheme (93/326).

Once the Commission has begun work on a proposal for an environmental law, the form of the legislation rarely changes. Where it does, however, it is more common for a regulation to be reformulated as a directive than vice versa. Member states prefer directives because they are flexible and leave it to national governments to decide how best to achieve the goals, while the national bureaucrats involved often prefer regulations because they do not demand transposition into national law, which itself can be a complex process. In the case of EU chemicals legislation adopted in the early 1990s, for example, the directives were so complex that they were difficult to transpose into national law, with the result that several of the national officials involved asked the Commission unofficially to focus in future on regulations, since they did not need to be transposed.

3   *Tertiary rules.* These take a variety of forms. Firstly, the EU issues Recommendations and Opinions, but since they have no binding force, it is debatable whether or not they are actually sources of EU law. They are often used to make a point about the development or implementation of EU policies, and sometimes have indirect legal effects.

Secondly, rulings by the European Court of Justice can have an important effect on how regulations, directives and decisions are understood or implemented. The most fundamental contributions made by the Court in the environmental field came out of case 91/79 in 1980, establishing the legitimacy of Community environmental measures, and case 240/83 of 1985, establishing that environmental protection was a core policy concern of the Community (see Chapter 2).

Thirdly, direction is also provided by a variety of additional 'soft laws', such as action programmes, strategies, declarations, green papers (designed to stimulate discussion on an issue or problem), white papers (outlining policy positions) and conclusions of meetings. As well as the action programmes, EU environmental policy has been guided by multiple green papers, such as those on the urban environment (1990), remedying environmental damage (1993), energy policy (1994), noise policy (1996), biodiversity, energy efficiency, integration of the environment with other EU policies (all 1998), and environmental liability and chemicals policy (1999). As noted in Chapter 2, there has also been a growing emphasis in recent years on the development of sectoral strategies, such as those addressing acidification, biodiversity and energy efficiency.

Finally, as is the case with governments everywhere, much of what the EU institutions do can be put down simply to custom. For example, there is no legal obligation on the Commission to work with interest groups in the development of legislative proposals, yet consultation has become the norm. Similarly, there is no mention of the working groups in the Council of Ministers (see Chapter 5) anywhere in the treaties, yet they are arguably one of the most important elements in the EU policy-making process.

Policy principles

The key parameters of EU activities in the field of environmental policy have been set by a series of principles outlined in the treaties. There are now 14 such principles, some of which are legally binding requirements, but most of which are no more than general goals. Some predate the Single European Act, but most were introduced and/or elaborated upon by the SEA, Maastricht and Amsterdam. They often appear noble in spirit, but the terms and concepts they introduce are rarely defined or explained, and while they have normally been intended to provide greater focus, they have occasionally created new ambiguities, sometimes appear contradictory, and have occasionally raised new questions about the objectives of EU environmental policy.

Listed in the order in which they emerged in the treaties, those principles are as follows:

1 *The polluter pays principle.* This is the oldest of EU environmental principles, outlined as early as 1973 and the First EAP: 'The cost of preventing and eliminating nuisances must in principle be borne by the polluter' (First Environmental Action Programme, *Official Journal*, 1973, C112, 1, 6). Furthermore, several early pieces of EU law incorporate the principle, such as directive 75/442 on waste, which imposes the costs of safe waste disposal on the producer, an arrangement sometimes described as the 'producer responsibility' principle. The principle implies that the costs of preventing or making good on environmental damage must not be passed on to the taxpayer or the consumer, and must not be covered by public funds, but that the entity responsible for actually or potentially damaging the environment must meet the costs of repair or of avoiding damage. It is based on the argument that charging polluters the costs of taking action will be an inducement for them to invest in less damaging methods and technology.

The argument has several flaws. First, an industry obliged to meet the costs of preventing or repairing environmental damage will almost inevitably pass the costs on to the consumer through higher prices for its products; in this regard, polluters will almost always be able to avoid paying. Second, the principle only works if the precise source of the damage can be firmly established; unfortunately, most environmental problems have multiple causes and sources, making it difficult to determine responsibility. For example, while some water pollution is caused by distinct and identifiable 'point sources' such as factories, much is also caused by multiple 'non-point sources' such as chemical runoff generated by agriculture and road vehicles. Finally, the growth in the funds that have been made available by the EU to help with environmental management projects in recent years actually runs counter to the principle; it is not the polluter who is paying in these cases, but the EU taxpayer. In short, it is difficult always to apply in practice.

2 *The principle of sustainable development.* This is a concept that has become a central environmental policy principle only since the SEA, although it could be argued that a tenuous link can be made back to the goal outlined in Article 2 of the Treaty of Rome for 'a harmonious development of economic activities, [and] a continuous and balanced expansion'. The notion was given greater clarity with Article 130r(1) of the SEA, which held that Community environmental action should ensure a 'prudent and rational utilisation of resources', a phrase that had often been used elsewhere as a definition of the meaning of sustainable growth or development (see McCormick, 1995, pp. 179–80). Maastricht went a step further in Article 2 by stipulating that 'sustainable and non-inflationary growth respecting the environment' was a 'task' of the Community, but left many environmentalists disappointed by its failure to establish sustainable development as one of the general policy goals of the EU (Wilkinson, 1992). This concern was addressed in the Treaty of Amsterdam, where Article 2 was amended to make 'balanced and sustainable development of economic activities' one of the tasks of the Community.

Unfortunately, the notion of sustainability has always been hard to pin down, prompting much debate about its meaning (see Collier, 1997, for example), and questions about the differences (if any) between sustainable 'growth' (a term used in Maastricht) and sustainable 'development' (used in the Fifth EAP and Amsterdam). While the treaties do not define the concept, the definition developed by the 1987 World Commission on Environment and Development (the Brundtland Commission) is the one now most commonly used by policy-makers and academics: 'Development that meets the needs of the present without compromising the ability of future generations to meet their own needs' (World Commission on Environment and Development, 1987, p. 43). While this definition was used in the Fifth EAP when it was adopted in 1993, the Environment DG in its mission statement in 2000 chose to express the idea as the 'preservation of the rights of future generations to a viable environment' (EDG Web page, 2000).

3 *A high level of protection.* Introduced by the SEA, this requires that the Commission, in its internal market proposals relating to health, safety, environmental protection and consumer protection, 'will take as a base a high level of protection'. Interestingly, the requirement was not directed at the Council when it came to adopting such measures, thereby creating a loophole by implying that the Council could water down Commission proposals in these areas. Another loophole was created by outlining the principle in Article 100a(3) rather than in the new Title VII on the environment, thereby implying that it related only to environmental laws that had an impact on the internal market. Since the clause derived from the concerns expressed by several member states during the negotiations on the SEA that majority voting could lead to a lowering of standards in areas such as environmental protection, it was interpreted by some as meaning that the Commission was expected to take as its starting point the rules in effect in the most stringent member states (Vandermeersch, 1987).

Maastricht removed these loopholes by adding the principle to Article 130r(2), and by specifying that 'a high level of protection' would now be Community policy, not just Commission policy. However, it added new loopholes by charging that the Community 'shall aim at a high level of protection *taking into account the diversity of situations in the various regions of the Community*' (emphasis added). Furthermore, it begged the question of how 'high' should be defined, and how it could be distinguished in this context from 'low' or 'moderate'. Also, Article 100a(4) of the SEA (which was not changed by Maastricht, or substantially by Amsterdam) allows member states exceptions from a Community measure adopted by a qualified majority vote 'on grounds . . . relating to protection of the environment'. In short, the principle is almost impossible to legally enforce.

4 *The prevention principle.* Introduced by SEA Article 130r(2), this encourages the Community to initiate action in such a way as to protect the environment by preventing problems emerging. (In some respects, this was already happening as a result of directive 85/337 on environmental impact assessment, adopted two years before the SEA came into force.) This is a goal that makes economic sense, because cure is usually more expensive than prevention. However, it depends for its effective attainment on reliable scientific data and improvements in the gathering and exchange of information. In fact, since the Community is required to take account of 'available scientific and technical data' in preparing its action related to the environment (see point 8 below), it could be argued – by the Community, by a member state, or by an industry – that nothing should be done in the absence of absolute proof of the existence of problems with undesirable environmental consequences (Jans, 1996a). Krämer (1995, p. 54) points out that only the English version of the treaty said that preventive action 'should be taken'; the absence of that phrase in all other languages suggests that the principle is weaker than it seems.

5 *The proximity principle.* Introduced by SEA Article 130r(2), this argues that environmental damage 'should as a priority be rectified at source' rather than further down the line, for example by setting emissions standards rather than air or water quality standards, or by requiring that the producers of hazardous waste dispose of it nearby rather than shipping it further afield. In the latter case, this would prevent affluent communities from shipping waste to poorer communities, reduce the risks of accidents during transport, and make it easier to monitor the handling of waste.

The development of the principle has been traced back to the 1975 directive on waste (75/442), which was in turn modelled on German federal waste law, which placed responsibility for waste disposal capacity plans on the *Länder*, several of which banned the import and export of waste (Bering, 1996). The issue of transfrontier shipment of wastes moved to the top of the EU environmental agenda in the 1980s, eventually becoming part

TABLE 3.1　*Changes to Article 174(2)*

In regard to environmental policy, this Article (formerly 130r(2)) is one of the critical elements of the treaties. Changes made to it under the SEA, Maastricht and Amsterdam provide an illustration of the changing priorities of EU policy.

In the Single European Act, the Article read as follows:

Action by the Community relating to the environment shall be based on the principles that preventive action should be taken, that environmental damage should as a priority be rectified at source, and that the polluter should pay. Environmental protection requirements shall be a component of the Community's other policies.

It was amended by Maastricht to read as follows:

Community policy on the environment shall aim at a high level of protection taking into account the diversity of situations in the various regions of the Community. It shall be based on the precautionary principle and on the principle that preventive action should be taken, that environmental damage should as a priority be rectified at source and that the polluter should pay. Environmental protection requirements must be integrated into the definition and implementation of other Community policies.

In this context, harmonisation measures answering these requirements shall include, where appropriate, a safeguard clause allowing Member States to take provisional measures, for non-economic environmental reasons, subject to a Community inspection procedure.

It was amended by Amsterdam to read as follows:

Community policy on the environment shall aim at a high level of protection taking into account the diversity of situations in the various regions of the Community. It shall be based on the precautionary principle and on the principles that preventive action should be taken, that environmental damage should as a priority be rectified at source and that the polluter should pay.

In this context, harmonisation measures answering environmental protection requirements shall include, where appropriate, a safeguard clause allowing Member States to take provisional measures, for non-economic environmental reasons, subject to a Community inspection procedure.

(The integrative principle described at the end of the first paragraph of the Maastricht version was moved to a new Article 3c, now Article 6.)

of the debate over the single market programme and prompting a 1992 Court of Justice decision on the question of whether or not hazardous wastes were 'goods' that could be traded. While the EU has committed itself to ending hazardous waste exports outside the EU in line with the Basel Convention on the control of the movement of wastes, the Court of Justice has issued decisions which seem to uphold the possibility of exports, creating some confusion (see Chapter 6).

6   *The integration principle.* Undoubtedly the most important and far-reaching of all the basic principles, this was introduced with the stipulation in the SEA that 'environmental protection requirements shall be a component of the Community's other policies' (Article 130r(2)). It was a key theme in the Fifth EAP (published in 1992), and was taken a step further in Maastricht with the charge that such requirements 'must be integrated into the definition and implementation of other Community policies'. Its importance was confirmed by Amsterdam, when it was deleted from the section on the environment, moved up to the Preamble to the treaty, and made into a separate Article 6.

There are only three other EU policy areas to which the same principle applies: consumer protection, culture and health. However, while the integrative clause seems to elevate these areas into a special class by themselves, its implications are open to debate. On the one hand, there is clearly no need to investigate the environmental implications of every single European policy or law; where, for example, is the environmental dimension in policies on worker mobility, European citizenship or telecommunications? On the other hand, which of the remaining areas of policy activity are realistically subject to the provision and which are not, and who decides?

Furthermore, Jans points out that it is unclear what is meant by 'environmental protection requirements', that questions have been raised as to whether or not the clause implies that environmental policy has a measure of priority over all the other EU policy areas, and that nothing is said in the treaties about how conflicts between environmental protection and the goals of other policy areas should be resolved. Finally, it raises the interesting legal question of whether or not the legitimacy of an action of the Council or the Commission in, for example, the fields of transport, agriculture or industrial development could be questioned on the basis that it infringed or did not fully take into account all the environmental implications (Jans, 1996a).

Environmental Data Services concluded in early 1998 that while integration had been a theme of Community policy statements for many years – particularly in relation to agriculture, energy, transport, industry, taxation and the structural funds – it had 'failed to make much headway due to the lack of adequate institutional mechanisms for promoting environmental appraisal of policies from an early stage within both the European Commission and the Council of Ministers' (*ENDS Report* 276, January 1998, p. 47). What effect the new provision in Article 6 of the Treaty of Amsterdam will have remains to be seen. (For further discussion, see Chapter 4.)

7 *The derogative principle.* Qualified majority voting (QMV) obliges all EU member states to adhere to the requirements of EU law where QMV is used, no matter what the cost. This could mean a substantial economic burden on poorer states obliged to meet the same environmental standards and goals as the richer states. Hence the SEA began to introduce the possibility of derogations (that is, exceptions to the general rule) when Article 130r(3) said that the Community should take account of 'environmental conditions in the various regions of the Community . . . [and] the economic and social development of the Community as a whole and the balanced development of its regions'. Maastricht amended Article 130r(2) to allow policy to take into account 'the diversity of situations in the various regions of the Community'.

These changes meant that there was clearly no requirement that the EU develop a uniform policy for all member states, thereby contributing to the emergence of a multispeed Europe. For example, Directive 88/609 on air pollution from large combustion plants temporarily imposed less stringent requirements on Spain so that its plans to develop new generating capacity would not be handicapped. Equally, acid pollution controls and the EU response to climate change imposed different emission reduction targets on different states. The trend on acidification policy is now away from uniform emission limits and towards a critical loads policy based on taking action aimed at dealing with problems in those parts of the EU worst affected by acidification (see Chapter 8).

8 *Taking account of scientific and technical data.* SEA Article 130r(3) introduced the idea that the Community, in 'preparing its action relating to the environment [changed by Maastricht to 'policy on the environment'] . . . shall take account of available scientific and technical data'. The clause was introduced at the insistence of the Thatcher administration, which was at that time in the dying stages of its refusal to admit that there was scientific evidence that British industrial emissions were a major cause of the problem of acid pollution. It could in fact have gone much further, and insisted that no measure would be taken without clear scientific evidence that it would contribute towards the alleviation of a problem (Vandermeersch, 1987), but it did not.

The term 'shall take account of' does not compel the EU to factor scientific data into its calculations, nor to provide hard proof of a link between cause and effect; indeed, such a requirement would undermine the preventive and precautionary principles. The clause also offers a legal opt-out to member states opposed to action, which can use it to argue against a law or policy on the grounds that the science is debatable or unclear. The ambiguities have prompted the EU to expend considerable effort on research, working with research and monitoring bodies inside and outside the EU, establishing first CORINE and then the European Environment Agency, and making information exchange a central component of several pieces of EU environmental law. For example, directive 90/313 on the freedom of access to information on the environment mandates free public access to all environmental information held by public authorities, and strictly limits the abilities of member states to deny access to such information.

9 *Benefit-cost calculations.* SEA Article 130r(3) introduced a call on member states to take account of 'the potential benefits and costs of action or of lack of action'. At any level of policy-making, such a goal is troublesome simply by virtue of the fact that it is easier to calculate the costs of action than of inaction. For example, it has been relatively easy to calculate the costs of reducing emissions of greenhouse gases (although even this is subject to debate), but almost impossible to calculate how much it will cost the European Union if nothing is done. It has also been impossible to calculate the theoretical benefits of the actions taken, particularly given the

doubts about the extent and the potential effects of climate change in the first place (see Chapter 10).

One area of Community environmental law in which costs have come to figure prominently has been the reduction of air pollution, where (in directives 84/360 and 88/609, for example), it was agreed that measures would be based around the best available technology not entailing excessive cost (BATNEEC). Once again, however, ambiguities have been built in – what exactly is 'excessive' cost? Presumably it can be taken to mean a point at which diminishing returns begin to show, but given the difficulties of placing a price on action as opposed to inaction, how can that point be established with any certainty?

10   *The subsidiarity principle.* This is a concept defined in Article 3b (now 5) as follows: 'In areas which do not fall within its exclusive competence, the Community shall take action, in accordance with the principle of subsidiarity, only if and in so far as the objectives of the proposed action cannot be sufficiently achieved by the Member States and can therefore, by reason of the scale or effects of the proposed action, be better achieved by the Community'. The principle has played an increasingly prominent role in discussions about integration generally since the early 1990s, but made its first modest appearance in the First EAP, which outlined five possible levels of action and emphasized the need – in regard to environmental policy – 'to establish the level [of action] best suited to the type of pollution and to the geographical zone to be protected'. It was first introduced to the treaties by the SEA, and exclusively in reference to the environment (SEA Article 130r(4)). It was then expanded to all Community activities by Maastricht when it was added to the list of principles at the beginning of the treaty.

Since competence over environmental policy is shared between the EU and the member states, it is clearly subject to this principle, but while transboundary issues and matters related to shared resources and trade are arguably better resolved at the EU level, it is debatable in many other areas which level is more effective. Member states with strong national bodies of environmental law may argue that action is better taken by the member states, but they may also want to protect themselves from emissions or waste from neighbouring states with weaker laws. Furthermore, should all EU environmental laws and policies apply to all member states, or only those experiencing the problem to which those laws and policies are a response?

All of this may be moot, however. Writing in 1995, Ludwig Krämer, then Head of Legal Matters and Application of Community Law in DGXI, noted that he knew 'of not one single environmental measure where the Council has decided or even discussed whether a measure could be better adopted at the Community level rather than at the level of the Member States' (Krämer, 1995, pp. 59–60).

11 *The international principle.* Introduced by Article 130r(5) of the SEA and strengthened by Maastricht Article 130r(1), this is the least ambiguous and troublesome of the underlying objectives of EU environmental policy. The SEA stated that the Community and member states would cooperate with third countries and international organizations, a clause that was deleted by Maastricht and replaced by the argument that one of the objectives of Community policy would be the promotion of measures at the international level to deal with regional or global environmental problems. This is an area where the EU – and the Commission in particular – has been active, both encouraging the compliance of member states with international treaties, and representing the EU in negotiations with other countries on the agreement of international treaties such as the 1985 ozone layer convention and the 1992 climate change convention.

12 *The proportionality principle.* Article 3b of Maastricht argued that 'Any action by the Community shall not go beyond what is necessary to achieve the objectives of this Treaty'. In other words, the obligations of EU law must be reasonably related to the objectives sought, and the EU must leave the member states with as much freedom of movement as possible. This could mean, for example, using minimum standards, allowing member states to impose stricter standards, using directives rather than regulations, using framework directives rather than more detailed and specific measures, and using non-binding recommendations and voluntary codes of conduct (Jans, 1996b). Unfortunately, since the objectives of the treaties are often very broad, it is often difficult to establish what actions are needed to achieve those objectives.

13 *The precautionary principle.* With roots in the German idea of *Vorsorgeprinzip* (von Moltke, 1987), this was added

under Maastricht to Article 130r(2), and in some respects strengthens the preventive principle by implying that the EU should take action even if there is a *suspicion* that an activity may cause environmental harm, rather than wait until the scientific evidence is clear. Where limits had previously been placed on action by the requirement that account should be taken of available scientific research, it has been argued that even tentative and indicative scientific data can now be sufficient grounds for taking measures to protect the environment (Jans, 1996a). At the same time, it is unclear just how the principle should be applied, or whose responsibility it is to draw attention to the grounds for suspicion.

Application of the principle has proved controversial, and EU policymakers have found it difficult to achieve a workable balance. In February 2000, the Commission was prompted to adopt a communication on the principle in an attempt to give it more clarity (European Commission press release, 2 February 2000). It emphasized that action taken under the principle should be 'proportionate to the chosen level of protection' (measures should be appropriately tailored), non-discriminatory in its application (comparable situations should not be treated differently), based on an examination of the potential costs and benefits of action or lack of action, and subject to review in the light of new scientific data. It also noted that 'the precautionary principle is neither a politicisation of science or the acceptance of zero-risk but . . . provides a basis for action when science is unable to give a clear answer'. Finally, it noted that while the principle was prescribed by Maastricht only to the environment, its scope was actually much wider.

14 *The safeguard principle.* Maastricht Article 130r(2) included a clause that allows member states to provisionally adopt stronger local standards than those outlined in EU law provided that they are for 'non-economic environmental reasons, subject to a Community inspection procedure'. This idea was repeated (in essence) in Article 130t, which allowed member states to maintain or introduce more stringent protective measures as long as they were compatible with the treaty, and the Commission was notified. The principle can be found in practice, for example, in directive 91/414 on pesticides (or 'plant protection products'): if a member state has reason to feel that a product authorized under the directive poses a risk to

human or animal health, or to the environment, it can restrict or ban sales of the product in its territory. The same is true of chemicals under directive 67/548, amended by 92/32.

Agenda-setting

While these are the underlying principles of EU environmental policy, or the formal objectives of that policy, it is also important to understand how the policy agenda is developed. Here the EU begins to move into the realms of informal inspiration, its work being driven by a combination of constitutional, political, economic and scientific opportunities and pressures.

Before the Commission can begin developing a proposal for a new law or policy, a problem must have been accepted as part of the agenda of European integration. In other words, a decision must have been made that it is within the powers, responsibilities and interests of the EU institutions to consider, propose and develop a response to that problem. The history of EU environmental policy in Chapter 2 suggests that policy concerns were initially very narrow, but that the agenda began to broaden in the 1970s, and expanded from one Environmental Action Programme to the next, driven by economic and political pressures and a redefinition of the objectives of European integration.

There is a common misconception that the European environmental agenda is dominated by the Commission, which generates proposals for new laws and policies within some kind of jurisdictional vacuum. However, while the Commission is responsible for proposing responses to problems, it has never had a monopoly on agenda-setting. As Environmental Data Services notes, 'whatever may be said about its ambitions, . . . [the Commission] is neither particularly large nor a fount gushing with new policy ideas' (*ENDS Report* 269, June 1997). Much of its work is generated and influenced by external political forces, notably the wishes of the governments of the member states.

Furthermore, it is important to appreciate that there is no single agenda, but rather that policy in the EU is driven by multiple agendas. In their study of agenda-setting in US government, Cobb and Elder distinguish between systemic and institutional agendas (1983, pp. 85–6). The former consist of all issues which are commonly regarded by members of the political community as meriting attention and as falling within the jurisdiction of government, and the latter as those issues under active and serious consideration by those in authority in particular institutions. The systemic agenda of the EU consists mainly of the goals outlined in the treaties, while institutional agendas can be found mainly in the work programmes of the principal European institutions. However, to these must be added the sub-institutional agendas of the directorates-general within the Commission, the national agendas of each of the member states, and the cross-national agendas of interest groups working in several member states but cooperating in their attempts to influence EU policy. Elements of all of these feed into and influence the sectoral policy agendas of the EU.

The impulses that drive the European environmental policy agenda come from a variety of sources, which are both internal and external to the EU institutions, formal and informal, predictable and unpredictable, anticipated and opportunistic, and structured and unstructured.

1 *Constitutional pressures.* The most fundamental impulse behind the setting of the EU environmental agenda can be found in the treaty obligations, the functional equivalent of constitutional obligations. In particular, Article 2 notes that 'sustainable and non-inflationary growth respecting the environment' is one of the tasks of the Community, and Article 3 describes 'a policy in the sphere of the environment' as one of the activities of the Community. These are broad and even ambiguous objectives; a 'task' or an 'activity' is very different from a 'responsibility' or an 'objective'. Furthermore, while the treaties outline many principles, they do not go so far as to list the specific responsibilities of the EU institutions relative to the member states. There is nothing in the treaties which says that the EU *must* develop a policy on the environment, and – as noted earlier – the EU has not developed a common environmental policy, nor even an EU environmental policy, but rather has developed a series of policies relating to different environmental issues.

Although they are not part of the 'constitution', the Environmental Action Programmes and the Work Programme of the Commission outline additional obligations that guide the actions of the Environment DG and other parts of the Commission with an interest in environmental issues. In fact, they amount to the *de facto* environmental agenda of the EU, because they list specific goals, and are subject to regular progress reports. In this sense, they provide the detail on the content of the EU environmental policy agenda that is so obviously lacking in the treaties.

2   *Pressures to harmonize.* While much of the Community's early activity in the sphere of the environment was driven by the pressures or the single market, the pressures to harmonize have since come less from the unexpected ramifications of economic integration, and more from what has become known as the leader-laggard dynamic (Haas, 1993, p. 138) and from the need to build a political consensus among the member states. 'Leader' countries are those with more stringent sectoral environmental measures and more ambitious policy goals, and whose governments are pressed by industry and public opinion to encourage other governments to adopt similar measures and aspire to similar goals. Meanwhile, 'laggard' countries are those which have adopted relatively weak environmental measures (or none at all) and which are more reluctant to accept stronger standards.

Wealthier northern member states such as Denmark, Germany and the Netherlands have earned a reputation – not always entirely merited – as the leaders (joined in 1995 by Finland and Sweden), while Greece, Italy, Portugal and Spain – and occasionally Britain and France – have come to be seen as the laggards. Governments and interest groups in leader states often complain that EU policy is not sufficiently ambitious, while there is relatively little political support in laggard states for the domestic policy changes required by EU law. It would even be fair to say that member states such as Greece and Portugal would probably have little in the way of domestic environmental policies were it not for the requirements of EU law.

The differences between the leaders and the laggards are usually explained by a combination of economic and cultural factors. In wealthier societies with a high standard of living, more people have more time to think about – and become concerned about – the extent to which their hard-won affluence is compromised by problems such as polluted air and water. In poorer societies, meanwhile, the costs of holding industry liable

to tightened environmental management controls and of promoting changes in the choices made by consumers may be seen
as a potential brake on economic development, and may thus
generate more opposition.

Leader states are credited with having created the pressure
for change either through developing national laws which
pose a threat to the single market, and demand a response
from the other member states, or through exerting pressure
for policy changes at the EU level. Examples include the
following:

- The most important element in the EU response to acid pollution was the 1988 directive limiting emissions from large
  combustion plants (88/609), which was not only modelled
  on a piece of German domestic law, but whose development
  and adoption were prompted largely by German political
  pressure.
- Part of the reason why the Commission began developing its
  controversial proposal for a carbon tax in the early 1990s
  was because Denmark, Germany and the Netherlands were
  considering the development of national taxes, and there was
  concern that these would interfere with the functioning of the
  single market.
- Domestic policy changes in Sweden and Britain in 1997–98
  led to pressure for a wide-ranging review of EU chemicals
  policy, the record on which had by then been modest at best.
- The EU began developing a directive on the recycling of
  electrical goods in 1998 mainly because similar laws were
  under development in Denmark, Germany, the Netherlands
  and Sweden.

Compelling as it may sometimes seem, the leader-laggard idea
must be treated with caution, for three main reasons. First,
words are cheap. As Keohane, Haas and Levy argue (1993,
p. 18),

> environmental politics is replete with symbolic action, aimed
> at pacifying aroused publics and injured neighbors without
> imposing severe costs on domestic industrial or agricultural
> interests . . . The environmental rabbit that is pulled at the
> last minute from an organizational hat may turn out to be
> illusory or ephemeral.

Second, it would be misleading to suggest that some countries consistently lead while others consistently lag. It is more accurate to argue that all member states have a mixed record on different issues at different times, with *tendencies* either to lead, to lag, or to come somewhere between the two. For example, Britain – or, more accurately, the Thatcher administration – proved an early laggard on acid rain, but became a leader once Thatcher changed her views in the later 1980s. It has also been a leader on marine oil pollution and climate change, so the common accusations that Britain has slowed down progress in developing the EU policy agenda are not entirely deserved.

Third, leader states may be good at suggesting policy initiatives, but may not have such a good record on policy implementation. For example, Germany is often described as a leader, but has only a middling record when it comes to notifying national implementation measures for EU environmental laws, while Ireland – usually described as a laggard – has one of the best such records in the EU (see Chapter 5).

3   *Legislative pressures.* Many new proposals for legislation come out of requirements or assumptions built into past laws. This is certainly the case with laws that include within them an obligation for amendment or review after a specified period of time, and is particularly true of framework directives, which set general goals with the assumption that more laws – known as daughter directives – will be developed later that provide more detail and focus. An example of a framework law was the 1996 directive on ambient air quality (96/62), which established air quality objectives for five key pollutants, adopted common methods and criteria for assessing air quality, and listed 12 pollutants that would need their own daughter directives. Work subsequently began on the development of daughter directives on sulphur dioxide, lead, benzene, carbon monoxide, heavy metals and other pollutants.

4   *Policy evolution and spillover.* Policy is rarely static, and the principles and goals of EU policy are constantly redefined as greater understanding emerges about the causes and effects of problems, as technological developments offer new options for addressing old problems, as the failure of existing policies demands new approaches, as the balance of interests changes within the member states, and as the po-

litical, economic and social priorities of European integration evolve. The broad impact of policy evolution can be seen in the manner in which the underlying philosophy of EU environmental policy has evolved from an emphasis on removing barriers to the single market to an emphasis on addressing environmental problems for their own sake, and finally to ensuring that environmental considerations are built into all EU policies. As this has happened, so the environmental agenda has broadened, new issues have appeared on the agenda, and new approaches to dealing with problems have been adopted.

For example, where the Commission in the 1970s and 1980s was developing policies dealing with specific problems and issue areas, it has recently begun moving towards an integration of these isolated responses into broader, inclusive policies. Hence, after pursuing separate sets of objectives in its attempts to improve air quality, the Commission in 1998–99 began talking about a broader strategic approach to air quality. Similarly, its approach to waste policy began with general waste management goals, shifted to attempts to reduce particular kinds of waste, and – when it was found that the waste problem was persisting, even becoming worse in some areas – began moving towards an integrated product policy aimed at reducing consumption, prolonging product life, and promoting reuse and recycling.

Policy agendas in general are driven in part by changes in understanding among policymakers about the causes and effects of the problems with which they deal. This is particularly true of environmental policy, where research may identify new problems, change our understanding of existing problems, or offer suggestions for new responses to existing problems. For example, the policies of the EU on the ozone layer and climate change grew out of changes in scientific understanding, and its policy on lead in fuel was given new direction by the realization that unleaded fuel was needed if road vehicles were to be fitted with catalytic converters, which were – in turn – a critical element in attempts to reduce vehicle emissions as part of EU policy on acid pollution.

5 *Pressures from EU institutions.* While the Commission has a monopoly over the development of new proposals for law, it is subject to various formal and informal pressures, including

suggestions from the European Council regarding the broad goals of EU policy; 'invitations' from the European Parliament (EP) and the Council of Ministers to develop new proposals; suggestions or demands from the EP or the Council of Ministers for changes in Commission proposals; and the impact of rulings by the Court of Justice on the content and nature of EU law.

With its powers over the adoption or rejection of new laws, the Council of Ministers is clearly a key source of pressure on the Commission. For its part, the EP plays a relatively limited role in agenda-setting and policy formulation, although it can draw the attention of the Commission to problems by submitting questions, generating 'own-initiative' reports and resolutions, or setting up committees of inquiry into breaches of EU law. Judge (1993) suggests that it is difficult always to be sure about the influence of the actions of the EP on agenda-setting, although he quotes cases where Parliamentary initiatives have had direct consequences: for example, a 1988 EP resolution led to the generation of the 1990 green paper on the urban environment, and the EP has taken the lead on the issue of banning imports of tropical hardwoods.

The Court of Justice is concerned primarily with interpreting the meaning of the treaties, so most of its impact on environmental policy has been focused on questions of implementation. However, it has had a fundamental impact on agenda-setting given that many of its rulings have broadened the responsibility of EU institutions over environmental policy, and have clarified the legal base of EU action and the legitimacy of European environmental law and policy.

6   *Requirements of international law.* During the 1970s, most European environmental law and policy was based on attempts to encourage cooperation among the member states. Since the 1980s, however, and particularly since the addition of the international clause to the treaties, the Commission has become increasingly involved in working with other international organizations on international policy development. The Council regularly gives it mandates to negotiate on international treaties on behalf of the EU, and the Commission also coordinates the implementation of such treaties among the member states. The first EU laws confirming the adoption of the terms

of an international environmental agreement were decisions 75/437 and 75/438 on the 1974 Paris Convention on the Prevention of Marine Pollution from Land-Based Sources. Only three more such laws were adopted in the next five years, but – following the Court of Justice decision on the AETR case (see Chapter 10) – the Community was adopting about three to five laws per year confirming the terms of international treaties, adopting a total of 54 such laws in the period 1990–99. Among the treaties adopted by the EU: the 1973 convention on trade in endangered species, the 1979 Bonn convention on migratory species, the 1983 international tropical timber agreement, the 1985 ozone layer convention, the 1990 Magdeburg convention on protection of the Elbe, the 1992 biological diversity treaty, and the 1994 Danube convention.

7   *Responses to emergencies.* A number of issues have moved up the EU environmental agenda in response to headline-making disasters, accidents and emergencies. The best known of these was the accident in 1976 at a chemical plant in Seveso, Italy, which was instrumental in encouraging the Commission to draft a proposal for a law obliging the manufacturers of toxic, flammable or explosive substances to take the steps necessary to prevent accidents. This was adopted in 1982 and became known as the Seveso directive (82/501). When barrels of waste which had gone missing following the accident were found in northern France in 1983, impetus was given to the development of a new directive on the control of the transfrontier shipment of hazardous waste (adopted as 84/631) (see Chapter 6).

In a similar vein, the 1986 explosion at the nuclear power plant at Chernobyl in the Ukraine encouraged the Community to take action to develop rules for the imports of agricultural products from third countries (regulation 1707/86 and subsequent amendments), and to make arrangements for the early exchange of information in the event of nuclear emergencies (decision 87/600). Similarly, the sinking of the ferry *Herald of Free Enterprise* in Zeebrugge harbour in 1987 (with the loss of 193 lives) provided an impetus for the Commission to propose the harmonization of the laws of member states on the monitoring of ships carrying dangerous goods in their territorial waters; the ferry had been carrying unknown quantities and types of dangerous cargo (Haigh, 1992a, p. 7.18-2).

EU environmental policy is driven by a variety of formal principles and obligations on the one hand, and by a variety of informal pressures and opportunities on the other. The principles are often little more than that, and while designed to provide clarification, have occasionally added confusion and ambiguity to the goals and methods of EU policy. Such confusion and ambiguity is a reflection of the nature of environmental problems (whose causes and parameters are difficult always to tie down), but it also reflects on the gap between the ideals espoused by the authors of the treaties and the realities of making policy in practice. For their part, the obligations have changed as the powers of the EU institutions have changed and as the relationships among those institutions have achieved greater clarity.

Chapter 4

Policy Formulation

A brief outline of the process by which environmental policy is made in the EU would read as follows: the European Council sets the broad objectives; the Commission generates draft laws and policies, and – through national bureaucracies – oversees the implementation of EU laws once agreed; the environment ministers and the European Parliament fine-tune the content of proposals and decide which will become law and which will not; and the Court of Justice ensures that EU law fits with the goals of the treaties.

As with all systems of administration, however, the formal outline of the policy process says little about the informal realities. The Commission does not develop proposals in a vacuum, but is subject to the influence of the internal and external forces outlined in Chapter 3. While the Environment Council and Parliament are responsible for deciding whether a new environmental law will be adopted or not, that decision has – in many respects – already been made as a result of the compromises worked out among competing interests at the policy formulation stage. Meanwhile, interest groups and corporations bring influence to bear from outside the formal policy structure.

This chapter examines the process by which environmental laws and policies are proposed and developed, and argues that the most influential actors in this process are: (1) the technical units of the directorates-general of the Commission where proposals are drafted and their core content is determined, and (2) the national and industrial sector experts with whom the Commission works on the development of proposals. Conversely, the weakest influences are the European Parliament, the environmental lobby and national enforcement agencies; the limited role of the latter in discussions on planning often leads to problems with implementation further down the line. The balance may be changing, however, thanks to the growing powers of Parliament and to efforts made in recent years to promote the activities of environmental groups, and to bring a greater variety of views to bear on the policy process from outside the EU institutions.

The argument is also made in this chapter that it is important to make a distinction between the formal and informal aspects of policy-making, or between actions taken because they are treaty obligations and habits that have emerged among European policymakers. To appreciate how the form and content of proposals for law and policy in the EU are moulded and adopted, it is important to understand the formal macro-policy system, but much more important to appreciate the cumulative role of informal meetings, exchanges of favours, unspoken understandings, coalition-building, package deals, the tension between the competing objectives of EU institutions and member states, the sharing of intelligence in hallways and cafeterias, and the reliance on short-cuts as a means of bypassing formal procedures.

Finally, the argument is made that the common criticism of the Commission for consulting too little and too late with external actors, and for cloaking in secrecy its early discussions on legislative proposals, is not entirely fair. There has been a steady democratization of the legislative process, and while there is a case to be made for even greater openness in that process, freedom of access to environmental decision-making within the Commission has already outstripped the ability of outside actors – notably NGOs – to take part in policy formulation.

The European Council

By its very nature, the European Council has always been the one EU institution least involved in the detail of policy, and the one most given to grand statements of intent and 'solemn' declarations. Nonetheless, many of those statements have come at critical junctures in the evolution of policy, and have both clarified the goals of – and given new direction to the work of – the other institutions.

While the Council has been most active in the fields of agriculture, the budget, the single market and related economic issues, and tends to steer away from discussions about more technically-oriented areas of EU policy, Johnston was quite wrong when she suggested in 1994 that 'other policy sectors, such as the environment, have been mostly untouched by the heads of government' (Johnston, 1994, p. 46). In fact, there have been a number of occasions – particularly in the 1980s and 1990s – when the Council has issued statements and declarations that have had a fundamental impact on the direction taken by EU environmental policy.

The first substantial contribution of the Council came before it had even been created, when the heads of government meeting in October 1972 issued their declaration that economic expansion was not an end in itself, that it should result in an improvement in the quality of life and standards of living, and that particular attention should be given to 'intangible values and to protecting the environment so that progress may really be put at the service of mankind'. The heads of government also called on the Community to develop a blueprint for a formal environmental policy by July 1973, the result of which was the publication of the First Environmental Action Programme, which set the foundation for all the policy developments that followed.

The Council focused on other issues during the remainder of the 1970s, but the combination of energy crises, social pressures and rising public interest in the member states pushed the environment back up the agenda, and the June 1983 European Council held in Stuttgart under the German presidency proved to be another landmark event. It not only played a key role in the development of the European response to acidification (see Chapter 8), but resulted in the adoption of a statement strongly in favour of accelerating and reinforcing action on pollution, which had a notable impact on subsequent air pollution laws.

Nearly two years later, leaders meeting at the March 1985 summit in Brussels concluded that environmental protection could contribute to improved economic growth and job creation, and that environmental policy should become part of the economic, industrial, agricultural and social policies pursued by the Community. This conclusion was to lead to the decision to make the integrative clause part of the SEA two years later, which was to have important ramifications for the role played by environmental considerations in EU policy more generally.

Subsequent statements at European Council summits (notably at Hanover in June 1988, Rhodes in December 1988, Dublin in June 1990 and Edinburgh in December 1992) helped nudge the development of law and policy and gave focus to some of the key objectives of EU policy. The Dublin summit was notable for a declaration on the 'environmental imperative' in which the heads of government outlined their belief that environmental action 'be developed on a coordinated basis and on the principles of sustainable development and preventive and precautionary action'. They also noted

> an increasing acceptance of a wider responsibility, as one of the foremost regional groupings in the world, [for the Community] to play a leading role in promoting concerted and effective action at the global level . . . [and its] special responsibility to encourage and participate in international action to combat global environmental problems. (*Bulletin of the European Communities*, no. 6, vol. 23, 1990, p. 18)

Environmental issues have since featured prominently on the agendas of the European Council, and the decisions of European leaders have given greater force and clarity to the objectives of EU environmental policy. Notably, the Council paid considerable attention in the late 1990s to the problem of global warming, which became one of the most contentious issues in negotiations between the EU, its member states, and its major economic competitors, notably the United States (see Chapter 10).

Initiation: the European Commission

The development of proposals for new EU laws and policies begins within the European Commission. Its most significant power lies in its monopoly on the proposal and drafting of new laws, but it also has a pivotal position as a broker of interests and a forum for the exchange of policy ideas (Mazey and Richardson, 1997), and as a mediator among the member states and the different EU institutions. Proposals are sent to other institutions and interested parties for discussion and amendment, and are then returned to the Commission which is responsible for overseeing and monitoring their implementation by the member states.

Public opinion on the Commission is generally negative, driven by a common misapprehension that the Commission is a large, powerful and inaccessible entity that is behind the growth in the regulatory burden on business, industry and citizens. In fairness, the Commission is neither large, powerful nor always inaccessible. While much of its work – like the work of bureaucracies everywhere – takes place out of the public eye, its employees liaise closely and often with interested outside parties. This is particularly true in regard to environmental issues – there are several channels through which interest groups, experts and national government ministries can work with the Commission in developing new laws, all of which must go through a lengthy and complex process of negotiation and elaboration.

While the Commission has substantially more power over initiating and influencing policy than do national bureaucracies, the final decision on the adoption of new laws rests with Parliament and the Council of Ministers, implementation is left largely to the member states, and the Commission has no powers of enforcement; instead, it tries to encourage policy implementation by national authorities. Furthermore, its work is guided and limited by the goals of the treaties, and the Commission must also answer to the other institutions (notably the Council of Ministers) and to the representatives of the member states in developing its legislative proposals.

At the top of the policy network are the 20 Commissioners, each of whom is given one or more policy portfolios for which they are responsible, and is supported by a *cabinet* of about seven to eight advisers. *Cabinets* play a central role in Commission policy-making, help coordinate policy, broker competing interests inside and outside the Commission, and are a key target for lobbying by sectoral and national interests (Donnelley and Ritchie, 1997). As is the case with cabinets in national governments, there is a hierarchy of portfolios in the Commission, with those relating to the budget, the internal market, trade, agriculture and external relations being regarded as the most senior. The environmental portfolio is still seen as middle-ranking, partly because of its relative newness and partly because of the relatively low level of policy activity on the environment (compared, say, to the internal market). The portfolio was tied to a Commissioner for the first time in its own right only in 1989, since when there have been five office-holders: Carlo Ripa di Meana (1989–92), Karel van Miert (acting) (1992–93), Iannis Paleokrassas (1993–95), Ritt Bjerre-gaard (1995–99) and Margot Wallström (1999–).

The body of the Commission consists of its 23 directorates-general (DGs) (see Table 4.1). The functional equivalent of national government ministries, DGs house the bureaucrats appointed to carry out the daily tasks of administration for the EU. About two-thirds of Commission staff are career em-ployees (or *fonctionnaires*), who work alongside national experts seconded for a specific period to provide specialist input into the development of EU policy. The latter tend to come from industry or national government ministries, or occasionally from NGOs,

TABLE 4.1   *Directorates-General of the European Commission*

New name	Old number
Agriculture	VI
Budget	XIX
Competition	IV
Development	VIII
Economic and Financial Affairs	II
Education and Culture	X/XXII
Employment and Social Affairs	V
Energy and Transport	XVII/VII
Enlargement	–
Enterprise	XXIII
Environment	XI
External Relations	I/IA/IB
Financial Control	–
Fisheries	XIV
Health and Consumer Protection	XXIV
Information Society	X
Internal Market	XV
Justice and Home Affairs	–
Personnel and Administration	IX
Regional Policy	XVI
Research	XII
Taxation and the Customs Union	XXI
Trade	I

and are normally employed on one-year contracts, renewable twice. They are paid by their member states, given a per diem by the Commission, and are guaranteed that their jobs at home will be held open for them.

The DG most centrally – but not exclusively – involved in EU environmental policy is the Environment DG. Created in 1973 as the Environment and Consumer Protection Service of DGIII (then responsible for industrial affairs), it was raised to the status of a separate directorate-general in 1981 (DGXI). Its internal structure was overhauled in 1989 in response to its increasing workload, and in 1995 consumer protection was made part of a new DGXXIV, and civil protection was transferred to DGXI from DGV (employment, industrial relations and social affairs). As part of the Prodi reforms in 1999, directorates-general ceased to be known by their numbers, so DGXI was renamed the Environment DG (EDG). It has five directorates: A deals with general and international affairs, B with integration policy, C with nuclear safety and civil protection, D with environmental quality and natural resources, and E with industry and the environment (see Table 4.2).

Situated in the southern suburbs of Brussels in two separate buildings, the EDG in 1998 employed about 500 staff and operated on a budget of just over 140 million ecus. Just over half its employees were involved in policy development, and the rest in administration and translation. While there has been a tendency for some of the DGs to be 'captured' by one member state or another – for example, External Affairs has a British tilt to its staff, while the Internal Market DG has a German tilt – Environment has no significant inclination towards any one member state. Its staff tend to be technical specialists because of the nature of their work, and most of their business is conducted in English for the same reason. About two-thirds of its staff are *fonctionnaires*, and the rest are national experts working through secondments of up to three years.

Time has seen changes in the approach of EDG employees to their work. It is sometimes assumed that the EDG has a green bias to its work, and a sympathy for the work of environmental NGOs, but this is not entirely true. One long-time staff member noted that while the service had once been dominated by employees with strong interests in the environment, it had slowly become more bureaucratic and technically-oriented. For

TABLE 4.2   *Organizational chart of the Environment DG*

Commissioner	
Director-General	
Deputy Director General	
Directorate A	General and international affairs
	1 Inter-institutional relations
	2 Climate change
	3 International affairs, trade and environment
	4 Development and environment
Directorate B	Integration policy and environmental instruments
	1 Environmental action programme, integration, relations with the European Environment Agency
	2 Economic analyses and employment
	3 Legal affairs, activities related to legislation and enforcement of Community law
	4 Structural policy, environmental impact assessment, LIFE
Directorate C	Nuclear safety and civil protection
	1 Radiation protection
	2 Regulation and radioactive waste management policy
	3 Civil protection
Directorate D	Environment quality and natural resources
	1 Water protection, soil conservation, agriculture
	2 Nature protection, coastal zones and tourism
	3 Air quality, urban environment, noise, transport, energy
Directorate E	Industry and environment
	1 Industrial installations and hazards, biotechnology
	2 Chemical substances
	3 Waste management
	4 Industry, internal market, products and voluntary approaches

his part, he put the EU first on his list of priorities, the Commission second, the EDG third, and the environment fourth – he saw himself as much less an environmentalist than a bureaucrat. He also argued that this shift had allowed the Environment DG to be taken more seriously by other services; its credibility would be undermined if it was perceived as a proselytizing organization rather than a professional service working in the broader interests of European integration. At the same time, another staff member argued that the EDG was not so technocratic as to be immune to internal politics, and to the influence of rivalries, friendships and professional biases.

Fonctionnaires and national experts alike often bemoan the length of time involved in seeing a piece of legislation through from proposal to adoption. More senior *fonctionnaires* in the EDG recall how it was once possible to complete a project in two to three years, but that seven to eight years has now become the norm. One national expert recalled how he had assumed upon arrival that he might see at least part of his project through to completion before his three-year secondment was over, but soon discovered that the process was very slow-moving, thanks in part to shortstaffing in the EDG (a common complaint among its employees), but mainly to the need to ensure that all the member states, all other relevant services of the Commission, and all interested lobbyists had their input.

More time has also been added to the legislative process in the EDG by the introduction by the Single European Act of the integration principle. This gave the EDG a higher status, because it has become much more active since 1987 in working with other parts of the Commission, particularly those that were already involved in activities with an obvious environmental dimension. At the same time, though, it has greatly complicated the EDG's work, because it must now network with all these other elements of the Commission, and make sure that it vets proposals from other DGs with an environmental element, and that it passes its own proposals on to other DGs for comment.

The other DGs most actively involved in environmental matters include the following:

- Agriculture (formerly DGVI). As well as dealing with concerns arising from the environmental impact of the Common Agricultural Policy, Agriculture is involved in rural develop-

ment issues and structural policies relating to the development of poorer rural regions of the EU. It is also involved
in the development of laws and policies pertaining to
forestry, organic agriculture and environmentally-friendly
farming.
- Energy and Transport (formerly DGVII and DGXVII). Commission staff working on energy matters deal mainly with
  issues such as fuel supply, the energy market, EU cooperation
  with non-member states, trans-European energy networks
  and energy technology, but they also look at the environmental impact of energy use and the safe transport of radioactive material, and manage the EU programmes on limiting
  carbon dioxide emissions through improved energy efficiency
  (SAVE and SAVE II) and on promoting the use of renewable
  energy (ALTENER and ALTENER II) (see Chapter 10).
  For its part, EU transport policy is concerned mainly with
  competition rules and market operation, but the Common
  Transport Policy action plan (1998–2004) includes the development of environmental standards for transport. The development of trans-European transport networks also has an
  environmental impact, and the Energy and Transport DG
  monitors the development of policy on issues such as road
  vehicle emissions and the transport of hazardous wastes.
  Several pieces of law have also been developed on safety at
  sea with a view to controlling pollution.
- Fisheries (formerly DGXIV) is responsible for the Common
  Fisheries Policy (CFP), which includes the conservation and
  management of marine resources, and agreements with non-
  member countries and international organizations. The major
  goal of the CFP is to strike a sustainable balance between
  available marine resources and the methods used to exploit
  them. Conservation involves drawing up guidelines on the
  management of resources, development of proposals for total
  allowable catches (TACs), and undertaking research into the
  status of fisheries.

The work of the Commission has been bolstered since 1993
by the European Environment Agency (EEA). As noted in
Chapter 2, the EEA is not a policy-making or implementing
body, but is charged with collecting, analyzing and distilling
information on the environment produced by various other

agencies. It makes that information available to EU institutions (including the Commission) and member states, helps promote comparable data-gathering systems among the member states, identifies and develops new ideas for EU environmental legislation, draws up triennial reports on the state of the European environment (the first two were published in 1995 and 1998), promotes methods for the harmonization of methods of measurement, liaises with national, regional and international agencies, and coordinates the European Environment Information and Observation Network (EIONET). EIONET consists of a network of national organizations that help retrieve information for the EEA, and identify special issues that need to be addressed.

Headquartered in Copenhagen, the EEA had about 70 staff in 2000 and a budget of nearly 17 million euros. Membership is open to non-EU countries, but so far only Iceland, Liechtenstein and Norway have joined from outside the EU.

The Commission policy process

The process of policy development within the Commission has become so complex – and involves so many different actors – that it can take several years. Krämer argues that EU environmental regulations 'are adopted behind closed doors, without public participation' (1996, p. 297), but this is misleading. Adoption involves the European Parliament, to which the public has substantial access, and while the opportunities for direct public participation in policy *formulation* are limited, the views of many interested parties outside the Commission are considered. Policy formulation is so thorough that by the time a proposal is sent to the Council and Parliament for discussion, it has reached an advanced stage of development and has been seen by many different people. This is particularly true of the proposals coming out of the EDG; most are so technical in nature that they demand the sustained input of experts, and most of the critical changes to a legislative or policy proposal developed by the EDG have already taken place before the proposal is sent out for discussion.

Once a decision has been taken (normally by the Commission, the Council of Ministers or the European Council) to

initiate a response to a particular problem, the relevant technical unit within the EDG will normally prepare a background
position paper in an attempt to quantify the scale of the problem
and the potential costs and benefits. This is used as the basis for
discussion with experts from the member states, normally beginning with a Commission-sponsored advisory committee meeting
in Brussels. The Commission also usually hosts parallel discussions with other interested parties; these might include representatives from other DGs, industry, academia, NGOs and/or
international organizations. Because of the large numbers of
interested organizations – and in order to avoid partisan discussions – the Commission prefers to meet with pan-European
organizations rather than with national organizations or individual companies (Krämer, 1996, pp. 301–2).

The invitations to the member states are sent to the permanent representations of the member states in Brussels, which
then decide for themselves who to send to the meeting; they can
send experts if they wish, but tend to send government officials
from the relevant unit of the relevant national authority. The
permanent representations are used as intermediaries because
if the EDG was to send invitations directly to the national
environment ministries, it might be accused of playing to its own
constituency. By leaving the choice to the permanent representations, it is reasonable to expect that the views of the delegates
will reflect the views of the national governments. The hosting
of the meeting is not a treaty obligation on the Commission, but
rather is a form of political insurance and investment.

The early steps taken to develop an EU acidification strategy
illustrate the process. The Swedish government was the primary
champion of the idea, opening discussions at the Environment
Council in March 1995, just three months after Sweden's admis-
sion to the EU. The Swedes enlisted the support of the newly-
appointed environment Commissioner, Ritt Bjerregaard from
neighbouring Denmark. At its meeting in December 1995, the
Council – in the careful diplomatic language that flavours so
much EU activity – 'invited' the Commission to develop an acidification strategy, and the invitation was 'accepted'. The Swedish
government continued to press the case by sending a delegation to Brussels to lobby the EDG in May 1996, two weeks
before a Commission-sponsored advisory committee meeting of
member states.

The meeting was attended not only by representatives nominated by the member states (mainly appropriate bureaucrats from national environment departments), but also by representatives from several other DGs (such as agriculture and energy), from Norway, the secretariat of the European Free Trade Association (EFTA), the UN Economic Commission for Europe (UNECE, repository of the 1979 Convention on Long-Range Transboundary Air Pollution – see Chapter 8), the International Institute for Applied Systems Analysis (IIASA, the research body contracted by the Commission to provide the data upon which the strategy would largely be based), and from the European Environmental Bureau and groups representing the electricity, oil and chemicals industries.

Advisory committee meetings such as this are an opportunity for the Commission to test its ideas on interested parties, and for those parties to offer comments and suggestions, ensuring that proposals then move in a direction that maximizes their acceptability to the member states. Since it is usually already well-known among member states, other EU units and interest groups which proposals are in the pipeline, and since the Commission will informally have tested the ideas behind these proposals with interested parties, there are few surprises at these meetings and the discussion is relatively placid. The meetings usually herald a complex process of discussions involving the Commission and interested parties that may take another 18–24 months or longer, and involve several more meetings of the parties to discuss each proposal. In the case of the acidification strategy, at least two further advisory committee meetings were scheduled, and arrangements were also made to liaise with the IIASA and UNECE.

Proposals are usually drafted and developed by the head of the relevant unit within the EDG, or a middle-ranking staff member with specialist expertise. They are drafted with legal considerations very much in mind; senior staff will already be familiar with the requirements of appropriate language, but proposals are nevertheless vetted by the legal unit of each DG and by the Legal Service of the Commission to ensure conformity with the treaties. During the drafting process, the staff member responsible will keep in close touch with the Policy Group, which is something like a board of management of a DG. In the case of the EDG, this consists of the director-general and an assistant, the deputy director-general, and the unit directors. They meet weekly to review the various draft proposals working their way through the EDG. Once they are satisfied, the draft will be sent out for inter-service consultation: it will be copied to all other interested DGs for comment, with the EDG deciding which other DGs to target and consult. A proposal on water policy, for example, might be sent to Agriculture, Energy and Transport, Research, Regional Policy, and Health and Consumer Protection.

An ongoing problem within the Commission has been that of coordination, and of ensuring that different Commissioners and DGs know what the others are doing. This is a particular problem for the EDG, given its relatively lowly position in the Commission pecking order, which must be balanced against the requirement that environmental considerations are built into all relevant laws and policies generated by the Commission. Some DGs – such as External Relations and Agriculture – are well-established and powerful enough to override objections from other DGs (Spence, 1997), but the EDG is not. Some of the problems are addressed by the requirement that the staffer responsible for drafting a proposal keep in regular contact with opposite numbers in other DGs that might have an interest in the proposal, and by weekly meetings of directors-general and their deputies. However, the most important safeguard against inadequate coordination lies in the work of the *cabinets*.

As well as being seen by the director-general (and the appropriate staff member) in each DG, it has also become increasingly common in recent years for drafts to be seen (prior to inter-service consultation) by the relevant member of the *cabinets* of the interested Commissioners. For example, a proposal sent to the Transport DG will be read not only by its director-general, but will go to the *cabinet* of the Commissioner responsible for transport policy, and will be reviewed by the member of that *cabinet* responsible for environmental issues. For many years, no time limits were placed on other DGs for the return of comments, but since 1995 there has been a requirement that the proposal be returned within ten working days, thus greatly speeding up the development process. If written comments are sufficient, these will be incorporated into the draft proposal. There may be enough disagreements, however, to merit a meeting among staff members from the interested DGs, or –

more seriously and much more rarely – a meeting among the relevant Commissioners.

Once all the services have had their input, and compromises have been reached on content, the proposal will be sent to the Secretariat-General of the Commission, and circulated to the *cabinets* of each of the Commissioners, which have ten days to respond. At this point, discussion usually ceases to focus on the technical aspects of the proposal, and is driven instead by national political considerations and by the ideological leanings of the *cabinets*, whose *chefs* and deputy *chefs* in the past have often come from the same political party as the Commissioner and are subject to influence from the national party. Environmental proposals tend to have greater support from the *cabinets* of socialist Commissioners than those of conservatives or Christian Democrats. While Commissioners are not national representatives, it is not unknown for them to allow narrower national interests to influence their opinions, especially when they are relatively new to the office.

Every Monday, the *chefs de cabinet* meet to go through the accumulated proposals and to draw up an agenda for the meeting of the Commissioners on Wednesday. If no objections have been raised to a proposal, it is added to the agenda as an A point, and is normally adopted by the Commission without debate. However, it is more normal for environmental proposals to have not yet won universal support, so they are usually submitted instead to *ad hoc* meetings of special *chefs*: the members of each *cabinet* with responsibility for environmental matters. While the EDG officials who drafted the proposal might attend these meetings, they usually do not speak. Instead, they will more likely have kept in regular touch with the special *chef* in the *cabinet* of the environment Commissioner, even – if necessary – drafting a statement which the special *chef* can present to the *cabinet*.

If there are difficulties at this meeting, the EDG official will redraft the proposal for resubmission, perhaps as many as three or four times in the case of more troublesome proposals. It is more usual with environmental proposals, however, for the special *chefs* to agree in general, but to attach four or five questions to the proposal for discussion at a later stage in the decision-making process. Once a majority of the special *chefs* have expressed themselves in favour, the proposal will be placed

TABLE 4.3   *Stages in the EU environmental policy process*

1   *Agenda-setting (all institutions)*

- constitutional pressures
- pressures to harmonize
- legislative pressures
- policy evolution and spillover
- pressures from EU institutions
- international law
- responses to emergencies
- exchange of information

2   *Formulation (European Commission, directorates-general)*

- background position or discussion paper
- proposal developed by technical units within DGs
- advisory committee meetings with national experts
- advisory committee meetings with industry, NGOs, other interested parties
- legal services
- inter-service consultation
- *cabinets* of interested Commissioners
- Secretariat-General of the Commission
- *chefs de cabinet*
- College of Commissioners

3   *Adoption (Council of Ministers, Parliament, ESC, Committee of the Regions)*

- Secretariat-General of the Council of Ministers
- Parliament, ESC, Committee of the Regions for opinion
- permanent representations
- relevant national government agencies
- environment working group
- COREPER
- Parliament for opinion
- Environment Council for decision

4   *Implementation (Commission, member states)*

- governments of the member states
- relevant national government agencies
- European Commission
- Court of Justice (if necessary)

by the *chefs de cabinet* on the agenda for the next meeting of the Commission, which will debate the proposal and – if necessary – put it to a vote.

There is no guarantee that if a particular director-general supports the proposal, his/her Commissioner will also support it. There may be agreement at the technical level but not at the political level, because *cabinets* may have injected a political dimension into the consideration of a proposal by a Commissioner. It has even been known for *cabinets* to write the inter-service response to a proposal rather than the director-general of the interested DG. Influence may have been exerted on a Commissioner by an interest group, an industry or by ideological considerations, but these are commonly disguised in the final written response as concerns about the cost-effectiveness of the proposal, or some technical objection. For example, proposals on the sulphur content of liquid fuel and on volatile organic compound (VOC) emission controls put forward in the early 1990s were opposed by the Spanish, French and Italian Commissioners at the time, ostensibly on the basis of concerns about cost-effectiveness, but more likely because their national industries were opposed.

Consultation: the European Parliament and external actors

Typically, the early stages of legislative and policy development see the Commission consulting often with national government officials, for the obvious reason that it is the member states which ultimately give the EU its authority, and (through the Council of Ministers) ultimately make the decisions on which proposals are adopted and which are not. At the same time, the EDG also holds discussions with corporate interests and with Brussels-based industrial federations. These bodies play an important part in the development of environmental proposals, helped by several critical strengths that they bring to the bargaining table: they represent communities with specific interests, they are well-organized and funded, they are usually very effective at quantifying the costs and benefits of different policy options and at offering alternatives, they employ technical experts who can respond persuasively and authoritatively to the often detailed technical content of EDG proposals, and they have a vested interest in the negotiations given that they are centrally involved in the implementation of subsequent legislation and will often have to meet most of the direct costs.

So effective has the industrial lobby become at working with the EDG that something of a symbiotic relationship has developed between the two. The former offers technical input into the development of legislation in return for concessions (whether actual or implied), as a result of which the EDG has become adept at identifying relevant industrial groups and at bringing them into the policy formulation process. There are several dozen industrial federations based in Brussels, and dozens more based in other parts of the EU with the capacity to bring their resources to bear on policy discussions at very little notice. Examples include the following (Brussels-based) organizations:

- The European Chemical Industry Council (CEFIC). Representing the national chemical federations of 22 countries and 41 chemical companies, including Bayer, Hoechst, Novartis and ICI, CEFIC brings substantial influence to bear on any policy developments on competition and the internal market that might have an impact on chemicals. It claims to represent 40 000 large, medium and small chemical companies, employing more than two million people and accounting for about 30 per cent of world chemical production (CEFIC Web page, 2000).
- The European Crop Protection Association (ECPA). This represents 16 national associations (such as the British Agrochemicals Association) and 19 research-based chemical companies (including BASF, Monsanto and Zeneca) dealing with crop protection products (i.e., pesticides).
- The European Union of National Associations of Water Suppliers and Waste Water Services (EUREAU). Founded in 1975, this represents 20 national associations of water suppliers in the EU member states and three EFTA states, and describes its role as follows: 'to make [technical and scientific] knowledge and expertise available at Community level, to ensure that it is taken into proper account by European decision-makers' (EUREAU Web page, 2000).
- The European Petroleum Industries Association (EUROPIA). Representing the petroleum industry, and with a membership

consisting of 27 companies active in the EU (including BP Amoco, Elf Aquitaine, PetroFina, Shell and five US companies), EUROPIA was founded in 1989 to lobby on related issues. Its members accounted in 1999 for 95 per cent of EU refining capacity, and EUROPIA was active on issues such as the Auto-Oil programme, air quality, acidification and climate change.

• The European Automobile Manufacturers Association (ACEA). With a membership of 13 vehicle manufacturers (including BMW, Fiat, Ford, Renault and Volvo), ACEA was set up in response to the growth of EU activities on economic and technical issues of interest to the automobile industry. It claimed in 2000 that its companies employed 1.6 million people and had a combined production turnover worth 365 billion euros (ACEA Web page, 2000).

One of the tactics used by the Commission to achieve its objectives has been to develop voluntary agreements with industry under which goals are agreed without mandating any particular means of achieving those goals. This has seen the Commission developing ever closer relations with industry in order to work out the terms of such agreements. A notable recent example is the strategy agreed between European road vehicle manufacturers – represented by ACEA – and the Commission on the reduction of CO_2 emissions from road vehicles. Under the terms of international agreements on climate change, the EU has agreed to an 8 per cent reduction in CO_2 emissions by 2008–12 (see Chapter 10). Instead of developing appropriate regulations or directives – which would be handicapped by the lack of the kind of technology needed to achieve these reductions – the EU has instead developed a strategy based on working with industry and consumers to reduce emissions. At its core is an agreement with ACEA under which they have agreed to investigate marketing strategies and technical changes (including possibly using alternative fuels or new propulsion systems) aimed at producing smaller and more fuel-efficient cars (Bongaerts, 1999).

In contrast to the efficacy of industry, three other sets of interests – the European Parliament (EP), environmental interest groups, and national enforcement agencies (see Chapter 5) – are notable for their relatively modest role in the early stages of the development of policy and legislative proposals.

The European Parliament

The steady growth in the powers of the EP is well-known and understood; a combination of the cooperative powers provided to it on environmental matters by the SEA, the growing (if still modest) presence of Green MEPs, the use of Article 95 (formerly 100a) on environmental legislation (which requires the Council to cooperate with the EP), and the new powers given to the EP by Maastricht and Amsterdam have made it a more significant actor in the environmental policy process. However, it still lacks one of the defining powers of a conventional legislature: the ability to generate proposals for new laws. Hence it is involved less in policy formulation than in making changes to policy proposals once they have left the Commission.

The EP would play a greater role in policy formulation if it was to send representatives to the early planning meetings hosted by the EDG, but this it rarely does, for three main reasons. First, there is the practical concern that its members and their support staff lack the time to be present at every planning meeting in every part of the Commission. Second, there is the constitutional matter that Parliament is not required to define or defend its position until it is presented with a finished proposal from the Commission. While informal soundings are occasionally taken by the Commission, senior members of the EDG have been quoted as arguing against the idea of bringing the EP into pre-legislative discussions (Judge, 1993, pp. 192–3). Finally, few MEPs have the kind of detailed technical knowledge and background that is often required of participants in the development of environmental legislation. As EP administrator Sylvie Motard put it (1996), Parliament 'is traditionally much more at ease discussing human rights than pondering the control of VOC emissions resulting from refueling operations at service stations'. On the few occasions when they are involved in the development of proposals, MEPs and their staff are able to offer little constructive input, and the Commission officials chairing organizational meetings may find themselves frustrated by the challenge of trying to summarize in an hour a proposal that may have taken many months to develop and may run to many pages.

There has been little evidence to date to suggest that the growing number of Greens in national governments and the

European Parliament has had a notable impact on EU environmental policy. However, this is likely to change if present trends continue. In 1997, Greens served in only two EU governments, those of France and Germany. By 1999, they had become members of the Belgian, Italian and Finnish governments as well, and the June 1999 European elections saw the Greens increase their share of EP seats from 29 to 37 – Greens were elected from every EU member state except Denmark, Greece, Portugal and Spain.

The absence of MEPs from the critical early stages of the development of new laws in the Commission means that their role in initiating or influencing the formulation of proposals is marginal (Williams, 1991, p. 160). However, this is not to suggest that Parliament is entirely absent from the early stages of the policy process. On the contrary, it often plays a useful role in articulating concerns about environmental issues (Arp, 1992, 10–14), which it does in several ways:

- By submitting questions to the Commission and the Council of Ministers which require written or oral answers, and either seek information or request action. The number of questions posed by Parliament has grown, and those on environmental issues have made up a substantial proportion at times (they made up more than 10 per cent of all questions asked in January–April 1988, for example, but had tailed off considerably by 1997, in part due to the reduction in the number of new legislative proposals coming out of the Commission).
- By generating 'own-initiative' reports and resolutions, and by reporting on the Commission response. For example, EP reports in 1984 and 1988 raised the issue of chlorofluorocarbons (CFCs) and the ozone layer, and while the long-time chairman of the environment committee, Ken Collins, admits that the proposals were considered unrealistic at the time, he argues that their terms were met by subsequent legislation (Collins, 1995). Meanwhile, a 1982 resolution played a key role in prompting the Commission to respond to the problem of imports of baby seal skins and products, leading to the ban imposed by a March 1983 directive (83/129).
- By generating pressure for improved implementation of EU laws. Since 1984, the Commission has published annual

reports to Parliament on the implementation of law and its own monitoring efforts, in response to which Parliament has occasionally demanded more information. It also carries out its own studies on implementation, such as the 1988 Environment Committee report on water legislation.

- By setting up committees of inquiry into breaches of EU law. The first ever such inquiry was set up in 1983 to look into the disappearance of barrels of toxic waste from the Seveso plant in Italy (see Chapter 6).

A combination of such tactics has meant that the EP has had an impact on the development of laws dealing with major industrial hazards, the transfrontier shipment of waste, landfill, the eco-labelling scheme and the implementation of EU environmental law (Judge, 1993, pp. 190–1), but such examples are few and far between. On the whole, the EP plays a role that is more reactive than proactive.

Environmental interest groups

Also failing to live up to their full potential are environmental interest groups, or non-governmental organizations (NGOs). Groups were slow to appreciate the implications of the evolving Community environmental programme and to begin actively lobbying the Commission. This was certainly the case with the experience of the Campaign for Lead Free Air (CLEAR) in Britain, which launched its campaign to have lead removed from petrol in Britain in early 1982, apparently unaware either of the content of existing Community law on lead in petrol, or of the importance of lobbying the Commission. The campaign very quickly picked up on the significance of Community law, however, lobbied the Commission as well as the British government, and was instrumental in a change of policy in Britain in 1983 (Haigh and Lanigan, 1995).

In his study of EU water policy, Richardson (1994) suggests that the EDG had been assisted in its deliberations by 'a politicised, mobilised, and effective constituency of environmental groups', but this is a debatable proposition. Krämer (1996, p. 297) is probably closer to the truth in his assertion that environmental NGOs 'are underrepresented in Brussels and lack resources, know-how and expertise in successful lobbying'. This certainly seemed to be the consensus among those interviewed for this study – there was a general admiration for the professionalism of individual members of NGO staff, but there was also agreement that NGOs had only limited influence. To be fair, they face a number of structural and logistical problems that put them at a disadvantage when compared to industry and industrial federations.

First, the environmental lobby in Brussels is small. There are only seven pan-European environmental NGOs with offices in Brussels, with a combined full-time staff of about 30 people (although there are many other lobbying organizations which include staff members with an interest in environmental issues, or whose interests include the environment; for example, the European Bureau of Consumer Unions, and the Environment and Development Resources Centre). The seven groups – which meet together on an *ad hoc* basis about two to three times each year, and are known informally as G7 – are as follows:

- The European Environmental Bureau (EEB). The oldest of the groups working at the European level, the EEB was founded in 1974 with the help and support of the Community, and for many years was the only environmental interest group working in Brussels to influence Community policy. The EEB is an umbrella body which acts as a conduit for contacts between NGOs and the EU. In 2000, it had 130 NGO members from 24 countries, which it claimed represented about 14 000 member organizations with a combined membership of more than 11 million (EEB Web page, 2000). Its main goal is to bring together NGOs in the member states in order to strengthen their collective impact on EU policy.
- Friends of the Earth Europe (FoEE), which set up a Brussels office in 1986 and now represents FoE groups in 27 European countries.
- Greenpeace International, which set up its Brussels office in 1988, and now represents 19 national Greenpeace organizations.
- The World Wide Fund for Nature (WWF), the European policy office of the international conservation organization founded in 1961. The Brussels office was opened in 1989, mainly because WWF had an interest in Community development assistance, and hoped to encourage the EC to tighten

its environmental requirements in the disbursement of that assistance, and to ensure that some of the funds were spent on conservation and development projects. It has subsequently shifted its focus to Europe, and to promoting co-operation among national WWF offices (Long, 1998).

- Climate Network Europe (CNE), an umbrella body founded in 1989, and representing 60 groups with a common concern for climate change and energy policy. CNE has been particularly active in providing technical inputs to the debate on the issue of climate change.
- The European Federation for Transport and the Environment (T&E), an umbrella body founded in 1992 and representing 25 groups interested in environmentally-sound transport issues.
- Birdlife International, the regional office of a UK-based umbrella body that was founded in 1993 and brings together organizations in 88 countries with an interest in promoting the protection of birdlife.

The problem of unfulfilled potential is best exemplified by the record of the EEB. It could be an active and effective representative of NGO opinion (particularly if it really represents as many people as it claims), but it had a reputation in the first half of the 1990s for poor leadership. Concerns about its effectiveness were sufficient, for example, to encourage Greenpeace in 1991 to withdraw all its national organizations from membership of the EEB. The Bureau has also had to adjust itself in the last decade to working with other NGOs – until 1988 it had a virtual monopoly on lobbying activities in Brussels. To be fair, the task of pulling together and trying to synthesize the collective interests and priorities of thousands of local, national and regional NGOs with a stake in EU policy is daunting.

The second problem faced by Brussels-based environmental NGOs is the common perception both inside and outside the Commission that the technical expertise of NGOs does not measure up to that of industrial groups, and that they lack the ability to discuss the costs and benefits of policy options in real terms. Much of the problem stems from their relative lack of resources, as illustrated by the position during early debates over climate change policy; one business lobby alone – the Union of Industrial and Employers Confederations of Europe

(UNICE) – had more staff in its secretariat than all the environmental NGOs combined (Skjaerseth, 1994, p. 31). Similarly, while environmental groups in 1993 had only one full-time expert on biotechnology among them, the industrial lobby had a Senior Advisory Board sponsored by 31 corporations, including giants such as Bayer, Ciba-Geigy, Du Pont, Hoechst and Unilever, whose resources were at the disposal of the Board (Rucht, 1993).

One EDG official argued that NGOs are good at offering criticism, but not so good at offering constructive alternative suggestions, in large part because of their variable grasp of the often complex technical details involved in an EU proposal. Another EDG veteran – and a former special *chef* – noted that industrial groups are wealthy, can pay good salaries to attract the kind of staff most effective at getting their message across to the Commission, are good at identifying the Commission staff developing proposals of interest, have the facts and figures needed to back up their arguments, and 'can take you out for a decent lunch'. NGOs, by contrast, have few resources and relatively few technical specialists.

The third problem stems from the fact that the umbrella organizations are dependent for much of their support on their member organizations, most of which still focus more on trying to influence policy at the national rather than the European level. There is also relatively little cross-national cooperation among interest groups, leaving organizations such as the EEB and Climate Network Europe like hubs at the centre of rimless wheels. Accepting support from the Commission offers little comfort, because it raises questions in the minds both of NGO staff and of Commission staff about their independence. When a group such as the EEB depends on the Commission for as much as 60 per cent of its funding (more than 500 000 ecus in 1995 – EEB Web page, 1998), questions must be raised about its autonomy.

The fourth problem faced by NGOs is that the compartmentalized nature of policy-making within the Commission requires that they be able to monitor and respond to policy developments in multiple DGs (Mazey and Richardson, 1993). One EDG staff member noted that NGOs tend to focus on the Environment DG, have not yet adapted to the integrationist idea that the environment affects other policy areas, and have devoted relatively little attention to the Agriculture or Energy and Transport DGs, for example. NGOs are fully aware of the problem, but lack the resources to respond. As one NGO staff member put it, the scope of the environmental debate has broadened to include several different directorates-general, and while his organization receives many invitations to take part in advisory meetings, he has to turn many of them down because he lacks adequate staff numbers. He notes that while there has been an 'explosion' of activity among DGs, the NGO structure has not been able to respond. The frustration is evident in the comment of a staff member from another NGO, who said she was not always confident that the Commission kept her group informed of what it was doing.

Brussels-based NGOs have responded to these problems in two main ways. First, they have tried to avoid the details and have instead looked at the bigger picture by trying to influence the outcome of reviews of the environmental action programmes, or through their well-publicized attempts to promote greater attention to environmental matters during the debates leading up to Maastricht (WWF *et al.*, 1991) and to the 1995–96 intergovernmental conference (Stichting Natuur en Milieu, 1995). Second, they have worked together informally towards dividing responsibilities, based on their particular interests. So instead of every group trying to chase every issue, Climate Network Europe has focused on energy and climate issues, Birdlife International on agriculture and land use, Greenpeace on oceans and the atmosphere, the EEB on standards, and the WWF on forestry and the structural funds. Anyone from the Commission or the media who contacts any one of the major groups will likely be referred – if necessary – to the appropriate staff member in another group.

NGOs have several important cards that they could play (for further discussion of this argument see Mazey and Richardson, 1993), but there is little indication to date that they are fully exploiting their potential strengths, which include the following:

• The ability to influence the political agenda in Brussels by building strong pan-European coalitions, and mustering the considerable forces of the thousands of regional, national and local NGOs active in the EU. Unlike industry (which is often limited by narrow agendas and conflicts of interest), NGOs are capable of taking a coordinated pan-European view of their long-term interests, providing a balance to the narrower views of the Commission.

• The ability to be of service through the provision of information. The EDG is small, it relies frequently on outside sources for expert technical information, and does not have the resources to adequately monitor compliance with EU law (see Chapter 5). National groups in particular could exert more influence by more actively assisting the EDG (and other parts of the Commission) with the provision of technical information, and in using their national bodies to act as watchdogs over compliance.

The EU has been instrumental in recent years in attempts to broaden the base of input into its deliberations on the environment. Most notably, it set up an informal General Consultative Forum on the Environment in 1993 (decision 93/701). Made up of members appointed by the Commission on the basis of suggestions from interest groups, the Forum was designed to provide advice on policy development from a variety of different sectors; its members came from interest groups, industry, business, consumer groups, local and regional authorities, trade unions and academia. The remit of the Forum was changed in 1997 by decision 97/1, under which it was renamed the European Consultative Forum on the Environment and Sustainable Development (or the European Green Forum). It has the same kind of membership, but its scope was broadened to include sustainable development (a consequence of changes introduced by the Amsterdam Treaty), members have been added from several non-EU states (the Czech Republic, Lithuania, Norway and Poland), and it has been provided with an independent chairman; Thorvald Stoltenberg was the first person appointed to the position.

Special interests also have a more formal influence on legislative proposals through the work of the Economic and Social Committee (ESC) and the Committee of the Regions. The former ensures the involvement of selected economic and social groups in EU policy-making, and counts among its 222 members representatives of environmental and consumer groups. Although consultation by the Council of Ministers and the Commission with the ESC on environmental legislation is optional, the ESC does have a Section for the Protection of the Environment, Public Health and Consumer Affairs (Section IV) that has been instrumental in changes to laws dealing with issues such as air pollution. While the Council has no obligation to do anything more than take the ESC's opinion into account, and its real significance is questionable, it does have one notable advantage: it has a number of technical experts among its members, and sets up its own working groups to which additional experts are invited to give evidence, so it can provide useful specialist comments on a proposal.

For its part, the Committee of the Regions (CoR) began work in 1994 with the same basic structure as the ESC, although in a more purely advisory role. It was set up in order to involve regional and local authorities more directly in EU policy-making, and can give opinions to the Council and the Commission on specified issues where regional interests are at stake, including transport, public health and implementation of the European Regional Development Fund. It also has 222 members, divided into eight permanent committees, including one dealing with land-use planning, the environment and energy.

While it is true that the Commission has consulted with an ever-widening variety of external interests on the development of new laws and policies on the environment, the influence of those interests is skewed in favour of bodies and agencies that can either offer the Commission the kind of technical input it needs, and/or are most likely to be directly affected by the content of such new laws and policies. Hence, while corporate interests and industrial federations offer technical advice on proposals, which can have the effect of influencing the content of those proposals to suit their needs and objectives, environmental groups have fewer resources available to them, and are thus not so well-placed to influence the formulation of EU policy.

Chapter 5

Policy Adoption and Implementation

While many of the technical aspects of environmental law are determined and resolved during the formulation phase, political and administrative matters come to the fore during adoption and implementation. Adoption is in the hands of the Council of Ministers and the European Parliament (EP), the former representing national interests, and the latter ostensibly representing the interests of voters, but in fact involved in an ongoing struggle to win more powers for itself. Meanwhile, the Commission is responsible for overseeing implementation, but to do this must work with national governments and environmental agencies, and must carry out its oversight responsibilities with no direct powers of enforcement. Finally, the European Court of Justice both provides clarification on the meaning of EU law, and is available to help the Commission with implementation – a member state that is suspected of infringing an EU law can be referred to the Court, which can impose a fine if the problem is not resolved.

Adoption has become more complex and time-consuming as the EP has won new powers relative to the Council of Ministers, and as the codecision procedure has made the two institutions into colegislatures. The EP has become more forceful in offering amendments to proposals from the Commission, to some extent making up for its relatively limited role in the development phase outlined in Chapter 4. The EP's Committee on the Environment is one of the biggest and most active of parliamentary committees, and has developed a reputation for encouraging the Commission and the Council to be more ambitious in the goals set by environmental law.

For its part, implementation remains the weakest stage in the EU environmental policy process, with continuing concerns about whether laws are fully, effectively or correctly transposed into national law, and implemented at the national level. Such problems have the unfortunate effect of undermining the credibility of EU environmental policy; while there is no question about the productivity of the EU institutions, the policies and laws they adopt mean little unless they are effectively implemented. Part of the problem lies in the relative novelty of EU environmental policy and the lack of an explicit legal base until the passage of the SEA, which Macrory (1992) argues contributed to the development of a climate in which policy-makers focused more on developing new laws than on implementation. Only in recent years has more attention focused on the need to improve the record with implementation. It was given new emphasis in the Fourth EAP, a 1990 European Council declaration spoke of the need to resolve persistent difficulties in implementation, and in 1992 a process called IMPEL was launched under which national enforcement agencies meet biannually with DGXI to exchange information and experience.

Political and administrative problems remain, however, including the difficulty of reconciling EU legislation with existing national and sub-national laws and regulations, the complexity of the administrative machinery in several member states, and the lack of a structured system by which records on implementation can be reported back to the Commission. Occasional suggestions have been made for increasing the powers of the Commission, and perhaps even creating an EU environmental inspectorate, but they have consistently been rejected by the governments of those member states opposed to giving the Commission greater powers.

Adoption I: the Council of Ministers

Once a proposal has been accepted by the Commission, it is translated into all the official languages of the EU, is published in the *Official Journal of the European Communities*, and is sent to the Council of Ministers, which not only subjects the proposal to its own complex internal decision-making process, but must also refer it to Parliament before taking a final decision on adoption. The Council is the primary meeting place for the ministers of the member states, the point at which the interests of the member states most obviously intersect with those of the

EU as a whole, and the institution ultimately responsible for deciding (in conjunction with Parliament) what will become EU law and what will not. As Article 145 of the Treaty of Rome puts it, the Council shall 'have power to take decisions'.

When a proposal has been received from the Commission, it is copied to the permanent representatives of the EU member states, who pass it on to the relevant national ministries for comment. Each member state maintains a permanent representation in Brussels, which is effectively an embassy to the EU responsible for representing national interests and feeding information back to national governments. These have diplomatic staffs that vary between 10 and 80 in number, the size being influenced by a combination of the size of the member state and its proximity to Brussels; states at a greater distance tend to maintain bigger delegations (Hayes-Renshaw and Wallace, 1997, p. 223). All the permanent representations include one or two councillors with responsibility for environmental affairs. This is a significant change from 1993, when only five member states had environmental councillors; the increase in numbers is a reflection of the increased workload of the Council in the field of the environment.

Meetings of the Council are organized and serviced by the Committee of Permanent Representatives (COREPER), which plays a vital role in preparing Council meetings and forging compromises (Hayes-Renshaw *et al.*, 1989, pp. 119–37). COREPER comes together as a group in two main committees: COREPER II consists of ambassadors or permanent representatives, and deals mainly with economic and external affairs, while COREPER I is made up of their deputies and oversees arrangements for all the other (mainly technical) councils, including the Environment Council. COREPER, in turn, is helped by the Secretariat-General of the Council, made up of eight directorates-general with specific responsibilities; the environment comes under Directorate-General D (Research, Energy, Transport, Environment and Consumer Protection) which has about six or seven staff members. The Commission staffer responsible for drafting the proposal stays in close contact with a member of the environment directorate-general so as to keep abreast of its progress. The continuity and lack of national bias within this small group allows it to identify and respond to possible conflicts and contradictions, helping smooth the work of the Council. However, in contrast to the situation in the Commission during the development of proposals, negotiations within COREPER and the Council of Ministers take place almost entirely outside the public domain.

Before COREPER considers a proposal in detail, it is sent to a working group of technical experts (a *groupe de travail*), which examines and discusses the finer points of the proposal and prepares the way for the final Council decision. Depending on its workload and on the attitude of the member state holding the presidency, the working group may start on the proposal before hearing the opinion of Parliament (Krämer, 1996). There is nothing in the treaties about working groups, and they are the least-known element of the Council system, and yet they are probably the most vital; they represent national interests, consist of technical experts and specialists, and are the focus for most of the discussion and negotiation on Commission proposals. Middlemas (1995, p. 243) describes them as 'the backbone of European integration, . . . [responsible for] performing the vital and frequently time-consuming technical groundwork for what will eventually become a piece of European legislation or policy'. Most of the negotiation and bargaining among the member states and with the Commission takes place within these working groups, so there is usually little left to discuss by the time a proposal reaches the ministers themselves.

The environment working group consists of environment *attaches* to the permanent representations, and experts brought in from the national ministries. Most of these individuals will probably already have attended the advisory meetings organized by the Commission, and so will be familiar with most of the proposals. Because of the technical nature of many environmental proposals, the environment working group arguably has more influence on the final Council decision than does COREPER or the environment ministers.

The number of times each group meets depends on the volume of work coming its way, but the environment group typically meets three times each week. Under the chairmanship of the delegate from the member state holding the presidency of the EU, the group normally begins deliberations on a new proposal with a *tour de table*, allowing each group member to state his or her general opinion on the proposal. The Commission staffer responsible for drafting the proposal is then invited to give a brief presentation, and will usually attend all subsequent meetings of the working group at which the proposal is discussed. The group goes through each proposal point by point, and continues its negotiations until a consensus is reached, or until the chair decides that the lack of agreement – or the need for political instructions – suggests that the proposal should be sent, unresolved, to COREPER.

The Commission plays a critical and active role in this process. Not only does it have the theoretical right to withdraw a proposal if it is unhappy with the discussion in the working groups, but it also has the right to amend a proposal at any time, and can thus help (or hinder) the process of discussion. Since most environmental proposals are technical in nature, they have been thoroughly discussed by the time they reach the Council, so the likelihood of withdrawal is marginal. The Commission goes to considerable trouble to map out the likely progress of the proposal through the Council, will already have given notice of its intentions in its annual legislative programme, and will often be responding to specific requests from the Council for new legislation. Since the working groups have a 'rolling programme' of work (few proposals will be introduced, discussed and adopted in the life of one six-month presidency), collaboration between successive presidencies is critical. Hence the Commission will even meet with ministers or senior bureaucrats from member states holding the next two or three presidencies in order to discuss current or future proposals and to learn more about the priorities of each of these member states.

It is obviously in the interests of a member state to ensure that proposals working their way through the Council during its presidency make significant progress and (preferably) are adopted. A presidency receives no credit for investing hard work in the development of a proposal that is adopted only during the term of its successor. Each member state learns from the Commission which proposals are likely to be on the Council agenda during their presidency, and will be inclined to push to the top of its agenda those which stand the greatest chance of being adopted during its six months at the helm. Much also depends upon the country holding the presidency and the resources it is prepared to invest in ensuring progress; some member states (such as Italy) will try to soldier through with a skeleton staff in their permanent representation, while others (such as Britain) may bring additional staff to Brussels several months in advance in order to maximize the productivity of their presidency.

The development of an environmental proposal is also very much driven by the negotiating styles of the representatives of each state, which can be affected by tradition, by the attitude of the home government towards European integration, and by the extent to which a member state depends on EU law. For example, while British governments have long had a reputation for running hot and cold on the idea of European integration, British civil servants are widely regarded as among the most efficient and effective at the EU level, and Britain has a reputation for taking its obligations under EU law seriously; one Commission employee used the word 'frightening' in describing the professionalism of British negotiators, a reflection of the extent to which the British government wishes to make sure that it reaches an agreement with which it can live. The Greeks, by contrast, are more relaxed, in part because Greece has relatively little national environmental legislation, and depends on the EU to fill in the gaps.

Some representatives are given a large margin of freedom on negotiations, while others are not. German representatives, for example, must clear their decisions both with the federal government and the governments of the *Länder*. While they may agree a line to follow at the beginning of negotiations on a new proposal, they must regularly refer to their home government regarding their position as the proposal changes form during discussions in the Council. This became particularly clear during an environment working group held during the German presidency in 1994, when – in the recollection of one Commission employee – 'the German president spent more time out of the room on the phone to Bonn getting instructions than he spent in the room negotiating'.

The atmosphere in sessions of the environment working group (as in almost all meetings of COREPER and the Councils) is usually relaxed and informal. Staff on the permanent representations meet with each other often, they come to know each other well, and they can usually anticipate the positions their counterparts will take. This is especially true of environment working groups where much of the legislation under discussion is highly technical, which has the effect of building a strong sense of stability and identity (Westlake, 1995, p. 290).

The informality can be seen in the typical timetable of the environment working group, which usually meets every Monday, Wednesday and Friday in the Justus Lipsius building in Brussels. Although scheduled to begin at 9.00a.m., meetings rarely begin until closer to 9.30a.m., and are prefaced by the sight of clusters of delegates chatting and laughing and generally giving the impression of a group of people who know each other well and are used to each other's style and expectations. One working group in May 1996 was held the day after the announcement by prime minister John Major of a policy of non-cooperation in response to the crisis over the ban on British beef. The British delegate duly made a statement as instructed by his superiors, but the meeting then proceeded in (if anything) a more light-hearted and relaxed spirit than usual.

Once the working group has reached a conclusion on a proposal, it is sent to COREPER. If it has reached complete agreement, the proposal is listed as a Point I, and is not normally discussed further by COREPER. If agreement has not been reached, it is listed as a Point II and will be discussed by COREPER, which will send it back to the working group for further discussion, several times if necessary. Once a decision is taken to pass proposals on to the ministers for discussion, those on which agreement has been reached are listed as A points, and those on which disagreement remains as B points. The ministers adopt A points with no further discussion, but need to debate the B points. If they cannot reach agreement, they can send the proposal back to the working group with instructions that they consider it once again. A proposal can go back and forth between a working group and the ministers several times before the final decision of the Council (the common position) is reached, a process that may take as long as six to nine months.

Adoption II: Parliament

Before the Council of Ministers reaches its common position, it must send legislative proposals to Parliament for an opinion. This is arguably the most troublesome stage in the adoption process, particularly in the environmental field. As noted in

Chapter 4, MEPs are rarely involved in the early discussions within the Commission, so most are now seeing proposals for the first time and usually have to rely on Commission representatives to update them on the trend of discussions in the Council (Westlake, 1997). Since very few are experts on the technical content of proposals, and most have to involve themselves in a broad range of interests, they tend to be swayed by political considerations in reaching their decisions. To complicate matters, the workload of Parliament means that it is usually running several months behind on the consideration of new legislation. While it has the power to delay and even block legislative proposals, the overall influence of Parliament was described by Henning Arp in 1992 with terms such as marginal, limited, piecemeal, and 'hard to trace' (Arp, 1992, pp. 29, 44, 71). This is no longer quite so true today.

As in most legislatures based on the parliamentary model, most of the work of the European Parliament is done in committees. Parliament has 20 standing committees, including the Committee on the Environment, Public Health and Consumer Protection created in 1973 in the midst of the Community's new-found interest in environmental matters. Chaired for all but five years between 1979 and 1999 by Ken Collins, an MEP from the British Labour party, and since the June 1999 elections by Conservative MEP Caroline Jackson, this has become one of the biggest, most powerful and most active committees of Parliament, particularly since the Single European Act introduced the integrative principle into environmental policy. Parliamentary opinions are reached in meetings of the committee, attended by Commission officials prepared to field questions and explain the rationale behind proposals. The committee develops a report on the proposal, and offers suggestions for amendments where necessary, which are made public and discussed in parliamentary plenary session.

For most of its early life, Parliament's influence on legislation was limited to the consultation procedure under which it provided non-binding comments to the Council before it reached a common position in certain areas, including proposals on the environment, nuclear energy, agriculture and transport. The SEA introduced the cooperation procedure, which allowed Parliament to play a more active role by giving it the right to a second reading on issues relating to the internal market, social policy, and economic and social cohesion, and the power to reject the Council position by an absolute majority of MEPs. Maastricht introduced a codecision procedure under which Parliament was given the right to a third reading on laws in selected areas, compelling the Council to pay even closer attention to Parliament's opinion. With the decision under the terms of the Amsterdam treaty to all but abolish the cooperation procedure, the Council of Ministers and Parliament effectively became colegislatures.

Ludwig Krämer (1996) summarizes the attitude of Parliament towards environmental proposals as follows:

1 it routinely urges the Commission and the Council to be more ambitious, and to develop more progressive and efficient legislation;
2 it rarely challenges proposals that are more technical in nature;
3 it is a champion of NGO participation in the decision-making process;
4 it is more active than the Commission or the Council in introducing an environmental element into proposals in other areas, such as agriculture, regional issues and the internal market.

At the conclusion of a lengthy and complex process of amendment and counter-amendment, proposals are sent for a final decision to the ministers. The foreign affairs, economic and agriculture councils meet most often – about 10–15 times each year – while, among the remaining councils, the Environment Council is one of the busier, meeting four to six times annually in recent years (See Table 5.1). Almost every proposal from the Environment DG goes to the Environment Council, which also occasionally receives proposals developed in other parts of the Commission; for example, before it was wound up in 1999, DGIII (industry) was active in developing proposals on vehicle emissions.

After taking into consideration the views of Parliament, the ministers must act either by unanimity, by a simple majority or by a qualified majority. Environmental legislation was long subject to unanimous votes which allowed a single member state to block legislation, but – as noted in Chapter 2 – the SEA made environmental proposals subject to qualified majority voting.

TABLE 5.1   *Frequency of meetings of the Councils of Ministers*

	1975	1980	1990	1996
Agriculture	15	14	16	13
General Affairs	16	13	13	13
Ecofin	8	9	10	8
Fisheries	–	7	3	5
Telecommunications	–	–	2	5
Environment	2	2	5	4
Industry	–	–	4	4
Labour and Social Affairs	2	2	3	4
Transport	2	2	4	4
Development	3	1	4	3
Energy	2	2	3	3
Internal market	–	–	7	3
Justice and home affairs	–	1	1	3
Research	2	–	2	3
Budget	2	3	2	2
Consumer Affairs	–	–	2	2
Culture/audiovisual	–	–	2	2
Education	1	1	2	2
Health	–	–	2	2
Civil protection				1
Tourism	–	–	1	1
Catastrophe protection	–	–	1	–
Trade	–	–	1	–
Others	2	3	–	–
Total	57	60	91	87

Source: Annual Reports of the Council.

This significantly altered the nature of environmental policy-making by encouraging recalcitrant states to work harder towards reaching agreement with the other states for fear of being in a minority.

Legitimation and clarification: the Court of Justice

In its role as the constitutional guardian of the treaties, the Court of Justice has played the critical role of building the legal competence of the EU, reaching decisions, for example, that established that the founding treaties were more than international agreements, that Community law produced direct effects and individual rights which national courts must protect, and that Community law should be directly and uniformly applied in all the member states. Its primary contribution to the development of environmental policy has been threefold: consistently supporting the view that the EU should have competence in the field of environmental policy, backing up the Commission in the sometimes difficult job of overseeing the implementation of EU law in the member states (see later in this chapter), and clarifying the meaning of key elements of the treaties.

As discussed in Chapter 2, the Court made important contributions in 1980 with *Commission* v. *Italy* (Case 91/79), which established the legitimacy of Community environmental measures and upheld the validity of using Article 100 as a basis for those measures, and in 1985 with *Procureur de la République* v. *ADBHU* (Case 240/83), which established that environmental protection was a core policy concern of the European Community. The former decision was backed up by a series of six Court decisions in 1982 (*Commission* v. *Belgium*, Cases 68–73/81) confirming the legitimacy of using Articles 100 and 235 as the basis for environmental law. The latter were fundamental to the development of EU environmental policy, because environmental protection had not been listed in the treaties as either a Community policy or a Community objective, but their effect was to put it on a par with all the objectives listed in the treaties. Hartley notes that the Court was ruling according to what it thought the law *ought* to be rather than what it was (1988), and Koppen suggests that the ruling had an impact on the discussions then being held that would lead to the amendments made by the SEA (1993).

The question of the relationship between free trade and environmental protection was raised in *Commission* v. *Denmark* (Case 302/86), otherwise known as the Danish bottles case. The Danish government had introduced legislation requiring the use of returnable containers for beer and soft drinks. Only 23 such containers were approved, the idea being to make sure that all containers would be taken back by retailers regardless of where they had been bought. No metal containers were allowed, and non-approved containers would only be taken back by the retailer who had sold the product (Koppen, 1993). The law may have greatly increased the volume of containers that were recycled within Denmark, but it also made it difficult for non-Danish producers to export their beer and soft drinks to Denmark. The Commission felt that the law was a form of disguised discrimination against non-Danish producers and a barrier to trade under Article 30. It argued that it was important to establish

> whether and to what extent the concern to protect the environment has precedence over the principle of a common market without frontiers since there is a risk that Member States may in future take refuge behind ecological arguments to avoid opening their markets to beer as they are required to do by the case-law of the Court. (ECR, 1988, p. 4611)

The Court repeated the substance of its decision in the ADBHU case that environmental protection, as one of the Community's essential objectives, could be used to justify certain limitations on the principle of the free movement of goods, but argued that the derogation from the free market principle had to be proportionate to the end to be achieved. It concluded that while the Danish return scheme was acceptable, the limit placed on the number of permitted container shapes was disproportionate and therefore infringed Community law. The 1985 directive on liquid containers (85/339), which required member states to draw up programmes for reducing the quantity of containers of liquids for human consumption found in waste for disposal, was a direct result of the decision.

Implementation: the Commission and the member states

If measured by the production of new laws, policies, white papers, green papers and action plans on the environment, there is no question that the EU institutions have been fertile parents. However, productivity means little unless policy intent is translated into practical action, and unless EU law is transposed into – or implemented at the level of – national regulatory systems. Here the record has been much less impressive. Responsibility for implementation rests with the member states, whose performance is monitored – under Article 211 – by the Commission. The varied levels of transposal and enforcement of EU law have been a matter of growing concern for EU institutions, within which there has been an expanding debate on how to improve application.

Implementation is a three-step process (Collins and Earnshaw, 1993, pp. 215–16). First, European law must be transposed or incorporated into national law. This is not simply a question of ensuring that every element of the directive is transposed into national law, but also involves making sure that the national legislative and administrative framework is suitable for the attainment of the goals of the law. In particular, the Commission must make sure that the goals of the law are being applied throughout the territory of every member state.

The second step involves practical implementation and measurable results. In order for national and local authorities to comply with the content of the law, relevant authorities may have to be strengthened, plans developed and investments made. In other words, member states must create the necessary administrative, technical and scientific infrastructure to protect and improve the quality of the environment. EU laws contain requirements that member states report back to the Commission regularly on the measures taken, but the record on this varies from one state to another (see Table 5.2), and the reports rarely say anything about how well or how badly the state is doing in terms of meeting the goals of the law.

The final step in implementation involves monitoring the application and effect of each law. It is the states which, under Article 10, must take 'all appropriate measures, whether general or particular, to ensure fulfilment of the obligations arising out of this Treaty or resulting from action taken by the institutions of the Community', and, under Article 175(4), must 'finance and implement the environment policy'. However, it is the Commission which must encourage them, and sometimes cajole them. Article 211 of the Treaty stipulates that the Commission is responsible for ensuring the application of EU law, with the ultimate authority – if needed – to deliver a reasoned opinion and bring infringement proceedings against member states.

In terms of transposal, regulations offer fewer problems than directives because they are directly applicable and so do not need to be transposed, although they may occasionally need

TABLE 5.2   *Notification of national implementing measures for environmental laws*

	% of directives applicable for which measures had been notified				
	1994	1995	1996	1997	Average
Denmark	100	98	98	100	99.0
Netherlands	98	98	98	99	98.3
Ireland	97	95	96	98	96.5
Sweden	–	94	95	97	95.3
Luxembourg	93	92	96	98	94.8
France	94	95	93	96	94.5
Austria	–	92	94	97	94.3
Germany	91	94	96	94	93.8
Spain	86	90	94	99	92.3
UK	82	93	94	96	91.3
Greece	85	88	91	97	90.3
Portugal	82	87	94	97	90.0
Finland	–	87	86	96	89.7
Italy	76	85	85	97	85.8
Belgium	85	83	86	87	85.3

Source: European Commission, *Annual Report on Monitoring the Application of Community Environmental Law*, various years.

supplementary national law. However, regulations made up only 30 per cent of the environmental laws adopted by the end of 1999, while directives made up nearly 42 per cent of those laws, and included among their number some of the most important and far-ranging pieces of environmental law adopted by the EU. Since most directives are not directly applicable in the member states, additional implementing measures need to be agreed by each of the national governments within a timeframe that is usually built into the directive. It is not enough for a national government to send out a circular announcing that it has adopted a directive, or to change the administrative structure of its environmental agencies – a national law or regulation must be passed, it must be published in an official government document so that everyone subject to the law is familiar with its content and goals, and the Commission must be notified of the action the member state plans to take.

Once a directive is adopted, the Commission sends a formal letter to each member state reminding them of the deadline for transposal into national law. Three months before the deadline, a second letter is sent out to those states which have not notified the Commission of their plans for transposal. Many problems and outstanding questions are resolved at this stage, mainly through informal discussions between the Commission and officials of the member states, but if the deadline expires and a member state has still not provided the Commission with this information, the Commission can bring infringement proceedings against the state under Article 226.

The Commission begins by sending the member state a 'letter of formal notice', outlining the grounds of the suspected infringement and giving two months to respond (although the deadline is usually longer in practice). If the member state does not respond, or the Commission is dissatisfied, then the Commission – usually after a substantial exchange of correspondence – delivers a 'reasoned opinion' in which it outlines its position on the legal issue involved. Reasoned opinions are delivered for failure to notify the measures taken to incorporate directives into national law, for non-conformity of the measures taken, for infringement of the treaties or regulations, or for the incorrect application of directives.

Among the directives that have been most often affected by problems of transposal is 85/337 on environmental impact assessment, which has proved difficult because of the many different kinds of project that are affected and the number of national government agencies involved. Complaints regarding 85/337 focus mainly on the quality of impact assessment studies and the failure of competent authorities to act on opinions expressed at public inquiries. There have also been problems with water directives, with regular complaints about water quality, and with waste legislation and concerns about illegal dumping, bad disposal practices and water pollution (European Commission, 1996, pp. 26–8).

The sources of problems with transposal are many and varied. The Commission itself puts delays in transposal down to difficulties inherent in the administrative structures of the member states – Finland, for example, would have a better record were it not for the Åland Islands, which are autonomous and have to arrange their own transposal measures, and the same is true of Britain and Gibraltar. Several member states have also had trouble keeping up with amendments to the more technical laws, particularly those on chemicals. The Commission blames non-conformity between national and EU law on the existence of two or more legal systems in several member states, and the difficulties that arise in amending national environmental law because of the effect it has on provisions in a variety of other areas, such as agriculture, transport and industry (European Commission, 1998, pp. 51–2).

Collins and Earnshaw (1993, p. 217) note a related set of problems. First, the range and complexity of existing national laws can make it difficult to adapt them to the requirements of EU law; second, concepts contained in many directives may be defined differently in different member states; and third, national and subnational administrative systems vary by member state. For example, Germany is a federation where the national and *Länder* governments must cooperate on transposal and implementation, while regional governments have more autonomy in Italy, Belgium and Spain than they do in Britain or France. Fourth, differences in 'legislative culture' will mean some member states take longer than others to agree new national laws; and finally, member states may occasionally decide that it is politically expedient for some reason to drag their feet on transposal.

Despite such difficulties, most outstanding problems are resolved following the issuance of reasoned opinions, but if the member state still does not comply within the period set by the Commission, the matter can be referred to the Court of Justice. This rarely happens but, when it does, environmental laws figure prominently; for example, problems with 14 environmental laws were referred to the Court of Justice in 1997, and with 15 in 1998. Since 1997, the Commission has been using its powers under amendments to Article 228, through which it can refer a case to the Court of Justice with a request that a financial penalty be imposed; 15 environmental cases reached the Article 228 stage in 1997, most of which were settled by the end of the year.

Unfortunately, the body of EU environmental law has grown much faster than the resources of the Environment DG, which lacks the staff numbers to monitor the transposal and implementation of every law in every member state. Furthermore,

Article 226 powers can be directed only at national governments, not at any of the other bodies and organizations
involved in the application of environmental law. The
Commission occasionally convenes meetings of national representatives and experts to monitor progress, and also carries out
its own investigations using its contacts in national government
agencies. However, it has had to fill in the gaps by becoming an 'enforcement entrepreneur', meaning that it has had to
engage the help of national and local governments, interest
groups, the European Parliament, and even European citizens
in supervising the process by which member states implement
that law.

The Commission in general has to rely heavily on the complaints system introduced in the 1960s to measure progress on
completion of the common market. This allows anyone – a government, an elected official, an interest group or an individual
– to lodge a complaint with the Commission, or to petition the
European Parliament if they suspect that a member state is
not meeting its obligations under European law. Key sources of
complaints include the following:

- The governments of member states themselves will occasionally report on other governments that are not being as aggressive as themselves in implementing law.
- Interest groups, the media and private citizens are an important source of information. Unfortunately, the Commission
  notes that many complaints from these sectors are prompted
  by a lack of information or misunderstandings about mainly
  procedural matters, and that such complaints can often be
  dealt with more efficiently within the member states (Commission, 1996, p. 10).
- Parliament has had a long history of being interested in implementation, dating back to a 1983 resolution requesting
  that the Commission submit annual reports on the failure of
  member states to fully implement Community legislation
  (*Official Journal*, C68, 14.3.83, p. 32). This led to the submission of the first *Annual Report on Monitoring Application of Community Law* in 1984, a document which has since
  become the standard source on the matter. Individual MEPs
  also raise complaints about environmental matters through
  oral or written questions.

- A new avenue for complaint was created with the establishment in 1994 under the terms of Maastricht of the office of the European ombudsman, who has the power to conduct inquiries into charges of maladministration against Community institutions (except the Court of Justice and Court of First Instance).

Useful though they may be as a means of drawing attention to problems that the Commission might otherwise have missed, complaints are not an entirely reliable measure, and the system suffers at least four drawbacks. First, it is unstructured, leading the Commission to conclude that although such information is valuable, 'sole reliance on such ad hoc and unverifiable reporting systems and sources of information could have severely detrimental consequences for the environment in the longer term' (European Commission, 1996, p. 5). Second, many of the problems drawn to the attention of the Commission are found not to be infringements because there is no relevant legal base (European Commission, 1998, p. 49). Third, the number of complaints is influenced by the political culture of different member states, and by their varied relationships with the EU. The fact that a large number of complaints is registered in a particular member state may reflect less a problem with implementation than a high level of environmental activism and political protest. Finally, complaints are difficult to prioritize – they may not necessarily be made about the most serious or the most urgent cases.

The *Annual Report on Monitoring Application of Community Law* has shown in recent years that suspected breaches are more common in the field of environmental policy than in any other field of European law (see Figure 5.1). The problem is one both of transposing EU law into national law properly and on time, and of actually applying the new laws. The former is relatively easy to measure because member states are required to keep the Commission informed of the action they have taken. The latter is more difficult because the Commission lacks an environmental inspectorate and must rely instead on complaints and whistleblowing.

Overall, Denmark regularly has the best record on implementation, which Collins and Earnshaw (1993, p. 219) put

FIGURE 5.1 Cases against which infringement proceedings were underway, by sector, February 2000

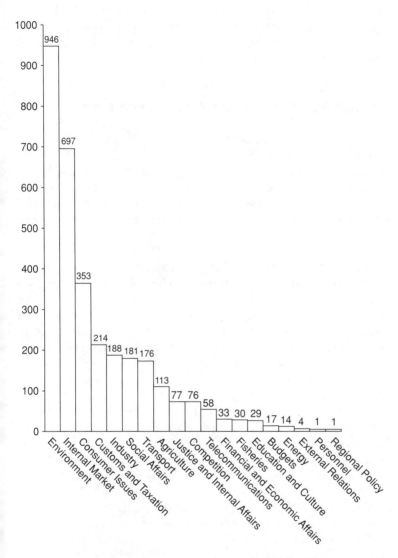

down to its high level of public and official environmental awareness, its effective implementation and monitoring systems, and the close involvement of the Danish parliament (via COREPER) in negotiating and adopting new environmental laws. The largest number of complaints are directed against Spain, Germany and France, and the least against Luxembourg, Finland and Sweden. In terms of topics, nature conservation and environmental impact are the most common subjects of complaint, while waste and air/water pollution are the subjects of the least (Commission, 1998, p. 53).

Preconditions for successful implementation

The process of implementation is straightforward in theory, but practice is another matter – whether at the European, the national or the local level, the implementation of law and policy is prone to numerous problems. Adapting to the European case the list developed by Hogwood and Gunn (1984, pp. 198–206), the preconditions for the successful implementation of policy include the following:

1   *Constraints must not be imposed by circumstances external to the implementing agencies.* There are many such constraints in the EU, ranging from political opposition to the varying economic and social priorities of different member states (and even of different regions within the member states), to disparities in the structure of national environmental policy structures and institutions. For example, some member states have an extensive body of national law and long experience with different means of achieving the goals of environmental management, while others do not. Equally, environmental regulation may be a relatively high priority for states with progressive domestic policies (such as the Scandinavian states), but a relatively low priority for poorer southern states which might see environmental regulation as a barrier to their industrial development plans.

Further constraints are added by differences in policy styles among member states. For example, the sanctions used in enforcement vary across the member states, with a preference for civil actions in some and for administrative remedies in others (Baldwin, 1995, pp. 258–9). Similarly, member states approach negotiations on law and policy with different values. Some member states – such as Germany, Greece and Italy – prefer strict rules, while others – such as Denmark, France and the

Netherlands – take a more pragmatic approach based more on informal cooperation and interaction (Siedentopf and Ziller, 1988, p. 63). The British have a preference for specific and achievable goals; their dislike of grand schemes was illustrated during a meeting of one environment working group in May 1996 when – to laughter – the British representative argued in favour of more detail in the proposal under discussion, quoting his 'Anglo-Saxon nervousness about aspirational objectives'.

2 *Adequate time and resources must be made available.* Laws and policies may fail simply because they are too ambitious, because the goals set are unrealistic, or because actors in the policy process fail to make their contribution. The problem is compounded in the case of the EU because member states know that they can be enthusiastic participants in negotiations on new laws, because there are so many options available to them to drag their feet when it comes to the actual implementation of those laws. They also know that the process of negotiation is becoming longer, that there is often a lengthy time-lag between the time a law is adopted and the time its goals are supposed to be met, and that further delay can be added through selective reporting on the steps they are taking to comply, and through the heavy workload that faces the relatively small number of lawyers working in the Environment DG (Williams, 1995, pp. 365–8). Public access to information has also been a key resource that was long missing from the legislative process. This was addressed in part by directive 90/313 on freedom of access to environmental information, which has helped provide more information on the state of the environment and has helped promote the complaints process.

The difficulties caused by actors failing to play their part are illustrated by an example reported by the Court of Auditors in 1992: while many water purification plants had been built in towns and villages in the EU with support from structural funds, many were not actually functioning because local authorities lacked the funds needed to maintain them (Court of Auditors, 1992).

3 *There should be a direct relationship between cause and effect, with few intervening links.* The more complex the relationship between cause and effect, the more chance there is of a policy failing. Few policy areas are more complex than

environmental management, which must take into account complex ecological relationships, varying climatic and geographical conditions and constant changes in scientific understanding. EU regulations directed at very specific problems – such as contaminants in feedstuffs, or trade in endangered species of wildlife – have a better chance of succeeding than more ambitious and broadbased directives, or the more technical EU laws such as those on chemicals and biotechnology.

4 *Dependency relationships should be minimal.* In other words, the perfect situation is one in which there is a single implementing agency, or – if there are multiple agencies – the central agency has minimal dependency on the others. This is clearly not the case with EU environmental policy, where the Environment DG must not only work with other DGs in order to ensure that the environmental impact of all laws and policies are taken into account, but the Commission must depend on national and local governments to transpose EU law into national law, on national and local government agencies to oversee implementation on the ground, and on a complex network of watchdogs to measure the process of implementation. Policy areas such as agriculture and transport have the benefit of being associated with relatively well-defined constituencies, and implementation is made easier because there are specific vested interests involved. This is not the case with the environment, however, where industry, agriculture and transport have lobbies that can oppose regulation, or can ensure that it is watered down, and – except for the small environmental lobby in Brussels – there are no institutions to defend the general interests of the environment (Krämer, 1995, p. 132).

The number of authorities involved varies from one law to another, so while it is relatively easy to measure implementation in some areas, it is more complex in others. For example, Haigh (1996) points out that implementing directives on lead in petrol has been relatively easy: petrol is made and distributed by a limited number of oil companies; transposal of directives has been achieved mainly by national law without the input of regional or local authorities; national laws have been written and agreed relatively quickly; once a standard has been set it has been relatively easy to ensure that it is met and for all competing products to be analyzed; and it has been relatively easy to prove the link between the reduction of the lead content of petrol and the lead content of the air. By contrast, implementing emissions standards has been much more difficult because of the number of sources that need to be authorized and monitored.

5   *Objectives must be understood and agreed upon.* When target dates and quality standards are set, the objectives of EU law are relatively unambiguous. For example, it is fairly clear what was meant in directive 88/609 on emissions from large combustion plants: sulphur dioxide emissions had to be reduced across the EU as a whole by 1998 by 58 per cent, using 1980 as a baseline, and nitrogen oxide emissions had to be cut by 30 per cent. However, European environmental law and policy is peppered with ambiguities, beginning with general goals (such as 'improving the quality of life') and moving through the objectives and methods of specific pieces of law. Perhaps the most famous ambiguity built into EU environmental law was the idea of reducing pollution using 'the best available technology not entailing excessive cost', an idea whose definition – argues Krämer (1995, p. 142) – can be interpreted differently from one member state to another, from one industry to another, and even from one company to another. Under the circumstances, it can be difficult to compare progress across member states.

6   *Tasks should be listed in the correct sequence.* In other words, in moving towards agreed objectives it is important that the tasks to be performed by each participant are specified in complete detail and perfect sequence. This is the case with EU regulations, which are binding in their entirety on all member states, and are directly applicable in the sense that they do not need to be turned into national law; hence the goals and the methods are the same for all member states. However, directives set goals and objectives but leave it up to the member states to decide how to achieve those objectives. This creates ambiguities that sometimes make it difficult for the Commission to be sure about the relative progress being made by different member states.

7   *There should be perfect communication and coordination.* This is only likely to happen either where government is heavily decentralized and key decisions are taken at the local level, or in a unitary system where national government has direct control over the agencies responsible for implementation. It is least likely to be found in an entity as complex as the European

Union, where the powers of the EU institutions relative to the member states are constantly changing, and where the member states use different administrative systems.

8   *Those in authority can demand and obtain compliance.* The fundamental problem here is that the Commission has responsibility without authority. As the 'guardian of the treaties' it is responsible for ensuring that EU law is applied, but it lacks the necessary staff numbers, funds or – most importantly – powers to impose sanctions and penalties beyond those that come under Articles 226 and 228.

Numerous suggestions have been made for improvements in the efficacy of enforcement, including the establishment of a green police, an EU environmental inspectorate, or an inspection audit scheme by which national agencies could be inspected (see below), but most involve an expansion in the powers of the Commission and an increase in its staff numbers and budget, ideas which are routinely rejected by member states opposed to the expansion of Commission powers (Collins and Earnshaw, 1993, pp. 238–9). Inspection bodies and sophisticated control mechanisms have been created to oversee policy on competition, fisheries, veterinary issues, customs and regional policy, but these are all policy areas for which the EU has greater competence and where an increase in Commission powers is less politically troubling to the member states.

The regulation creating the European Environment Agency (1210/90) included an article stipulating that a review should be undertaken after two years to discuss the possibility of giving the EEA more powers over monitoring compliance with law and policy. The regulation came into effect in 1993, and the review was undertaken in 1995, but the EEA remains essentially a data-gathering body. Nevertheless, its work has led to improvements in the quality of data on the state of the environment, which has made it easier for the Commission to monitor progress, to develop a clearer picture of the extent of environmental problems and the effects of EU law, and to be more sure about the accuracy of reporting by member states.

To the list developed by Hogwood and Gunn, at least four more requirements can be added arising out of the particular circumstances of the EU:

9   *Policies must be implemented evenly.* As interpreted by the Court of Justice, Article 10 obliges member states to make whatever provision for enforcement is effective, proportionate and equivalent to that for the national laws of a member state. This has resulted in a wide disparity in the efforts and resources of environmental enforcement agencies, running the gamut from well-supported agencies monitoring the practical application of EU law to others doing very little, and from arrangements where agencies both inspect for compliance and make decisions on granting permits or bringing court actions (as in the UK and Denmark) to arrangements where these tasks are separated (as in the Netherlands) (European Commission, 1996, p. 9).

Differences in the aggression with which member states pursue the enforcement of different laws, and the enforcement practices and penalties they use, can create an unevenness in the level of implementation and cancel out the goal of harmonizing laws across the member states, creating a new kind of barrier to the internal market. Some member states may even see it as being in their interests to drag their feet on implementation so as to give them a competitive edge over other member states, or to appease a sectional interest at home (Cini, 1996, p. 26).

10   *Reporting on compliance must be reliable.* It is impossible to be sure about the efficacy of policy unless its effects are reliably reported back to the administering authority. Richardson suggests that there is a tendency to cheat in reporting, in part because of a desire on the part of member states to appear to be good Europeans, and in part to be able to spread out the costs of implementation over a longer period of time. He quotes the example of the 1976 bathing water directive; because Britain decided that only beaches with more than 500 people per mile qualified, it designated just 27 beaches for compliance with the directive, compared to 8000 in the other eight member states. At the same time, countries which had established a good record on compliance (such as France, Germany and the Netherlands) were found to be taking insufficient samples from their designated beaches (Richardson, 1996, p. 287). The quality of feedback may improve as the result of the system of questionnaires introduced by directive 91/692, which came into force in 1997.

11   *The actors involved must have the same priorities.* Unlike nation-states, where environmental problems are often seen in

national terms and where different levels or government generally see problems and solutions in a similar light, different EU
member states occasionally face different problems, and have
differing policy priorities. For example:

- Different member states have different administrative systems,
  and do not always have comparable domestic authorities
  responsible for environmental policy.
- Different member states have different perceptions about the
  most important environmental problems they need to resolve.
  Forest management is more important for Germany than for
  most other member states, while Britain is almost unique in
  the role played in ecology by hedgerows, and the British
  perhaps care more about the welfare of wildlife than do most
  other Europeans.
- Waste disposal is a major public concern throughout the EU,
  but the governments of some member states see the control
  or illegal waste dumps as the main element of the problem,
  while others focus more on emissions from waste incinerators (Commission, 1996, p. 2).

12   *Implementation should be considered at the same time
as policy formulation.* This is a point that has long been made
– among others – by the European Parliament, which in a 1988
resolution on EU water legislation noted the need 'for implementation to be considered at a much earlier stage in legislative
drafting' (*Official Journal* C94 11.4.88, p. 157). Similarly, a
House of Lords Select Committee in the UK in 1992 noted that
'too much [EU] environmental legislation is formulated and
drafted with insufficient attention to its eventual implementation' (House of Lords, 1992, p. 47). Part of the problem stems
from the fact that the national authorities most centrally
involved in implementation are rarely (if ever) represented at the
early development stages of legislation.

Improving the quality of implementation

The implementation of environmental law was low down the
list of priorities for the Commission in the 1970s and early

1980s, because it was too busy developing policies and building a body of law. It was only after the Seveso incident (1983–84) that the focus began to change. The committee of inquiry set up by the European Parliament censured the Commission

> for having failed to perform fully and properly its role of guardian of the Treaties . . . [and] for its failure to take the necessary measures vis-à-vis the Member States with regard to the implementation and application of [Directive 78/319 on the disposal of toxic waste]. (*Official Journal*, C127/67 14.5.84)

The number of DGXI staff dealing with implementation was subsequently increased; the Commission became more active in bringing cases before the Court of Justice; the first in what was to become an annual series of reports on the application of EU law was published in 1984; the issue of implementation was emphasized in the Fourth and Fifth EAPs, and it became the subject of a 'Declaration on the Environmental Imperative' adopted at the Dublin European Council in June 1990. The latter called on the Commission to conduct regular reviews and to periodically evaluate existing directives to ensure that they were adapted to scientific and technical progress, and to resolve persistent difficulties in implementation (*Bulletin of the European Communities*, 1990, vol. 23, no. 6, p. 18).

The Fifth EAP made provision for the creation of an implementation network that would allow for the 'exchange of information and experience and the development of common approaches at practical level, under the supervision of the Commission' (*Official Journal*, C138 17.05.93). The idea was conceived during an informal meeting of EU ministers in the Netherlands in October 1991. After further discussions, the EU Network for the Implementation and Enforcement of Environmental Law (IMPEL) was launched in late 1992. It brings national enforcement authorities together at biannual meetings chaired jointly by the Environment DG and the member state holding the presidency of the EU. Its goal is to improve implementation by encouraging the exchange of information and experience, developing a greater consistency of approach to implementation and enforcement, and improving communication among the Commission and the member states (Verkerk, 1996). IMPEL has encouraged the Commission to draw up fewer new laws and to concentrate instead on improving the efficacy of existing laws.

In November 1996 the Commission published a report offering suggestions for ways of improving implementation (European Commission, 1996); these included reducing disparities in inspection methods used by member states, setting minimum criteria for the handling of complaints, establishing guidelines for access to national courts, making sure that all proposals for new EU environmental laws were as clear as possible, and further developing IMPEL. The environment ministers responded in June 1997 by inviting the Commission to develop minimum criteria for national inspectorates (thereby dealing with the problem caused by disparities in the structure and approach of inspectorates noted in point 9 above), and by enhancing the status of IMPEL; it was given a secretariat, and its informal biannual meetings were formalized.

IMPEL responded in turn with a paper on ways of improving the inspection of industrial installations, which environment Commissioner Bjerregard decided to develop as a directive. Despite concerns about subsidiarity, Environmental Data Services noted the precedent offered by directive 96/82 on major accident hazards, which obliges member states to organize a programme of inspections for hazardous installations, and allows at least one inspection of a site per year if the competent national authority has not systematically appraised the accident hazards posed by that site (*ENDS Report* 277, February 1998, p. 43).

New environment Commissioner Margot Wallström placed implementation high on her list of priorities upon taking office in 1999. She threatened to 'name and shame' member states failing to meet targets for reductions in emissions of greenhouse gases in particular, noting that while she would prefer to be 'more of a consultant or adviser to member states' she might have to be more a 'policewoman'. She argued that existing member states needed to be role models for aspirant eastern European members, and warned that if governments consistently breached EU environmental laws they would risk delays in receiving regional aid funds. Finally, she warned that if national agencies proved incapable of enforcing laws, she would propose the creation of an EU environmental inspectorate (*European Voice*, 10–17 November 1999, p. 2).

PART II

POLICY OUTPUTS

Chapter 6

Chemicals and Waste

Particularly in industrialized countries, many of the most pressing environmental problems are ultimately chemical in nature: air and water pollution, toxic and hazardous wastes, pesticides and herbicides, chemicals in food and ecosystems, and so on. Just as such problems have been the focus of much of the environmental policy activity of national governments, so they have been high on the EU environmental agenda. If all the laws adopted by the EU on air pollution, water pollution and the control of wastes are included, then just over half of all EU laws on the environment are directed at some element of the chemical problem: managing the use of chemicals; limiting the release of chemical substances that have a harmful effect on human, animal and plant life; and controlling the shipment and disposal of chemical wastes.

The earliest EU chemicals legislation dates from 1967, and was motivated primarily by a desire to remove the obstacles posed to the common market by different sets of national regulations. During the 1970s, the focus shifted to consumer protection, with measures taken to ban or limit the commercialization of dangerous substances and preparations. By the 1980s, the Community was examining the links between chemicals and environmental management, since when the policy focus has shifted towards attempts to minimize the impact of chemicals on the environment.

The control of chemicals as such has been relatively narrowly defined, because while it has been the subject of about one in eight of all EU environmental laws, more than four-fifths of these are amendments to a body of just 19 laws directed mainly at controlling the use of dangerous substances, limiting the effects of accidents involving dangerous substances, controlling chemical exports and the import of banned or restricted chemicals, protecting consumer health and safety, and promoting research on the toxicity of chemical compounds. A further one in eight EU environmental laws have been aimed at controlling the use of pesticides but, again, most are amendments to a body of just 15 laws on pesticide residues.

The management and recycling of wastes have also been priority goals of EU environmental policy since the mid-1970s. As with all industrial societies, European states are large producers of waste, and the most common approach so far to dealing with that waste has been to place it in landfill. However, not only does this cause environmental problems, such as the contamination of groundwater and the generation of methane (a greenhouse gas), but suitable and inexpensive sites are difficult to find in a region as heavily populated as western Europe, and the creation of landfill facilities usually generates enthusiastic opposition from local communities.

Several member states have tried to circumvent their domestic problems by exporting waste to other countries, but this has proved controversial and has prompted a debate over the extent to which member states should become self-sufficient in waste management, and the extent to which they should be allowed to export waste to each other or to third countries outside the EU. Following the emergence of a consensus that they should control exports, and the agreement of a ban on exports to ACP countries, the EU has focused on attempts to reduce waste generation by using market forces to encourage manufacturers and consumers to minimize resource consumption, prolong product life, and encourage recovery and recycling.

Chemicals: the problem

Chemicals have been central to the development of industry and modern agriculture, and have made vital contributions to the efficiency of manufacturing, the productivity of farming, and the health and convenience of consumers. The vast majority of these chemicals are harmless to humans and the environment if used in the correct quantities, combinations and circumstances, and they have substantially improved the quality of life for most people. However, a growing minority are either toxic – meaning poisonous to humans, animals and plants – or hazardous, meaning that they pose an immediate threat to humans and the environment because they are corrosive, flammable or reactive (that is, they explode or give off noxious gases if mixed with other chemicals).

Chemicals have only become a significant environmental issue with the chemical revolution that has taken place since the late 1950s, which has seen the number of chemical compounds in regular use in industrialized countries leap from less than 10 000 to well over 120 000. Most are synthetic, and ongoing research has ensured that anything between 200 and 1000 new compounds are added to the list each year. Unfortunately, understanding of the actual or potential effects of these chemicals lags far behind the rates at which they are being developed, in large part because testing is an expensive and often lengthy process – thorough studies may need decades of research. While it is relatively easy to determine which chemicals are corrosive, flammable or reactive, it is much more difficult – and takes much longer – to test them for their longer-term toxic effects on humans or the environment.

Selected chemicals have been implicated in harm to wildlife and ecosystems, and in human health problems as varied as allergies, birth defects, cancer, damage to key organs, fertility problems and mental impairment, but information on actual or potential effects varies from one chemical to another. Furthermore, such effects change with different combinations of chemicals, and different people and environments are impacted differently by different chemicals, over different periods of time. The European Environment Agency notes that data on emissions are scarce, and that the threat posed by chemicals remains unclear because of the lack of knowledge about their concentrations and about the manner in which they move through and accumulate in the environment (EEA, 1998, p. 109).

At the core of the issue of chemicals policy is the troubling problem of risk assessment (see Rosenbaum, 1998, pp. 122–44). Unlike many other areas of public policy, environmental management causes politics to overlap in many places with science, creating a relationship that often has unhappy results. Risk assessment involves determining the point at which an activity – in this case the use of chemicals – ceases to be useful and begins to become harmful or dangerous. Unfortunately, the timetables and motives that drive the work of scientists and policymakers rarely coincide. Scientists need time to develop certainty about the effects of chemicals on the environment, they are interested primarily in facts (although science is not always value-free), and much of the data they generate are based on the study of individual chemicals in laboratory conditions. By contrast, policymakers need to move more quickly (many are looking no further than the next election), are often driven by subjective issues such as ideological bias and concerns about whether or not a law can be enforced, and must develop policies to address the effects of the interaction of multiple chemicals in varied conditions.

Under the circumstances, the formulation of policy is often complicated by differences of opinion between scientists and policymakers, and – in the absence of scientific certainty – policies must be developed on the basis of information that is incomplete at best, and highly questionable at worst. Risks are often assessed and determined more by subjective political judgement than by objective scientific certainty.

Chemicals: the policy response

The complexity of the issue of chemicals in the environment has undermined attempts either by EU institutions or by the governments of the member states to approach it in anything more than a rather piecemeal fashion. Changes in domestic policy in Sweden and Britain in the late 1990s not only highlighted the somewhat *ad hoc* nature of EU policy, but also coincided with increasing demands from several member states for a more proactive approach aimed at phasing out the use of hazardous chemicals. However, until a more global approach is developed to addressing the impact of chemicals on the environment, EU policy will continue to be based on four main priorities developed mainly in the 1970s and 1980s:

The handling of chemicals

Directive 67/548 on the classification, packaging and labelling of dangerous chemicals is often – but wrongly – described as the first piece of Community law on the environment. (Strictly speaking, that honour belongs to directive 59/221 on ionizing radiation, which preceded the 1967 law by eight years.)

In its original form, directive 67/548 was not an 'environmental' law at all, but was instead an attempt to harmonize legislation on products which happened to have implications for the welfare of the environment. The recitals to the directive say nothing about the environment, instead referring to the importance of protecting workers and the public from dangerous substances and preparations, and of removing the 'hindrances' posed to the 'establishment and functioning of the common market ... [by] differences between the national provisions of the six Member States'. The word 'environment' appears nowhere in 67/548 nor in its first five amendments, and was only finally added with the sixth amendment to the directive, adopted in 1979.

Based on Article 100, the directive dealt mainly with the classification of dangerous chemicals, test methods and related procedures. It defined dangerous chemicals as those that were explosive, oxidizing, flammable, toxic, harmful, corrosive or irritant, and set out detailed rules applying to their packaging and labelling. The directive went on to become the precursor to a substantial body of law focusing on the control of chemicals; by the end of 1999 it had been amended nearly 40 times, and the list of substances covered by 67/548 and its amendments had become quite lengthy.

The sixth amendment to 67/548 – directive 79/831 – was important not just because it finally introduced an environmental dimension into the underlying justifications, but also because it introduced a preventive element into the control of chemicals; any producer or importer of more than one tonne of a new substance was required to register the substance with the competent national authority at least 45 days before it was marketed, and the registration had to be recognized by all other member states. To dispel concerns about variable national regulation requirements, standard testing methods and a system of information exchange were established. The directive also required the compilation of the European Inventory of Existing Chemical Substances (EINECS). Published in 1986, this contained a list of the nearly 100 000 chemical substances placed on the market in the Community between 1971 and 1981, none of which needed prior notification. The seventh amendment (93/67) extended the requirement for risk assessment to new chemical substances.

The First EAP noted that the regulation of classification, packaging and labelling was not enough for more dangerous chemicals, and that it might be necessary in some cases to ban or limit the marketing of chemicals. A proposal aimed at doing this began to be developed in the Commission in 1973, but by the time it was adopted by the Council in 1976 as directive 76/769, it had been watered down to cover only PCBs, PCTs and monomer vinyl chloride (VCM) (Johnson and Corcelle, 1995, p. 231). Subsequent amendments saw the Commission and the Council tentatively expanding the reach of 76/769 to other substances, but rarely more than one at a time:

- directive 79/663 imposed a ban on the use of dangerous chemicals in ornaments such as lamps and ashtrays, and the use of phosphate in textile articles such as pyjamas and undergarments;
- directive 82/806 banned the use of benzene in toys;
- directive 83/264 banned the use of two chemicals in textiles, and the use of three chemicals in objects designed to play jokes or pranks;
- directives 83/478 and 85/610 banned the marketing of blue and white asbestos and the marketing of products containing asbestos, including toys, paints, varnishes, smoking paraphernalia and filters;
- directive 85/469 limited the use of PCBs and PCTs.

In 1988, the principles underlying 67/548 were extended under directive 88/379 to the classification, packaging and labelling of dangerous preparations, meaning mixtures and combinations of several chemical substances. The main goal of the new directive was to arrange for the classification and labelling of preparations according to the degree of danger they represented, regardless of the use to which they were put. It did not require pre-marketing notification, but introduced classification by calculation as an alternative to animal testing, and information about each preparation had to be provided on a safety data form introduced by directive 91/155.

Accidents at chemical plants

Public safety became a focus for EU chemicals policy in the 1970s, prompted partly by the emerging influence of the

TABLE 6.1 *Key pieces of EU law on chemicals and pesticides*

67/548	Directive on dangerous substances. *Establishes harmonized system for the classification, packaging and labelling of dangerous substances.*
74/63	Directive on the content of animal feed. *Establishes maximum levels of pesticide residues in animal feed.*
76/769	Directive on dangerous substances and preparations. *Framework directive for the approximation of laws of member states relating to restrictions on the marketing and use of dangerous substances and preparations.*
76/895	Directive on pesticide residues. *Establishes levels for pesticide residues in and on fruit and vegetables.*
78/631	Directive on pesticides. *Establishes requirements for the classification, packaging and labelling of pesticides.*
79/117	Directive on pesticides. *Prohibits marketing of pesticides containing substances such as mercury or DDT.*
79/831	Directive on dangerous substances. *Amends 67/548 for the sixth time (introducing an environmental element into the recitals), and 78/631.*
82/501	Directive on accidental hazards of industrial activities (the Seveso directive). *Requires member states to establish procedures aimed at preventing and limiting effects of accidents due to industrial activities involving dangerous substances.*
88/379	Directive on dangerous preparations. *Establishes rules on the classification, packaging and labelling of dangerous preparations such as paints, solvents.*
1734/88	Regulation on export and import of chemicals. *Establishes a common system of notification and information.*
91/414	Directive on pesticides. *Harmonizes approaches to granting of market authorization for pesticides.*
2455/92	Regulation on import and export of chemicals. *Establishes system of notification and information on imports from and exports to third countries of chemicals banned or restricted in the EC.*
793/93	Regulation on existing chemical substances. *Establishes system for the evaluation and control of the risk of chemical substances marketed in the EC before September 1981.*
96/82	Directive on accident hazards (Seveso II). *Concerning control of major accident hazards involving dangerous substances. Replaces 82/501.*

environmental movement, but mainly by a number of high-profile accidents at industrial plants using chemicals. Among the earliest was the explosion in June 1974 at a chemical plant in Flixborough, near Scunthorpe in northern England. Owned by Nypro Ltd, the plant manufactured chemicals used in the production of nylon. A pipe in the plant developed a leak, and was removed for repair and replaced by a temporary pipe that was unable to withstand the required heat and pressure. A cloud of cyclohexane vapour was released and spread throughout the plant before exploding with a blast thought to be the equivalent of 15–45 tonnes of TNT; the plant was destroyed, and 28 people were killed and 36 injured (Center for Chemical Process Safety, 1994, pp. 10–12, 263–72).

Just over two years later, on 10 July 1976, another accident occurred at a chemical plant manufacturing pesticides and herbicides near Seveso in northern Italy. The rupture of a reactor vessel led to the release of a toxic vapour cloud containing a mixture of chemicals which included ethylene glycol and dioxin, a particularly unpleasant chemical that was used in pesticides and herbicides, and during the Vietnam war as the main ingredient in the defoliant Agent Orange. No-one was hurt, but the cloud contaminated the entire plant and nearly 2000 hectares in its vicinity, leading to the evacuation of nearly 800 people, a decision to slaughter all farm animals in the area, and the fencing-off of the most severely contaminated area around the plant.

Flixborough and Seveso underlined the potential dangers to public safety posed by accidents at chemical factories, prompting the Commission to begin drafting a proposal for a law aimed at preventing accident hazards through more effort to build safety features into chemical factories at the design stage. Directive 82/501 – otherwise known as the Seveso directive – encouraged plant operators, national and local authorities and the Commission to cooperate in identifying and controlling the risks of emissions, fires, explosions and other accidents in industrial plants. It obliged all manufacturers of toxic, flammable or explosive substances to take the necessary steps to prevent accidents and to limit the effects of accidents on humans and the environment. They had to notify control authorities whenever any one of a specified list of 180 substances was being used at their installations, and – in the case of an accident – immediately inform the authorities. The member state in which such an accident took place had to produce a complete report on the causes and effects of the accident.

The directive was amended twice (in 1987 and 1988) and was then thoroughly reviewed and replaced by directive 96/82, known as the Seveso II directive. This is aimed at encouraging the prevention of major accidents involving dangerous substances, and at limiting the consequences of such accidents if they occur. It covers both industrial activities and the storage of dangerous chemicals, and requires the operators of relevant industrial plants to notify local authorities of their activities and to develop accident prevention plans. Internal emergency plans must be developed by operators, external emergency plans by competent authorities, the plans must be regularly tested, and member states must place necessary controls on the siting of new plants to minimize the effects of accidents, and make changes (including new transport links) to existing plants.

To back up the legislation on accident hazards, the European Commission created the Major Accidents Hazards Bureau within its Joint Research Centre in Milan. The Bureau evaluates information from the member states, collects information and accident case histories, and disseminates information to member states, industries and local authorities.

Pesticides

Running parallel to these developments, a sub-family of laws has been adopted by the EU on pesticides and their residues in foodstuffs. The first of these came in 1974, when directive 74/63 established maximum levels of pesticide residues in animal feed, and was followed in 1976 by directive 76/895 which did much the same for fruit and vegetables. Directive 78/631 introduced the same kinds of requirements on classification, packaging and labelling as were contained in 67/548, but the Community went a step further in 1979 by banning the use of certain pesticides and related products, including DDT and compounds of mercury (79/117). Human health was again at the heart of directive 78/631, but environmental damage, particularly harm to birds and wildlife, was quoted as another motivation.

Relatively few pesticides were covered by the 1978 directive, and member states were allowed to ban other pesticides in their own territories and to establish maximum levels for pesticide residues in food, creating a messy situation in which inconsistent national laws and limits were allowed to coexist (Lister, 1996, p. 245). Directive 91/414 was thus adopted to create a harmonized Community system for authorizing active ingredients – of which there are an estimated 850 in use in the EU – and individual products. The plan was to evaluate all 850 ingredients by 2003, but progress to date has been slow.

Trade in dangerous chemicals

In the late 1980s, the Commission turned its attention to the export and import of dangerous chemicals. It began with the issue of restricting exports of chemicals already banned or restricted within the Community, many of which were still being manufactured and sold mainly to developing countries (Johnson and Corcelle, 1995, p. 255). Regulation 1734/88 set up a common notification system for the export of 21 chemicals, including mercury, PCBs, PCTs and DDT. In 1989, eight chemicals used in the development or production of chemical weapons were made subject to export authorization (regulation 428/89), and in 1992 regulation 2455/92 was adopted introducing a prior informed consent (PIC) scheme that complemented a joint scheme developed by the UN Environment Programme and the UN Food and Agriculture Organization. Exporters of listed chemicals were required to give their national authorities at least 30 days notice of their plans, the authorities then had to notify their counterparts in the country to which the chemicals were being exported, and the latter could refuse to import the chemicals, or could impose conditions.

The second half of the 1990s saw the beginnings of a wide-ranging review of EU chemicals policy, prompted in part by the Swedish government and a proposal put forward in 1997 by its Chemical Policy Committee for a phase-out of persistent and bioaccumulative substances (*ENDS Report* 269, June 1997, pp. 21–5). Britain had also begun internal discussions on the development of a policy for the sustainable use of chemicals. These national initiatives were symptomatic of a broader dissatisfaction among member states with the modest progress being made in EU chemicals policy, notably in the implementation of the programme introduced by regulation 793/93 for assessing and managing the risks posed by existing chemicals (*ENDS Report* 279, April 1998, pp. 39–40). The regulation was designed to improve the quality of information on chemicals marketed in the Community before September 1981, and the evaluation of the risks they posed to humans and the environment. It required submission of data on all the chemicals listed in EINECS, and risk assessment of priority chemicals.

Of the more than 100 000 chemicals that qualified under the regulation, only 111 had been listed for priority assessment, and no agreement on action had been agreed for any. In a paper developed by the British presidency for an informal meeting of the Environment Council in April 1998, it was concluded that there was 'still some way to go before the Community has an efficient, integrated approach to chemicals risk assessment and management'. A paper brought to the meeting by the governments of Austria, Denmark, Finland, the Netherlands and Sweden argued that the EU had no overall policy for chemicals with short- and long-term goals, lacked an overview of the results achieved by EU policy to date, and suggested the need for a new framework directive on chemicals. This would, among other things, place the burden of proof that a substance was harmless on the manufacturer, importer or user, and impose a duty on suppliers to inform consumers of the possible impact of chemicals on humans and the environment (*ENDS Report* 279, April 1998, p. 39).

At the June 1999 meeting of the Environment Council, ministers adopted a policy for chemical products based on three principles: accelerating chemical risk assessment procedures, improving access to information for public authorities, and increasing product safety. Useful though these might have been as general goals, they again underlined the need for the EU to move from individual tactical approaches to selected chemicals and chemical problems, toward a broader strategic approach to the issue of chemicals in the environment.

Waste: the problem

Waste is a problem largely confined to industrial societies, and is symbolic of their failure to use materials and energy efficiently.

As industrial and consumer demand and consumption have grown, as industrial production has increased and as consumers have acquired more disposable income, so the production of waste has increased. At least three issues have arisen as a result: how much of that waste can be recycled, how much must be sent for disposal, and should states be self-sufficient in disposal or is waste a 'good' that can be traded? If it *can* be traded, which countries are acceptable trading partners, and what guarantees can be made for the safety of wastes in transit?

The answers to these questions have been complicated by an ongoing debate over the meaning of the words 'waste' and 'disposal'. Almost anything can be regarded as waste if it is no longer of use to its owner, but much of what modern consumers think of as 'waste' is a resource that can be recycled or reused. If it cannot, however, then what options are available for disposal, and should 'disposal' be defined as destruction or safe storage? If waste is burned to generate energy, does that constitute 'recovery' or 'disposal'? When is waste hazardous, and how do we define 'hazardous'? Finally, what is the difference between 'hazardous' and 'toxic'? These are all questions that have muddied the waters as EU policy on waste has evolved.

Waste is produced at every stage of the industrial process, from the extraction of raw materials to their conversion into manufactured products and their final consumption. The extent of the problem is debatable, however, and trends are difficult to confirm, because wastes are defined differently from one state to another, data are collected in different ways, and the quality of that data is variable. The confusion is reflected in the figures: the OECD figure in 1997 for total waste production in OECD Europe was 2.225 billion tonnes (OECD, 1997a), but the totals in 40 per cent of those countries excluded agricultural and mining wastes, the biggest sources of waste in most industrialized countries. The EEA estimated that the total production of solid waste in Europe was probably at least four billion tonnes annually (EEA, 1998, p. 132). Meanwhile, statistics suggest that there was an increase in waste production during the 1990s, but at least part of the increase could have been the result of improved waste monitoring.

The biggest source of waste in the EU is mining and quarrying, which accounts for nearly half the total, the balance coming from industry (32 per cent), municipal sources (17 per cent) and energy (6 per cent). The production of municipal waste in the EU grew by 9 per cent in the period 1990–95, and by the mid-1990s stood at about 420 kg per person per year (about 40 per cent of which was packaging waste). While this was substantially below the figure for the United States – which produces more than 730 kg per person per year – it still placed a significant strain on local authorities as they sought the means for safe and effective disposal.

About 69 per cent of all municipal waste is buried in landfill, but an increasing proportion is incinerated (more than 25 per cent) or composted (10 per cent). Each of these options presents its own problems. Waste in landfill can give off gases such as methane and CO_2 (both implicated in climate change), can lead to chemicals and heavy metals being leached into water and soil, can be expensive where land is at a premium, and the development of landfill sites is often opposed by local residents (the NIMBY syndrome, or 'not in my back yard'). Meanwhile, incineration can lead to air and water pollution, is not an effective response to the problem of disposing of hazardous waste, and also comes up against NIMBYism. For its part, composting works only if hazardous substances are not introduced into the soil via the waste.

One option for dealing with waste is to prevent (or at least reduce) its creation by designing products with a view to reducing the generation of waste as a byproduct. Another option is recycling, but while recycling rates for plastics, paper and glass in the EU are improving, they vary considerably from one member state to another. In the case of plastics packaging, for example, Germany and Austria have a rate of more than 15 per cent, and Britain stands at about 7–7.5 per cent, while rates in Ireland, Portugal and Greece are less than 4 per cent (*ENDS Report* 289, February 1999, p. 16). No trend data are available for aluminium, steel, plastics or other materials, but in 1993, recycling rates for glass in the EU varied from 27–29 per cent (Greece, Spain, Portugal, Ireland and the UK) to 64–76 per cent (Denmark, Germany, the Netherlands) (Golub, 1996). Recycling usually offers compelling economies of scale for industry, but there is a limit to what can be profitably recycled. For the consumer, meanwhile, there are few (if any) economic incentives; recycling is usually a voluntary undertaking, and the volume of domestic wastes that are recycled depends largely on the creation of recycling schemes by entrepreneurs or local government.

While the reduction of municipal waste offers its own challenges, a more troubling problem is the management of hazardous waste: the chemical and radioactive byproducts of industry and energy generation, little of which can be recycled or destroyed, and most of which must therefore be placed into safe storage. Because disposal is expensive and not all countries have adequate disposal facilities, there is a temptation for producers to ship such waste to countries that either have such facilities or are prepared to store the waste.

Accurate figures on the size of the waste trade are hard to come by, because not every country compiles such data, different countries have different definitions of 'hazardous' waste, and such figures as exist take into account only legal waste transfers (Montgomery, 1995). Barely 1 per cent of all hazardous waste generated in industrialized countries is shipped across national frontiers, and the hazardous waste trade is restricted mainly to industrialized countries (UNEP, 1993, pp. 333–5). Nonetheless, the issue of transfrontier shipment has drawn much political attention in the last decade. In the EU, member states have disagreed over whether waste can be traded across borders, or whether all member states should become self-sufficient in disposal facilities.

Waste: the policy response

Waste management has become one of the priorities of EU environmental policy. The first laws in this area were adopted in the mid-1970s, but the development of EU policy has accelerated over the past decade, reflecting a rise both in political and public interest in the problem, and concern about the mixed record in bringing it under control. The emphasis of EU policy has been on waste prevention, recycling and reuse, improving disposal conditions, and regulating the transport of waste. However, despite the adoption of 85 laws and the elaboration of strategies and a broad variety of policy objectives, the EU does not yet have a common waste management policy. Policy activities have focused on five main areas as follows.

Waste management

Against a background of mounting waste production and the energy crisis of 1973, political opinion in the Community in the mid-1970s was in favour of reducing waste and using natural resources more efficiently. The first major legislative step was taken in 1975 with the adoption of the framework directive on waste (75/442), aimed at harmonizing national waste measures, and obliging member states to ensure that waste was disposed of without harm to human health and the environment. They were required to designate competent authorities to oversee waste disposal, and these authorities had to develop waste disposal plans, establish permit systems for waste disposal, treatment or storage installations, prevent the uncontrolled disposal of waste, and encourage the prevention of waste generation and the reuse of waste.

'Waste' was defined in the directive as 'any substance or object which the holder disposes of or is required to dispose of pursuant to the provisions of national law in force', and 'disposal' was defined as 'collection, sorting, transport and treatment . . . storage and tipping above or under ground [and] the transformation operations necessary for its re-use, recovery or recycling'. Selected categories of waste were excluded from the directive, including radioactive, mineral and agricultural waste. While the goals of the directive were noble, member states were given considerable latitude on implementation, as a result of which the directive led to few changes, and Lister describes it as 'an unfulfilled promise' (1996, p. 71).

In 1976, a consultative Committee on Waste Management was set up to provide the European Commission with advice on waste management policy. With a representative from the Commission and two from each member state, it met for the first time in March 1977 and developed a list of priorities, including toxic waste, waste paper and packaging. A directive on toxic and dangerous wastes was already under discussion, and this was adopted in 1978 as directive 78/319 requiring member states to reduce the creation of hazardous waste, encourage effective processing and recycling, and ensure safe disposal. An annex contained a list of 27 groups of wastes considered hazardous, including heavy metals, pesticides, organic halogen compounds and asbestos, but excluding radioactive wastes, explosives and other dangerous commodities. While it defined the substances in these 27 groups as 'toxic and dangerous' if they appeared 'in such quantities or in such concentration as to constitute a risk to health or the environment', it failed to give any guidance on the point at which a risk began to be posed. It was left to the member states to decide the quantities and concentrations.

Evidence that the directive was making little real difference to the handling of toxic waste eventually led to the development of a new directive (91/689) which added lengthy annexes containing lists of hazardous (as opposed to 'toxic and dangerous') waste, and imposing several requirements on member states regarding the handling, recording and disposal of hazardous waste. The term 'hazardous' was apparently chosen because it was wider and more comprehensive than 'toxic and dangerous' (Johnson and Corcelle, 1995, p. 194), and was defined as including any waste that was – among other things – explosive, flammable, irritating, harmful to human health, toxic, corrosive or mutagenic.

Reducing the creation of specific wastes

Several pieces of law were adopted during the 1970s dealing with particular kinds of waste. Among these was directive 75/439 on the disposal of waste oils, and directive 76/403 on polychlorinated biphenyls (PCBs) and polychlorinated terphenyls (PCTs). The waste oil directive was based on national law in West Germany, and on similar proposals then under discussion in France and the Netherlands. It encouraged member states to ban or control the pollution of water, soil and the air by regenerating waste oil or using it to generate energy, and to establish a waste oil collection and disposal system.

The Community also developed what was perhaps the world's most advanced regulatory regime for another very specific sector: the titanium dioxide industry. This was one of three industries that had been listed in the First EAP in 1973 as a desirable focus of Community regulation, the others being paper and pulp, and iron and steel. Titanium dioxide is used in paint and sometimes as a colourant, and was a source of often serious water pollution problems. It has been the subject of a series of directives, beginning with 78/176 and moving through several subsequent amendments.

Managing transfrontier shipments of waste

At the beginning of the 1980s, the question of how to deal with the movement of wastes across frontiers moved to the top of the political agenda, prompted by an interesting coincidence. In January 1983, the Commission had sent the Council a proposal for a directive aimed at providing cradle-to-grave supervision and control of transfrontier movement of hazardous waste within the Community. Just three months later, 41 barrels of hazardous waste containing dioxin, which had been collected following the 1976 Seveso accident and stored until they had disappeared in August 1982, were discovered in northern France. The discovery of the barrels emphasized the ease with which hazardous waste could be shipped across borders, and led to attempts to tighten the proposal, notably by the European Parliament which set up a committee of inquiry into the problem. After hearing from the Commission, independent experts and national ministers, Parliament came down in favour of the proposal being adopted as a regulation, and of member states being allowed to refuse imports of hazardous waste shipments. In the event, after several long negotiating sessions among the environment ministers, the proposal was watered down and adopted in December 1984 as directive 84/631.

The directive introduced a prior informed consent (PIC) procedure under which anyone wishing to ship toxic or dangerous waste (as defined in directive 78/319) from one member state to another – or into a member state from outside the Community – had to provide detailed information on the origin, composition and quantity of the waste, had to have a contract in hand with a consignee, and had to have notified the state that would be receiving the waste, which could object on grounds of environmental protection, public health, public policy or security. Unfortunately, a 'recycling loophole' was created by the legislation: in the case of shipments of recyclable waste, the states involved had only to be notified rather than to give consent, so a shipper could avoid the PIC requirement simply by saying that the waste was intended for further use and making the necessary arrangements with the recipient (Schmidt, 1992).

In the late 1980s, the issue of transfrontier waste shipments became part of the agenda of the single market programme. The 1985 Cockfield report mentioned the waste trade in the context

TABLE 6.2   *Key pieces of EU law on waste*

75/439	Directive on the disposal of waste oils. *Establishes requirements on the collection and disposal of waste oils; prohibits discharge into water and drainage systems. Revised by directive 87/101.*
75/442	Directive on waste. *Framework directive aimed at encouraging member states to prevent or reduce waste production and to encourage waste recovery. Key amendments made by directives 91/156, 94/3 and 99/31.*
76/403	Directive on the disposal of chemicals. *Establishes goals and procedures on disposal of PCBs and PCTs.*
78/176	Directive on waste from the titanium dioxide industry. *Places controls on the discharge, dumping, storage and injection of waste from the titanium dioxide industry.*
78/319	Directive on toxic and dangerous waste. *Harmonizes arrangements for disposal of toxic and dangerous waste, and encourages member states to reduce its production. Replaced by directive 91/689.*
84/631	Directive on shipments of hazardous waste. *Encourages measures for supervision and control of transfrontier shipment of hazardous waste.*
89/369	Directive on air pollution from new municipal waste incinerators. *Sets emission limits on dust, heavy metals, acid gases, hydrofluoric acid and sulphur dioxide from new municipal waste incineration plants.*
89/429	Directive on air pollution from existing municipal waste incinerators. *Builds on 89/369 by extending emission limits to existing plants.*
880/92	Regulation on eco-labelling. *Establishes voluntary award scheme for environmentally-friendly products.*
259/93	Regulation on waste shipments. *Establishes system to monitor, supervise and control the shipment of waste within, into and out of the EC.*
94/62	Directive on packaging and packaging waste. *Requires member states to establish return, collection and recovery systems, and to set targets for recovery and recycling.*
94/67	Directive on hazardous waste incineration. *Sets emission limits and establishes operating and monitoring requirements for incineration of most types of hazardous solid and liquid waste.*

of the free movement of goods and services, and the Commission warned of the 'large-scale waste tourism' that might result from the elimination of border controls (European Commission, 1989). Once again, a problem being addressed by the Commission was given graphic illustration by a headline-making event: the saga of the *Karin B* in 1987–88.

An Italian firm had arranged for a consignment of radioactive waste to be shipped for storage in Nigeria. When the Nigerian government discovered what was happening, they insisted that the Italian government remove the waste. The latter agreed to do this, and most of the waste was loaded aboard a German ship named the *Karin B*. Protesters prevented the ship from unloading in Ravenna (the port of origin), and it subsequently spent two months at sea being denied entry to ports in six EU states including Britain, Germany and France. It was eventually allowed to dock at Livorno, and its cargo was unloaded and arrangements made for disposal.

The *Karin B* was just one of several controversies involving shipments of waste to the South, which drew public attention to a relatively small problem; barely 2.5 million tonnes of hazardous waste was shipped from OECD states to non-OECD states in the period 1989–93 (OECD, 1997b). Nonetheless, the issue of hazardous waste exports to the South became the subject of discussions during 1988 between the Commission and the Environment Council, the Commission pointing out that the problem was covered in principle by directive 84/631 and its amending directive 86/279, which imposed tighter controls on the shipment of dangerous waste to third countries (Johnson and Corcelle, 1995, p. 206). In May, Parliament issued a resolution condemning the export of hazardous waste to the South, but the Commission had already decided to develop a new directive that would strengthen 84/631, provide a tighter definition of 'hazardous waste', and provide tighter rules for the transport of waste.

Meanwhile, the issue was on the agenda during negotiations leading up to the opening for signature in March 1989 of the Convention on the Control of Transboundary Movements of Hazardous Wastes and their Disposal (the Basle Convention). The goal of the Convention, which came into force in May 1992, is to minimize the generation of hazardous waste and to control transfrontier shipments. It established written PIC as a condition for export; recognized the right of every state to ban the entry or disposal of imported waste; and declared illegal any shipments that did not meet the terms of the Convention. A new dimension was introduced by the agreement reached in December 1989 under the terms of the Lomé IV Convention. The latest in a series of development and cooperation agreements between the Community and several dozen African, Caribbean and Pacific (ACP) states, Lomé IV was the first to make environmental protection a separate arena of EC–ACP cooperation, and included a ban on hazardous and radioactive waste exports from the Community to the ACP states, even those with facilities for storage or disposal.

Underlying these developments was the vexing question of whether or not wastes were 'goods' that should be allowed to be traded within the EU as freely as any other commodity. The proximity principle argued that 'environmental damage should as a priority be rectified at source', a concept which seemed to contradict the argument that producers of waste should be allowed to ship it to other countries. While it was undesirable in principle to use other countries as sites for waste disposal, there were several reasons why this was a common procedure: waste production occasionally outpaced the capacity of domestic facilities to process that waste, several EU countries lacked processing and disposal facilities, and it was sometimes cheaper to have the waste processed in another country.

A 1992 decision by the European Court of Justice – *Commission v. Belgium*, Case C-2/90 – added new confusion to the issue. Belgian law prohibited the deposit or discharge in the province of Wallonia of wastes originating anywhere else in Belgium or the Community. The Court argued that this might run counter to the provisions of Articles 30 and 36 of the Treaty of Rome (ensuring the free movement of goods and services), but refused to overrule the Belgian law on the grounds that waste disposal posed serious threats to the environment and thus merited strong controls, and also referred to the proximity principle. The confusion thus caused was not resolved until the Community adopted decision 93/98 bringing into effect the rules of the Basle Convention (Lister, 1996, pp. 121–2).

Concerned about the poor record of the member states in implementing existing waste legislation, the Commission in 1990 proposed a new regulation on the supervision of waste shipments. The negotiations that followed saw a division of opinion between states in favour of greater trade controls and those in favour of more liberal arrangements. There were suggestions – notably from France and the UK – that the member states should become more self-sufficient in waste management, thus reducing the need for transfrontier movements. This argument was opposed by the Benelux states and others on the grounds that they did not have the facilities to process all their waste, and relied on the freedom to ship waste to countries with such facilities. Nonetheless, directive 91/156 – which amended 75/442 and improved the definitions of waste and disposal – introduced the principle of self-sufficiency (Koppen, 1997) by requiring that the Community and the member states take care of their own waste disposal. Two years later, regulation 259/93 (a direct result of the Basle convention) gave effect to the terms of Lomé IV, banned the export of waste to third countries except under specified conditions, and allowed states the right to ban waste imports provided they informed the Commission. However, it allowed smaller or less affluent EU states to export any waste they could not process themselves to neighbouring member states.

As noted above, a key weakness of directive 78/319 on toxic and dangerous waste was that 'waste' and 'disposal' were not defined. In 1991, in response to a call by the Commission for a new strategic approach to waste management, directive 91/156 made key amendments to the original framework directive 75/442. Waste was now defined as any substance or object in specific categories listed in an Annex 'which the holder discards or intends or is required to discard'. However, the new clarity offered by the list was undermined by a loophole introduced in the final category in the Annex: 'any materials, substances or products which are not contained in the above categories'. The same problem arose with directive 94/3, which provided a list of wastes and became known as the European Waste Catalogue (EWC), but – after listing 15 different categories of waste – noted that waste could also be defined as 'any materials, substances or products' not included in the 15 categories. A 1997 Commission report noted that the classification of waste varied 'considerably' from one member state to another, and that no member state had incorporated the EWC into national law (European Commission, 1997).

Landfills

One issue with which the Commission wrestled throughout the 1990s was the management of landfills. Although they have long been the most popular approach to the disposal of wastes in western Europe, chemicals can be leached from unsuitable or badly managed landfill sites into the water table, posing a threat to human health and local ecology. Landfills can also give off noxious gases; for example, they account for one-third of the EU's emissions of methane, a major greenhouse gas.

In 1991, the Commission published a draft directive designed to regulate landfills by setting out systems of site classification and protocols for testing waste, and also to limit the amount of organic waste added to landfill, and thereby to reduce methane emissions. Considerable debate followed with much of the opposition coming from Britain, uncomfortable with the organic waste limits. The proposal was voted down by the European Parliament in 1996 because it allowed weak standards for the many small rural landfill sites in the EU (*ENDS Report* 256, May 1996). The Commission then developed a new draft which allowed biodegradable waste to be placed in landfills, but to be reduced in stages by 2010. This was adopted in 1999 as directive 99/31.

Reducing waste production

In 1992, the EU began looking at the environmental impact of products by launching a scheme aimed at reducing waste by using market forces to encourage manufacturers to make environmentally-friendly products. Established by regulation 880/92, the eco-label scheme develops a set of criteria for different product lines, and allows manufacturers who meet those criteria to display the official flower logo of the scheme on their approved products. The scheme is voluntary (it is up to the manufacturer to apply to have a product considered), it aims to stimulate supply and demand for environmentally-friendly products, and it was introduced in order to replace national eco-label schemes, thereby removing the risk that differences among those schemes may pose a barrier to the single market. All members of the European Environment Agency (the 15 EU member states and Iceland, Liechtenstein and Norway) are eligible to take part.

Ecological criteria are developed for each product line on the basis of an assessment of their lifetime impact on the environment; in other words, the complete life-cycle of the product is analyzed, from the extraction of raw materials to production, distribution and disposal. The Commission sets the criteria in discussion with *ad hoc* advisory groups of experts, and they are usually valid for a fixed period, normally three years. Applications from manufacturers go first to the competent national authority (usually the environment ministry or the national standards agency), and are then reviewed by a six-member Consultation Forum (with representatives from industry, commerce, trade unions and consumer and environmental groups), and then by a Regulatory Committee consisting of representatives of the member states. The Council of Ministers makes the final decision.

About 200 products had been awarded the label by the end of 1998, and criteria for nearly 20 product lines were operational by late 1999, including washing machines, paints and varnishes, personal computers, footwear, laundry detergents, refrigerators and dishwashers. Meanwhile, criteria for shampoos, rubbish bags and several other products were under development. While the scheme undoubtedly appealed to environmentally-conscious consumers, there were no data available regarding the effect of the label on sales of different products, or on the contribution of the scheme to the reduction of waste.

The second attempt to develop a policy on products came with the directive on packaging and packaging waste (94/62), which set targets for recovery and recycling (90 per cent by weight of packaging waste output to be recovered within ten years, and 60 per cent of that to be recycled), proposed that a marking scheme for packaging be set up, tried to ensure that products were designed to make recycling easier, and encouraged information and education programmes to alert consumers to the benefits of recyclable packaging.

In mid-1998, there were indications that the Commission was thinking about developing an integrated product policy in order to minimize resource consumption, avoid the use of hazardous substances, prolong product life, make reuse and recycling easier, and more tightly allocate responsibility and liability.

Based on the idea of looking at the life-cycle of products, it is aimed at replacing fragmented approaches to waste generation with a more coherent life-cycle analysis. Environmental Data Services of the UK noted that the idea was motivated by the realization that increased consumer demand had offset many of the contributions made by improved technology to lowering pollution levels and pressures on natural resources, that it was becoming more difficult to 'squeeze environmental improvements out of industrial processes', and that a closer examination of the effects of products throughout their life-cycles might provide a means to achieving significant reductions in resource use and the generation of pollution and waste (*ENDS Report* 281, June 1998, p. 23). A broad consensus was reached on the idea at the Environment Council in May 1999, heralding the development of a more global EU approach to waste, following the models being developed with air, water and acidification (see Chapters 7 and 8).

In early 2000, the following proposals on waste were working their way through the Commission and the Council:

- Prompted by legislation in the Netherlands, Germany, Denmark and Sweden, a directive was being developed on waste electrical and electronic equipment (WEEE) which would oblige retailers to take back a similar end-of-life product from households when selling a new one, impose obligations on manufacturers and importers to fund the collection and reprocessing of WEEE from retailers and households, and encourage member states to collect an average of 4 kg of WEEE per person per year from households. Critics charged that the programme would impose significant costs on manufacturers and retailers.
- A directive was under development on non-hazardous waste incineration. This would replace two directives adopted in 1989 (89/369 and 89/429), and would apply to all types of non-hazardous waste, including sewage sludge, clinical waste and tyres, as well as selected hazardous wastes (such as waste oils and solvents) excluded from the 1994 hazardous waste incineration directive (94/67).
- The Commission was looking at the problem of end-of-life vehicles (ELVs), of which about eight to nine million are discarded every year in the EU, producing about 1.9 million

tonnes of waste. A proposal for a new law was introduced in 1995 based around the idea of requiring auto manufacturers to ensure that 95 per cent of the parts used in all vehicle models approved after 2005 would have to be reused and 8 per cent recycled. For vehicles approved before 2005, the target would not apply until 2015. Member states would also have to encourage manufacturers to design vehicles in such a way as to facilitate dismantling, reuse and recovery, ensure the setting up of systems for the collection of ELVs, and prohibit manufacturers from shredding, incinerating or landfilling materials containing lead, cadmium, mercury or chromium from new cars sold after 2003.

The examples of chemicals and waste illustrate clearly the evolutionary nature of EU environmental policy, and the manner in which so much of this policy has begun with a focus on very particular goals and has broadened over time to take a more global approach to a series of related problems. They also show how the Community often set out to deal with problems relating to the single market, and ultimately began addressing environmental problems for their own sake. The EU does not yet have either a chemicals policy or a waste policy, but recent trends suggest that it is close to developing a broader set of objectives designed to address problems that are substantial in scope, and that have implications across the board of industrial activity.

Chapter 7

Air and Water Quality

The control of pollution has been at the heart of one of the oldest and most complete programmes of EU environmental law and policy. Since the first law on air pollution was adopted in 1970, and the first on water pollution in 1973, the EU has built an extensive body of law dealing with emissions into the air from road vehicles, fossil fuels and industrial plants, and with the protection of freshwater, marine water, surface water and groundwater. It began to take a more broad-ranging and strategic approach to pollution problems in 1996 with the adoption of an integrated pollution prevention and control directive. In the same year it adopted a framework directive on air pollution, and a proposal for an Auto-Oil programme designed to encourage the motor and oil industries to cooperate on the problem of vehicle emissions. In 1998 it began work on a broad-ranging water pollution control strategy.

The EC began addressing air quality issues in a fragmentary fashion in the early 1970s, again more out of a concern for the functioning of the common market than for the state of the environment. It went on to build a programme based around seven areas of activity: limits on emissions from road vehicles, controls on the content of fuels, limits on emissions from industrial plants, the control of acidification, rules on specific substances in the air (such as sulphur dioxide, lead and nitrogen dioxide), and contributions to international attempts to address depletion of the ozone layer and the problem of climate change. Only since the 1980s has environmental protection become the key motivation, and only since the mid-1990s has there been an attempt to build strategic approaches to problems such as acid pollution, or to build a broad-ranging policy on air quality.

While there have been notable achievements on air pollution – such as the European contribution to dealing with lead in petrol and acidification – the EU air quality programme has not been as complete as its response to water quality issues. EU water policy was initially based on concerns about human health, and about making sure that drinking and bathing water were clean enough for human use. In the 1980s the emphasis began to shift towards protecting the aquatic environment, and four main strategies have since been used: an effect-oriented approach based around the setting of quality standards for water intended for different uses; a source-oriented approach aimed at preventing pollution at source by setting effluent standards for dangerous substances; a product-oriented approach that sets standards for potentially pollutive commodities such as fertilizers and detergents; and the setting of design specification standards for boats and ships aimed at preventing oil pollution.

The major directives include lists of pollution limits, require states to designate 'types' of water to be covered, apply standstill rules requiring states to ensure that water quality becomes no worse, and require states to designate 'competent authorities' to inspect relevant waters (Sunkin *et al.*, 1998, p. 187). The general shift by the Commission towards a strategic approach to environmental issues has been reflected in water policy with the development of a framework water directive. Published in 1997, its goal is to provide an integrated approach to the protection of surface water, groundwater, estuaries and coastal waters, based around a system of river basin management districts to be established in every member state.

Air quality: the problem

Air pollution is almost exclusively the result of the burning of fossil fuels, particularly the coal used in many power stations, and the fuel used in road vehicles. As population has increased, so has the demand for energy, the number of vehicles on European roads, and the size of towns and cities. The result has been a reduction in air quality such that – to varying degrees – air pollution afflicts every city in the EU, and occasionally major towns and rural areas downwind from urban centres.

Industrial and agricultural activity produces a variety of chemical byproducts, the most problematic being the following:

- *Sulphur dioxide (SO₂)*. Produced when the sulphur present in fossil fuels is released and reacts with oxygen, SO_2 is one of the primary constituents in acid pollution, reacting with water to produce sulphuric acid and causing damage to human health, trees, rivers, lakes, soils, buildings and materials. The sulphur content of different fuels varies, running as high as 3 per cent in crude oil, and as high as 10 per cent in high-sulphur coal. Power stations and oil refineries account for 58–60 per cent of emissions in the EU, the balance coming from smelters and similar installations, and from natural sources such as decaying organic matter and sea spray.

- *Nitrogen oxides (NOₓ)*. A collective term for nitric oxide and nitrogen dioxide, NO_x forms when combustion oxidizes the nitrogen in fuel and some of the nitrogen naturally present in the air. Road vehicles account for about 63 per cent of emissions in the EU, and power stations for about 20 per cent, most of the balance coming from natural sources such as lightning and decaying organic matter.

- *Volatile organic compounds (VOCs)*. This is another collective term, covering a wide range of compounds containing carbon, and usually taken to include hydrocarbons and oxygenates such as alcohol. Some are carcinogens, and others can react with NO_x in sunlight to produce photochemical oxidants, or smog. VOCs are produced mainly by road vehicles (30 per cent of emissions in the EU), the chemical and petroleum industries, paints and glues, and the use of solvents in industrial processes (35 per cent of emissions in the EU) (EEA, 1995, p. 66), and by natural sources such as fires and decaying organic matter.

- *Ammonia (NH₃)*. This is mainly a byproduct of animal waste and fertilizer use, and is a particular problem in regions of the world such as western Europe where there is intensive agriculture. Like SO_2, NO_x, and VOCs, ammonia is a primary constituent in acid pollution (see Chapter 8), causing cloud water to become more alkaline and increasing the rate of conversion of SO_2 and NO_x to acids.

- *Suspended particulate matter (SPM)*. This is a collective term for solid and liquid material suspended in the air, varying in size from fine aerosols to particles in the form of dust. The major sources of SPM include forest fires and the burning of fossil fuels, and its danger lies more in the threat it poses to human health than to the environment. Large particles pose a minimal threat, but smaller particles contribute notably to respiratory problems.

- *Carbon monoxide (CO)*. Most CO emissions come from natural sources, but the balance changes in urban areas where most come from the incomplete burning of fossil fuels. CO has little environmental impact, but can cause health problems in humans, and can even be fatal.
- *Carbon dioxide (CO₂)*. Produced mainly by the burning of fossil fuels, CO_2 is the major pollutant implicated in the problem of climate change. Small amounts exist naturally in the atmosphere, but the use of fossil fuels has led to a 25–28 per cent increase in concentrations compared to pre-industrial times.
- *Hydrocarbons*. This is a collective term for organic compounds of hydrogen and carbon, including methane, ethane, propane, polyethylene and benzene. They pose a threat both to air and water quality.
- *Heavy metals*. These include lead, cadmium, mercury, copper and zinc, many of which are introduced to both air and water as byproducts of industrial activity, and almost all of which pose a threat to human health. Improved water treatment and the phasing out of leaded petrol have reduced exposure risks of some to humans, but emissions of others (such as cadmium and mercury) are increasing.

Several problems face the policymaker in dealing with air pollution. First, the damage caused to human health and the environment results not from a single pollutant, but from multiple pollutants acting in concert. For example, tropospheric ozone (found from ground-level to an altitude of 10–15 km, and a key element in smog) develops during the summer when nitrogen oxides and VOCs react in the presence of sunlight, and during the winter when SO_2, NO_x and particulates are trapped at ground level by cold air. Second, different people are affected differently by different levels and combinations of pollutants; hence lead is more of a threat to children than to adults, and smog is more troubling to people with breathing problems than to those without. Third, many of the substances that are defined as pollutants are naturally present in the air, the result of processes as varied as volcanic activity and the decay of organic matter.

Nonetheless, a combination of national and European emission reduction policies and changes in the structure of industrial production has led to some significant reductions in production and emissions of several key pollutants, notably SO_2, lead and chlorofluorocarbons (CFCs). Representing the figure for 1990 as 100, NO_x emissions in western Europe were down to 91 by 1995, VOC emissions to 89, SO_2 emissions to 71, and CFC production to just 11 (EEA, 1998, chapter 5). The EEA notes, however, that most of the emission reductions have resulted from measures aimed at large sources in the industry and energy sectors, and that there has been less success in reducing emissions from transport and agriculture. Goods transport by road in Europe increased by 54 per cent between 1980 and 1998, and passenger transport by car increased by 46 per cent between 1985 and 1998. This resulted in an overall growth in transport-related environmental problems, while the relative contribution of industry to problems such as climate change, acidification and tropospheric ozone declined (EEA, 1998, pp. 279–81).

Air quality: the policy response

The Community response to air quality problems began in the 1970s, but it was piecemeal, was prompted more by concerns about avoiding trade distortions than about protecting human health or the environment, and has always tended to lag behind the response to water quality problems. Although the first pieces of law on vehicle emissions (70/220 and 72/306) predate the first pieces of law on water quality (two directives on detergents in 1973), the body of laws on water quality built steadily during the late 1970s, and it was not until the 1980s that the EC began taking more concerted action on issues such as transboundary air pollution and threats to the ozone layer.

For Johnson and Corcelle (1995, pp. 126–7), the relative slowness of the Community response to air quality issues can be explained in part by the energy crisis of 1973 – the governments of the member states were loathe to agree air pollution controls given that light crude oil with a low sulphur content was relatively scarce and expensive – and by the opposition offered by the politically powerful energy and automobile

industries in western Europe, which proved effective at lobbying against change both with national governments and the
European Commission. There was also resistance to action
in West Germany, whose government was opposed throughout the 1970s to the development of pollution control laws
that might impose heavy costs on German industry. Finally,
because polluted water is generally more visible than polluted
air, it was tempting for the Commission to focus on water in
order more quickly to be able to point to the benefits of European policy.

The political and economic tides began to turn in the early
1980s as the energy crisis faded into history and public opinion
in Germany became increasingly vocal about the links between
air pollution and damage to forests (see Chapter 8). Once the
Commission began paying more attention to air quality – from
about 1983–85 – it built a substantial body of laws, some of
which have become lynchpins of the entire EU environmental
policy regime; notable among these is directive 88/609 on emissions from large industrial plants.

Unlike the approach to water quality control, which has been
based on a limited number of approaches, EU air quality control
has used or suggested a wide variety of methods, including the
following:

- The setting of product quality standards, such as the sulphur
  content of liquid fuels and the lead content of petrol. The
  first such piece of law was directive 75/716 on the sulphur
  content of gas oils (used mainly for domestic heating and
  cooking and for diesel-engined road vehicles). This and subsequent amendments steadily reduced sulphur content from
  more than 0.5 per cent by weight to 0.1 per cent in gas
  oil, and to 0.05 per cent in diesel fuel (the goal of directive
  93/12).
- The setting of air quality standards, notably those for sulphur
  dioxide, suspended particulates, lead and nitrogen dioxide.
  Directive 80/779 was the first piece of EC-wide law laying
  down mandatory standards. It set 'limit' values – which are
  mandatory – and 'guide' values – which are non-obligatory,
  and recommended as goals to which member states should
  aspire. Such values were set for concentrations of SO_2 and
  suspended particulates at ground level for different times of

the year. While the motive behind 80/779 was to protect human health, directive 85/203 on NO_2 was designed to protect both human health and the environment.

- The use of emission limit values, notably in relation to industrial plants.
- Pollution emission 'bubbles', or the establishment of upper limits on total emissions. This has been used, for example, in relation to SO_2 and NO_x emissions from large combustion plants.
- Monitoring programmes aimed at improving the quality of information about specific pollutants. These have been an element of many different air quality laws, most notably directive 92/72 on ground-level ozone. This requires member states to develop a network for the collection of information on ozone, the rationale being that the chemistry behind its formation is not fully understood. Suggestions by the European Commission that the directive include the eventual setting of limit values were dropped on the basis that several member states would not have been able to meet such values (Haigh, 1992, p. 6.15-2).
- Reductions by manufacturers in the production of pollutants, as in the case of CFCs (see Chapter 10).
- Substance-oriented approaches aimed at reducing the impact of pollutants such as asbestos on both water and air.
- More controversially, the idea of imposing 'green taxes' designed to make the price of services or goods reflect their environmental costs.

The first piece of Community legislation on air pollution was a 1970 directive setting standards for emissions of carbon monoxide and unburned hydrocarbons from motor vehicles (70/220). It was adopted in response to laws passed in 1968 and 1969 in Germany and France, respectively, which the Commission felt posed a threat to the functioning of the common market; there is no mention in the recitals to the directive of human health or environmental quality. The directive heralded a succession of amendments and elaborations; carbon monoxide and hydrocarbon limits were further reduced (74/290), emission limits were set for nitrogen oxides (77/102), limits for all three pollutants were reduced (78/665 and 83/351), limits for all three pollutants were further reduced to bring the

TABLE 7.1 *Key pieces of EU law on air quality*

70/220	Directive on road vehicle emissions. *Sets limits for emissions of carbon monoxide and unburned hydrocarbons from petrol-engined vehicles other than tractors and public works vehicles.*
72/306	Directive on emissions from diesel-engined vehicles. *Sets limits on the opacity of emissions from diesel-engined vehicles except tractors and public works vehicles.*
78/611	Directive on lead in petrol. *Sets maximum limits for lead content of petrol sold in the EC.*
80/779	Directive on sulphur dioxide and suspended particulate concentrations. *Sets limits for ground level concentrations of SO_2 and suspended particulates.*
82/884	Directive on lead in the air. *Sets limit values on concentrations of lead in the air, and mandatory sampling methods to be followed.*
85/210	Directive on lead in petrol. *Builds on 78/611 by requiring member states to make unleaded fuel available.*
88/609	Directive on large combustion plants. *Requires staged reduction of emissions of SO_2, nitrogen oxides, and dust from plants with a rated thermal input greater than 50 MW.*
92/72	Directive on air pollution by ozone. *Requires member states to establish network for monitoring collection of information and public warnings on ozone.*
96/61	Directive on integrated pollution prevention and control. *Requires application of best available technology to prevent or minimize air, water or soil pollution by industrial plants.*
96/62	Directive on ambient air quality assessment and management. *Outlines common methods and criteria for air quality assessment.*
99/30	Directive on air pollutants. *Sets limit values for sulphur dioxide, nitrogen dioxide, oxides of nitrogen, particulate matter, and lead in ambient air.*

Community into line with US standards (88/76), emission limits were set for particulates (88/436), and limits were set for small cars (89/548).

Along the way, three important changes took place. First, by the early 1980s, free trade was no longer the main rationale behind reducing vehicle emissions, and the recitals for directive 83/351 quote the argument made in the First EAP for 'account to be taken of the latest scientific advances in combating atmospheric pollution'. Second, while early directives were based on the idea of 'optimal harmonization', meaning that member states were not obliged to adopt the emission standards, directive 89/548 introduced mandatory standards that were designed to be at least the same as those in force in the United States. This paved the way for the introduction of three-way catalytic converters, the devices that are fitted to vehicle exhaust systems to reduce emissions of hydrocarbons and carbon monoxide. When directive 91/441 extended the limits in 89/548 to all new model cars, catalytic converters became mandatory on all new cars from 1993. Third, while EC policy on vehicle emissions in the 1970s was based on regulations developed by the UN Economic Commission for Europe (see Chapter 8), rising concern in Germany about the effects of pollution on forests led to the Community taking more control over the development of its own new proposals.

The Community had also begun addressing the problem of lead in air, starting out modestly with directive 77/312 requiring member states to set up screening programmes in order to establish the lead content of blood in the population. The following year, directive 78/611 set limits on the lead content of petrol. This again came at the prompting of West Germany, which had limited the lead content of its petrol to 0.4 grammes per litre with effect from January 1972. In response, the Commission set up two committees to study the health and technical aspects of lead emissions from motor vehicles. Their work concluded that the member states allowed significantly different levels of lead in petrol, and while there was no immediate public health problem, action should be taken to prevent an increase in airborne lead levels as vehicle use increased, and to remove another technical barrier to trade (Haigh, 1992, p. 6.7-2).

When West Germany announced a further reduction in the lead content of its petrol to 0.15 g/l with effect from January

1976, the Commission responded with the proposal that was eventually adopted as directive 78/611, requiring upper limits of between 0.15 and 0.4 g/l. This was followed in 1982 by a directive setting maximum limits for lead concentrations in the air (82/884), which took six years to work its way through the system in large part because of opposition from the British government, which argued that the scientific evidence that prompted the proposal was incomplete (Haigh, 1992, p. 6.6-2). Member states were given five years to meet the limits, and were required to ensure that monitoring stations were operating wherever people were likely to be exposed to lead in air for long periods or where limit values might not be reached.

A new directive on lead in petrol (85/210) was adopted relatively quickly, in large part because of a change in attitude by the British government, prompted on the one hand by recommendations in favour of reduced lead by the Royal Commission on Environmental Pollution, and on the other hand by a public campaign orchestrated by the Campaign for Lead Free Air (CLEAR). There was also support from West Germany, which at that point was beginning to realize that unleaded petrol was a requirement for the use of catalytic converters on vehicle exhausts, which were in turn part of the strategy to deal with acid pollution by reducing emissions of nitrogen oxides. Directive 85/210 established limits for the lead content of petrol in order both to reduce air pollution by lead and to prevent barriers to trade resulting from different limits in different member states. It allowed member states to continue selling leaded petrol, but required them to reduce the upper limit to 0.15 g/l as soon as possible. Two years later, directive 87/416 allowed member states to prohibit the marketing of low-octane leaded petrol.

The effect of these changes has been significant, with more progress made on reducing emissions of lead in the EU than of any other air pollutant bar CFCs. For example, lead emissions from petrol between 1990 and 1996 fell by 50 per cent in Britain, by 80 per cent in the Netherlands and Germany, and by 98 per cent in Denmark, Finland, Norway and Sweden (EEA, 1998, p. 112).

Despite this success, and despite the contribution made by EU law to the reduction of other pollutants, the Commission by the early 1990s had begun to realize that its approach to air quality had its weaknesses, among which was a poor record on compliance. There were particular problems with the air quality directives, including differences in measuring and reporting requirements, differences in the criteria used by member states to designate zones where extra time was needed to meet limit values, a failure by every member state to apply guide values, and differences in the methods used to provide information in the event that limit values were exceeded (European Commission, 1995). In response, the Commission began work on a new ambient air quality framework law, which was adopted in September 1996 as directive 96/62. This set new EU-wide air quality objectives for SO_2, SPM, lead, NO_2 and ozone, adopted common methods and criteria for assessing air quality and making the results publicly known, and required that member states draw up action plans listing the measures they proposed taking. It also listed 12 pollutants for which daughter directives would need to be developed, setting limit values and 'alert thresholds' (levels beyond which there is a risk to human health from brief exposure, and requiring immediate action by member states).

A series of daughter directives was listed in 96/62, with timetables. A draft of the first – covering SO_2, lead, fine particulates and NO_2, and based on World Health Organization guidelines – was published in October 1997, approved by the Council of Ministers in 1998, and adopted in 1999 as directive 99/30. A second draft directive – on benzene and CO – was published in late 1998, a year behind schedule, and a third – on polyaromatic hydrocarbons and heavy metals, including cadmium, arsenic, nickel and mercury – was published in late 1999.

While directive 96/62 took care of several of the weaknesses inherent in the older separate directives, a number of its elements have been called into question (Lefevere, 1997). First, it had been suggested that a standstill clause be included, prohibiting a deterioration in air quality in zones with good levels. However, this was left out at the behest mainly of southern states such as Spain, which argued that it would be an unfair restriction on industrial development in areas with good air quality. Instead, the directive says that member states 'shall maintain the levels of pollutants . . . below the limit values and shall endeavour to preserve the best ambient air quality, compatible with sustainable development' (Article 9). Second, questions have been raised about whether or not it is a good idea to set uniform air quality objectives for the entire Community, rather than setting higher goals for more vulnerable regions. Third, surprisingly little allowance is made in the directive for dealing with the resolution of cross-border pollution, specifically for giving states the ability to work with neighbouring states when the latter are contributing to the failure of the former to meet their limit values.

Also under development in the late 1990s was a proposal first mooted in 1992 for an Auto-Oil programme aimed at bringing together the Commission and the oil and motor industries to investigate ways of reducing vehicle emissions and promoting cleaner fuels in the most cost-effective manner by 2010. What were then DGIII (industry), DGXI and DGXVII (energy) were all involved in developing the programme, which was innovative in the sense that rather than being drawn up mainly within the Commission, it was developed in consultation with the oil industry (represented by EUROPIA) and the car industry (represented by ACEA). Not surprisingly, both groups felt that the bulk of responsibility should fall on the other, with ACEA arguing that it could not build low-pollution cars unless oil companies produced cleaner fuel, and EUROPIA arguing that car companies could produce cleaner engines with existing technology and fuels (Coss, 1999).

The Commission proposal on Auto-Oil was adopted in June 1996, and immediately ran into a stumbling block when it was revealed that it would cost the motor industry 4.1 billion ecus per year for 15 years, and the oil industry only 770 million ecus. The smaller cost for the oil industry was put down to its more effective lobbying, and to the fact that while the oil industry was dealing with a single product, motor manufacturers were competing with each other (*Financial Times*, 17 February 1998). Problems also arose in the Council of Ministers, where poorer southern states argued that the proposals would place a major strain on their domestic oil industries, and in the European Parliament, where members felt that the proposals did not go far enough, and proposed more than 100 amendments.

Following ten weeks of discussion in early 1998 at a conciliation committee bringing together members of the EP and the Council, agreement was finally reached in July on a heavily amended Auto-Oil programme. It introduced a series of measures against air pollution from passenger cars and light commercial vehicles, and new measures on the quality of petrol and diesel fuels, all of which would be achieved with amendments to directives 70/220 and 93/12:

- Mandatory limit values were laid down for emissions of CO, hydrocarbons, NO_x and suspended particulates, aimed at reducing emissions by 60–70 per cent by 2010, from 1990 levels; southern states were given longer to comply.
- On-board diagnostic systems – designed to monitor the emissions of vehicles and warn drivers if they were polluting too much – would be mandatory on all new passenger vehicles with petrol engines starting in 2000, and for diesel-powered vehicles starting in 2003.
- Tax incentives were to be allowed on all new series production vehicles which complied in advance with the limit values.
- The sale of leaded fuel was to be prohibited with effect from 1 January 2000, although a member state could ask for an extension to 2005 if it could show that the ban would result in 'severe socio-economic problems'. Most member states met this deadline with time to spare, but Italy asked for a three-year extension, and Greece and Spain for five-year extensions. Officials in the EDG were not persuaded by their arguments about 'socio-economic problems', and environment Commissioner Margot Wallström suggested that it would set a dangerous precedent (*European Voice*, 28 October–3 November 1999, p. 5).
- A two-stage programme was agreed for tightening fuel quality requirements aimed at reducing the sulphur content of petrol and diesel; stage one began in 2000, and stage two is to begin in 2005.
- Car manufacturers would build vehicles with cleaner engines beginning in 2000.
- A proposal for a directive on emissions from heavy vehicles was to be discussed.
- A review of the programme would take place before the end of 1999 that could lead to stricter fuel standards with effect from 2005.

The Auto-Oil programme was followed by Auto-Oil II, designed to expand the agreement on emissions controls to sources of pollution not covered by the first programme – these include motorcycles, outboard motors, air compressors and other petrol-driven machinery and tools. Where motor manufacturers bore much of the burden for Auto-Oil I, the follow-up programme is likely to affect oil producers more squarely.

While different levels of progress have been made in each of the seven main areas upon which EU air quality policy has focused, approaches to each have developed independently. This has become a matter of concern to policymakers in recent years, and there are now signs that the EU is moving more in the direction of developing a single clean air policy (*ENDS Report* 288, January 1999, pp. 46–7). The trend was already suggested by the 1996 framework directive on air quality, Auto-Oil I and II, and the acidification strategy discussed in Chapter 8. By late 1998, the European Commission was suggesting that it might be better to integrate all these approaches and that the EU might consider developing an air quality strategy at five-year intervals. Each five-year cycle would begin with a review of the latest evidence of the threats posed to air quality and progress in improving air quality. The nature of air pollution would then be modelled and data collected on the cost-effectiveness of emissions reductions by source and member state, and finally proposals would be made for air quality objectives and an implementation strategy. The proposal was still under discussion as this book went to press.

Water quality: the problem

The management of water is a multifaceted issue. While policy on air deals exclusively with the quality of the air we breathe, water comes in several different forms (as groundwater, as surface freshwater or saltwater, and in precipitation) and must be managed differently according to the multiple roles it plays in our lives: it can be used for drinking, recreation, fishing, irrigation, raising crops, generating power and as a transport medium; it is a habitat for animal and plant species; and it must also be managed for its role in flooding and soil erosion. Furthermore, while pollution is the only man-made threat to air quality, water is threatened both by pollution and overexploitation (the EU has dealt more with the former than with the latter).

Water pollution in industrialized countries comes mainly from six sources:

- Agriculture has become a cause of pollution as farming has intensified, the use of chemical fertilizers and pesticides has expanded, and the volume of animal waste has grown. Rainfall runoff from farmyards and land treated with chemicals carries potassium and nitrogen compounds down into the groundwater and into neighbouring rivers and lakes, and water used for irrigation can also become polluted with salts, wastes and chemicals.

  Of particular concern is the effect on groundwater; not only is it thought to account for about two-thirds of the public water supply in the EU, but reductions in pollution take years to be reflected in improved quality because of the time it takes for pollutants to move through groundwater. Guide levels for nitrates are thought to be exceeded in groundwater beneath more than 85 per cent of agricultural land in Europe, maximum concentration limits are exceeded beneath about 20 per cent of agricultural land, and the evidence from different kinds of aquifers in different parts of Europe suggests that pollutant concentrations are growing (Stanners and Bourdeau, 1995). On a brighter note, pesticide use has either stabilized or fallen since 1985, although this is in part a reflection of the increasing efficiency of the active ingredients used in pesticides (EEA, 1995, p. 81).

- Domestic sources contribute to the reduction of water quality through the generation of sewage. The quality of surface water (mainly rivers and lakes) has improved in the EU as the proportion of the population connected to municipal waste water sewage treatment plants has increased. This has reduced the amount of organic matter being released into surface water, the presence of which can lead to deoxygenation, the release of ammonium, and the decline of fish and aquatic invertebrates and organisms. However, most of the improvements have come in northern states, where more than 80 per cent of the population is connected to sewage treatment plants. There has been less progress in southern states, where only about half the population is connected (EEA, 1995, pp. 81–2).

- Industry is a source of chemical pollution – notably from steel plants, the pulp and paper industry, metal foundries and oil refineries – and can also interfere with ecosystems by releasing warm or hot water into rivers and streams. Accidental oil and chemical spills are also a problem, often causing the kind of extensive damage that can never be fully repaired.
- The mismanagement of toxic and hazardous waste disposal can lead to chemical pollutants entering the water supply.
- Transport causes problems mainly through runoff, which washes oil, other petroleum products and heavy metals such as lead and cadmium off road surfaces and into rivers and streams, or leaches them down into groundwater. With the growing volume of traffic on European roads, this source is expanding.
- Air pollution can also have an impact on water quality, not only from direct discharge as pollutants fall on water, but also through adverse chemical processes set off by the introduction of pollutants into water. This is particularly true of acid precipitation, which can kill fish and other aquatic life, harm the birds and mammals that feed on fish, and pollute drinking water supplies.

Some water pollution comes from point sources such as individual factories, and from accidental releases such as oil and chemical spills, but since these sources are relatively easy to identify, they are also relatively easy to manage. Unfortunately, most of the pollutants affecting water quality come from non-point sources such as the cumulative effect of agricultural runoff, which is more difficult to control. The deterioration in water quality has effects on aquatic ecosystems, interferes with aquatic food chains, leads to the loss of wetlands and can cause eutrophication: excessive amounts of nutrients in a body of water stimulate the growth of plants, cause algal blooms, and drive out the natural animal and plant life.

Water quality: the policy response

Water pollution control is one of the oldest and most completely developed sectors of EU environmental policy. Its evolution can be roughly divided into three phases. The first came in the

1970s, was motivated more by concerns about human health than about environmental protection, and focused on setting water quality objectives (WQOs) which defined the minimum quality requirements needed to limit the cumulative effect of pollution, and to ensure no damage to human health (and later to the aquatic environment). After a pause in the 1980s, a second phase of legislation – including 1991 directives on urban waste water treatment and the control of nitrates used in agriculture – placed more emphasis on setting emission limit values (ELVs), or the maximum quantities of pollutants that could be discharged from particular sources. The third phase began in 1996 with a fundamental rethink of Community policy, agreement on the need for a more global approach to water quality management, and the development of a framework water directive designed to offer a more strategic approach to water quality issues.

Phase I (1973–80)

The First EAP identified water as an issue on which priority action was needed, and the development of a Community policy on water quality can be dated from the almost immediate adoption in 1973 of a directive on detergents and their biodegradability (73/404). Motivated by concerns that phosphate-based detergents posed a threat to water quality, and that different national laws on detergents posed a threat to free trade, it was prompted by the visible and increasingly widespread problem of foaming in rivers caused by the use of detergents which could not be broken down by sewage treatment. The directive prohibited the marketing and use of detergents containing surfactants in four categories that had biodegradability levels of less than 90 per cent. (Surfactants are surface-active agents, or substances which reduce the surface tension of liquids, allowing the formation of bubbles.) A supplementary 1973 directive (73/405) established standardized methods for testing detergents and their biodegradability.

The broader legislative framework on water quality control was laid down with two key laws adopted in 1975 and 1976. The first of these was the surface water directive (75/440), which was designed to ensure – in the interests of protecting public health – that surface water abstracted for use as drinking water met certain standards and was adequately treated, and to improve the quality of rivers and other surface waters used as sources of drinking water. It established three mandatory WQOs for surface water, stricter quality goals, and standardized methods for treating drinking water. Member states were required to draw up plans of action and were given ten years to improve water quality with the ultimate objective of meeting the quality goals.

These goals were expanded by the drinking water directive (80/778), which set standards for the quality of water intended for human consumption or for use by food producers; it listed more than 60 water quality standards and guidelines for water quality monitoring. This has since been the fundamental law relating to the quality of water for human consumption, although it has proved controversial because of the difficulties member states have had in meeting its requirements (Lister, 1996, p. 133).

The second major piece of early EU legislation was the bathing water directive (76/160), which was again motivated more by concerns for human health than for the state of the aquatic environment (the word 'environment' appears among the recitals, but the directive is clearly aimed mainly at the comfort of swimmers and bathers). The directive required improvements in the quality of bathing water (fresh or seawater), mainly by ensuring controls on the disposal of sewage. It set mandatory WQOs, stricter quality goals, and standardized measurement methods for bathing water, giving member states ten years to meet the targets set. A contentious issue arose during the development of the directive over the definition of bathing water. Early drafts suggested that it was water where bathing was either authorized or tolerated, but since there are very few parts of the European coastline where bathing is not tolerated, monitoring would have proved an expensive proposition (Haigh, 1992, p. 4.5-2). The wording was subsequently changed to define bathing waters as areas 'in which bathing is explicitly authorized by the competent authorities of each Member State, or bathing is not prohibited and is traditionally practised by a large number of bathers'.

The first law aimed at protecting the aquatic environment (rather than human health) was the framework dangerous substances directive (76/464), designed to eliminate the pollution

TABLE 7.2   *Key pieces of EU law on water quality*

73/404	Directive on detergents. *Framework directive prohibiting marketing of detergents not meeting specified levels of biodegradability.*
75/440*	Directive on drinking water. *Establishes standards and treatment requirements for surface water intended for abstraction for use as drinking water.*
76/160	Directive on bathing water. *Establishes values for the quality of bathing water, particularly with goal of reducing presence of sewage.*
76/464*	Framework directive on water pollution. *Establishes framework for elimination/reduction of pollution of inland, coastal or territorial waters by dangerous substances. Introduces concept of best available technology (BAT) and produced several daughter directives.*
77/795*	Decision on exchange of information on surface freshwater quality. *Establishes common procedure for exchange of information on the quality of surface water in the Community.*
78/176	Directive on waste from the titanium dioxide industry. *Places controls on the production of waste from the titanium dioxide industry.*
78/659*	Directive on quality of fresh waters. *Establishes quality objectives for rivers and other fresh waters needing protection or improvement in order to support fish life.*
79/923*	Directive on water quality. *Requires member states to designate coastal and brackish waters needing protection or improvement to support shellfish, and to establish pollution reduction.*
80/68*	Directive on groundwater pollution. *Prohibits or regulates direct and indirect discharges of dangerous substances into groundwater.*
80/778	Directive on drinking water quality. *Establishes quality standards for water intended for drinking or for use in food and drink manufacture.*
91/271	Directive on urban waste water treatment. *Establishes standards for the collection, treatment and discharge of urban waste water, and controls over the disposal of sewage sludge.*
91/676	Directive on water pollution from nitrates. *Requires action on pollution of water from nitrates in inorganic fertilizer and manure.*
Forthcoming	Framework directive on water (to replace all laws marked*)

by dangerous substances of inland surface waters, territorial waters and internal coastal waters, and to reduce pollution caused by less hazardous substances. It came as a response to several international conventions then undergoing development – such as the 1976 Convention for the Protection of the Rhine against Chemical Pollution – and the need to ensure coordinated implementation of these conventions. It defined 'pollution' as the direct or indirect discharge by humans of substances or energy that cause hazards to human health, harm to living resources or aquatic ecosystems, or that damage amenities or interfere with the other legitimate uses of water. The directive included two lists of hazardous substances: list I (sometimes called 'the black list') included mercury, cadmium, hydrocarbons and carcinogens, and list II ('the grey list') included metals such as lead, copper and chromium, and cyanides, fluorides and nitrites. Prioritizing these substances proved contentious, so it was not until the early 1980s that daughter directives began to be adopted on specific substances, such as mercury (82/176 and 84/156) and cadmium (83/513). Even by the mid-1990s, barely 1 per cent of the 1500 substances listed in the framework directive had been subjected to specific values and targets, all of them from the black list (Lister, 1996, p. 146).

The idea of developing daughter directives for specific pollutants failed to take into account the potential effects of a mixture of different pollutants (an issue that was later addressed in the 1996 integrated pollution prevention directive). The efficacy of the directive was also undermined by the setting of unrealistic deadlines, and by the provision that member states could set either WQOs or ELVs. All member states preferred the latter except Britain; since it has short, free-running rivers and nothing, for example, as long as the Rhine, it argued that the absorptive capacity of rivers should be taken into consideration, and that water quality standards were preferable. A compromise was reached by which both approaches were to be included in daughter directives, but reaching agreement on the specific limits for specific substances proved much more difficult than was originally anticipated. Haigh (1992, 4.2-1) argues that the 'parallel' approach weakened EU policy on dangerous substances in water, and slowed agreement on daughter directives.

The 1976 directive was followed in 1980 by the supplementary groundwater directive (80/68), which had the same principles but stricter goals, and took a preventive approach to controlling water pollution. Leaching from landfills and storage sites has combined with waste disposal to pose a major threat to the quality of drinking water (about 70 per cent of which is extracted from underground sources in the EU), and of water used for amenities and recreation. The directive contained bans or restrictions on direct or indirect discharges of nearly 30 substances, contained in two lists. Two controversial exceptions were allowed, however: it did not apply to domestic waste from dwellings not connected to a sewage system and outside the area in which groundwater is used for human consumption, nor to discharges of radioactive substances or small quantities of List I and List II substances. Later the same year, Directive 80/778 became the first to set quality standards for drinking water, the issue again being public health rather than environmental protection.

The First EAP proposed the development of a source-oriented approach to water pollution, in which laws were developed that targeted specific industries. Several such industries were identified, but the European Commission worked up proposals relating only to two: pulp and paper, and titanium dioxide (a white pigment used in paints and other products). Member states were too concerned about protecting the interests of national pulp and paper industries to reach agreement on the former, so work proceeded only on the latter, resulting in directive 78/176. This and several subsequent amendments were aimed at preventing, progressively reducing and eventually eliminating all pollution from this source. The directive was prompted by a squabble in the early 1970s between France and Italy over the dumping of waste from a titanium dioxide factory at Scarlino in Italy, resulting in the creation of 'red mud'.

Ecological and economic motives were combined in laws adopted in 1978 and 1979 on the quality of waters supporting freshwater fish and shellfish. The first of these (78/659) required that WQOs be set for designated freshwater areas in order to improve environmental quality for fish, specifically salmonids (salmon and trout) and coarse fish. The second (79/923) did the same for shellfish, requiring that member states designate coastal and brackish waters which needed protection or improvement in order to support shellfish.

The EU has been less active on developing laws relating to marine pollution, preferring to work instead within the parameters of international agreements (not always successfully), and to rely on decisions rather than regulations or directives. Most of these decisions have been a result of the Commission signing international treaties on behalf of the EU: they include the 1972 London Convention on the dumping of wastes at sea, the 1972 Oslo Agreement on the North Sea, the 1974 Helsinki Convention on the Baltic Sea, the 1976 Barcelona Convention on the Mediterranean, and protocols to these and other conventions. An attempt was made by the Commission in 1976 to develop a directive on waste dumping at sea (modelled on the London and Barcelona conventions), but it failed mainly because the member states felt that the existing conventions were sufficient.

Lister (1996, p. 168) argues that the EU has been most successful where it has dealt with problems involving specific industries, and where there has been a broad consensus for action. It has been less successful where the member states have failed to agree on the urgency of a problem, or where the regulatory issues have been more broadly framed. He notes that the difficulties of confronting political differences among the member states, and of complex issues relating to implementation, led to a 'regulatory pause' in the late 1980s and early 1990s on water quality management. Part of the problem was a scientific and political debate over the relative merits of the water quality objectives and the emission limits values approaches. In order to regain some legislative momentum, recent policy proposals have moved in the direction of combining both approaches.

Phase II (1988–95)

Despite the initiatives taken in Phase I, there were still significant gaps in the Community approach to water pollution. In 1988, a ministerial seminar was held in Frankfurt to review Community water policy and to make suggestions for improvements that needed to be made and gaps that needed to be filled.

One of the first pieces of law to emerge following the 'pause' was the urban waste water treatment directive (91/271), which was also the first major piece of water pollution law to be based on the new legal authority provided by the Single European Act, rather than the old Articles 100 and 235. The directive used the ELV approach to reduce the pollution of freshwater, estuaries and coastal waters by setting conditions for the treatment and discharge of domestic sewage, industrial waste water and rain-water run-off.

The directive was based on environmental arguments rather than a public health rationale, the recitals mentioning the need to 'prevent the environment from being adversely affected by the disposal of insufficiently-treated urban waste water', and making a distinction between sensitive and less sensitive areas. It required that all urban areas with a population of more than 2000 should have waste water collection systems by the end of 2000 (areas with less than 15000 people) or 2005 (areas with more than 15000 people), and should have introduced controls on the disposal of sewage sludge and banned the dumping of sewage sludge at sea. The directive arose out of concerns about the amount of untreated sewage finding its way into European fresh and coastal waters: in several EU states, the majority of urban waste water or sewage was being dumped into the sea untreated – for example, 70 per cent of waste water in Belgium, 80 per cent of the sewage in Portugal, and 90 per cent of the sewage in Britain (Haigh, 1992, p. 4.6-4).

In addition to trying to impose controls on water pollution from industrial processes, the EU had begun trying to address the impact of agriculture on water, notably through laws on the content of fertilizers and the control of nitrate pollution. The early rules on fertilizers established requirements for labelling, and placed limits on the quantities of chemicals such as boron, cobalt and manganese in fertilizer. The main nitrate directive (91/676) was focused more on reducing water pollution caused by the storage and use of inorganic fertilizer, and required that member states identify the areas most in danger of nitrate pollution, and develop action plans to prevent the problem becoming worse. It was prompted by the need to 'protect human health and living resources and aquatic eco-systems and to safeguard other legitimate uses of water'.

Phase III (1996–)

By the early-1990s, the Commission, Parliament and the Council had all begun thinking about the need for a more global approach to water policy, rather than the continued development of a series of laws dealing with discreet areas. Much of the existing law was out of date and was criticized by Parliament for being often contradictory (European Parliament, 1996, p. 52).

There were several indicators of the emerging change in approach. A 1992 Council resolution called on the Commission to draw up a detailed programme for the protection of groundwater, which resulted in the publication in 1996 of a draft Groundwater Action Programme. In 1993 the Commission proposed a directive on the ecological quality of water aimed at requiring member states to monitor water ecology and identify potential sources of pollution. The Fifth EAP (published in 1993) argued that the Community should take account not only of the quality of water but should ensure that it was available in quantities that were sufficient to allow sustainable development without upsetting the natural equilibrium of the environment.

In mid-1995, the need for a more global approach to water policy was emphasized by severe winter flooding in northern Europe and a long drought in southern Europe. In June, the Environment Council and the European Parliament called on the Commission to review water policy in light of the Fifth EAP. In its Communication, the Commission argued that the four goals of sustainable water policy were to provide a safe and secure supply of drinking water, to provide enough water to meet the needs of industry, agriculture, fisheries, transport, energy generation, recreation and other economic sectors, to ensure that water quality and quantity were sufficient to meet the needs of the aquatic environment, and to ensure that water was managed so as to prevent or reduce the adverse impact of floods and droughts. A consensus emerged that the proposed directive on water ecology should be broadened into a framework water policy directive.

The Commission report acknowledged that these four goals were not always compatible, and argued that a sustainable water policy was one which achieved a balance between the four objectives. At the instigation of the Commission, a two-day Water Conference was held in Brussels in May 1996, attended by about 250 delegates representing member states, local and regional government, regulatory agencies, the water industry, agriculture, consumers and the environmental lobby. The main conclusion of the conference was that water policy was fragmented, and that there was a need for a single piece of framework legislation to pull together the achievements of the previous 20 years.

In response, the Commission published a proposal in February 1997 for a framework water directive which incorporated all existing requirements, coordinated all the different objectives of water policy and the measures so far taken, and allowed for increased public participation in developing water policy. The directive would for the first time provide an integrated framework for the protection of surface water, groundwater, estuaries and coastal waters. It was to encourage cooperation between different member states by using management based on river basins rather than administrative or political units. Its major principles and features included the following (Europa Homepage, 1999):

- A system of river basin management districts will be established in each member state, with each district including more than one river basin, and groundwater and coastal waters being assigned to the 'nearest or most appropriate' basin. Management plans will then be developed, specifying what actions are needed to implement the environmental objectives for each basin. The plans are due to be in place within ten years, and fully operational within 16 years. These will help generate information in a standard format that can be easily analyzed and compared.
- There are four basic objectives: the protection of aquatic ecology, the protection of specific habitats, the maintenance of clean drinking water, and the protection of bathing water. All four need to be integrated for each river basin, with the aquatic ecology objective being applied to all bodies of water.
- Member states are to be allowed to use 'green taxes' to achieve the goals of the directive, the goal being to prevent the over-abstraction of water, to encourage more efficient use

of water, and to ensure that the environmental costs of water use are borne by the user.

- Because not all bodies of water are used for the same purpose, specific protection zones are to be established within each river basin, subject to more stringent protection according to the uses made of them.
- Groundwater should not be polluted at all, so direct discharges into groundwater should be banned, and groundwater should be monitored so that changes in chemical composition can be detected, and man-made pollution addressed.
- WQO and ELV approaches should be used in combination.
- In the interests of balancing the priorities of different groups, promoting transparency and improving the record on implementation, arrangements must be made for the participation of citizens, industry, NGOs and other interested parties. These will include exchange of information among water professionals, and biannual conferences to exchange views and experiences.
- EU water legislation will be rationalized by replacing several Phase I directives: 75/440, 76/464, 77/795, 78/659, 79/923 and 80/86.

Grant Lawrence, Head of the Water Unit in the EDG, described the proposal as 'the final pillar of our water policy. When it is put into place it will support and give architectural coherence to the whole water policy edifice. It forms the framework that will apply to water policy . . . for a good part of the [21st century]' (*Enlarging the Environment* (DGXI), no. 2, 1997). The Environment Council meeting in March 1999 reached unanimous agreement on the proposal, but because it was subject to the codecision procedure it was expected to undergo more change during negotiations between the Council and Parliament. It was still under discussion as this book went to press.

An integrated response to pollution

Until the mid-1990s, the tendency with EU environmental policy was to approach air and water quality issues separately, a philosophy which overlooked the fact that pollutants do not exclusively affect one medium or the other, and that controls on pollution in one medium could result in pollutants being released into the other. The Fifth EAP listed integrated pollution prevention and control (IPPC) as a priority for EU policy, so the Commission developed a proposal for a new directive in this area during 1991–93. Britain took a leading role in the discussions, a staff member from the UK Department of the Environment overseeing the preparation, and the proposal being based heavily on the integrated pollution control system used in the 1990 Environmental Protection Act. Several other member states – notably Germany – did not enter the debate until later in the process, by which time they were faced with a proposal whose principles ran counter to their traditional domestic approaches to pollution control (Schnutenhaus, 1994).

The philosophy behind IPPC was that pollution problems should be prevented or solved altogether rather than simply being transferred from one medium to another. The proposal was adopted in 1996 as directive 96/61, in which pollution is defined as

> the direct or indirect introduction as a result of human activity, of substances, vibrations, heat or noise into the air, water or land which may be harmful to human health or the quality of the environment, resulting in damage to material property, or impair or interfere with amenities and other legitimate uses of the environment.

The directive promotes the use of best available techniques (BAT), and is based around the issuance of permits for industry, setting emission limit values for all installations.

In 1997, a five-year programme to prepare technical guidance on the industrial processes covered by the directive was launched, aimed at developing 'best available techniques reference documents' (or BREFs) that competent agencies could take into account when developing their controls (*ENDS Report* 268, May 1997, p. 39). Under the terms of the directive, an Information Exchange Forum was set up consisting of representatives from member states, industry and NGOs, which monitors the work of a small European IPPC Centre based in Seville, Spain. BREFs are developed by the centre for specific sectors (it began with the cement and lime, iron and steel, and pulp and paper sectors), and these are then passed on to the Forum and to the Commission for their views. Once approved, they are published by the Commission, and local agencies are expected to use them as guidance in developing their responses to integrated pollution control.

The IPPC approach was the logical outcome of nearly 30 years of policy development in the fields of air and water quality control, during which it had become clear that there was a limit to what could be achieved by approaching the two different sectors separately. The development of air and water quality control strategies was a reflection of the global approach to limiting pollution in these two areas, and while these pulled together all the sectoral approaches developed by the Community in the 1970s and 1980s, they were tactical responses that overlooked many of the interrelationships between cause and effect in the threats posed to air and water. The integrated approach to dealing with air and water quality issues pushed EU policy onto a new level of maturity.

Chapter 8

Acidification

Particularly since 1985, the European Union has developed a substantial legislative and policy response to acidification which can be credited largely – but not wholly – with leading to major reductions in emissions of the pollutants involved (mainly sulphur dioxide and nitrogen oxides). A multinational programme to reduce acidifying pollutants in Europe began in 1975 under the auspices of the UN Economic Commission for Europe (UNECE), predating the EU response by eight years, but while the former was unable to encourage action by Britain – the biggest producer of sulphur dioxide in western Europe – EU legislation was able to encourage Britain to take the necessary action in 1988.

EU environmental policy on acidification has been driven by tensions caused by a variety of political and economic pressures, including different levels of affluence (wealthier member states have tended to be more willing to respond than poorer member states, which have been concerned that emissions reduction requirements would interfere with their economic development plans) and differences of opinion between member states creating their own acid pollution problems and those affected more by activities in neighbouring states. For example, while Austria and Sweden imported 93 per cent and 92 per cent respectively of their sulphur deposition in the 1980s, and so were more actively in favour of international cooperation, transboundary pollution was thought to account for only 20 per cent and 14 per cent respectively of deposition in Britain and Spain, two of the member states which proved least supportive of joint action (European Commission, 1995, p. 2057).

Although the causes and effects of acid pollution were identified and understood as early as the mid-19th century, it was not until the 1960s that new research encouraged the governments of industrialized states to respond substantively to the problem. The earliest and most enthusiastic proponents of anti-pollution measures were downwind states such as Sweden and

Norway. Prompted largely by the unwillingness of upwind states such as Britain and Germany to address transboundary pollution by limiting their emissions, the European Community was able to do little beyond placing modest limits on the sulphur dioxide and nitrogen oxide content of fuel. The most telling pressures for change meanwhile came from agreements brokered by the UNECE.

It took a domestic policy reversal in Germany in 1982–83 – induced by a combination of the growing power of the Greens, strategic considerations within Germany's political parties, and new evidence about the extent of forest death – for the balance of opinion within the Community to change in favour of a response. When it came, the Community's draft 1983 directive on reducing emissions from large combustion plants was to be modelled largely on a 1982 domestic German law. However, it took another five years – with most of the opposition coming from the Thatcher administration in Britain – for agreement to be reached on the content of the EC directive, which was finally adopted in June 1988.

Since then, emissions of acid pollutants in the EU have fallen significantly, the body of legislation dealing with acidification has expanded, and the EU has begun to develop a broader strategic approach to the problem based less on source-led percentage reductions of emissions, and more on effects-based reductions that take into account the different level of sensitivity of different environments to acid pollution.

Acidification: the problem

Acid pollution is one of the major long-term environmental costs of the agricultural and industrial revolutions. The burning of coal, oil or natural gas by power plants, industry and road vehicles – combined with agricultural intensification – produces several primary pollutants such as sulphur dioxide (SO_2), nitrogen oxides (NO_x) and ammonia, which undergo chemical reactions that can produce secondary pollutants such as nitrogen dioxide (NO_2, formed mainly by a reaction between nitric oxide (NO) and oxygen). These primary and secondary pollutants can be converted in the atmosphere, on the surface of buildings, inside plants, animals and humans, or below ground, into sulphuric and nitric acids.

Depending on a variety of biological, chemical and meteorological factors, soils, forests, lakes, rivers, animals, plants and buildings are susceptible in varying degrees to the effects of these pollutants, acting alone or in conjunction with other factors. Several of these pollutants also contribute to other environmental problems: nitrogen oxides, for example, are an ingredient in the creation of ground-level ozone (which is harmful to human health) and in threats to the ozone layer, and also contribute to eutrophication – the harmful build-up of nutrients and organic material in lakes (for more details, see McCormick, 1997).

The first signs of a link between the burning of fossil fuels and acidification were identified in Europe and North America in the mid-19th century, but there was to be no significant scientific or political response until the mid-20th century, when postwar economic reconstruction and expansion led to a doubling of demand for fossil fuels in Europe and North America, and new levels of consumption in Asia and Latin America. The world now relies on fossil fuels for 90 per cent of its commercial energy supplies: oil 41 per cent, coal 28 per cent, and natural gas 21 per cent, with the balance coming from nuclear power, hydropower and other sources.

As consumption increased, so pollutive emissions grew and acidification worsened. Accelerated research following the Second World War confirmed the existence of a problem with local, national and international dimensions, with the greatest emissions coming from the industrial centres of Europe and North America, and the most serious damage occurring downwind of those centres. The major chemical elements in the problem are as follows:

- Sulphur dioxide, produced mainly by power stations and other industrial plants which use fossil fuels, and by metal smelters, oil refineries and district heating installations. As noted in Chapter 7, power stations and refineries account for more than half of SO_2 emissions in the EU, with the worst pollution coming from a relatively small number of point sources, mainly power stations. The 100 biggest emitters (one-third of them in western Europe) between them accounted for 42 per cent of European SO_2 emissions in 1994, with the ten biggest alone accounting for more than two million tonnes of SO_2 emissions each year (Barrett and Protheroe, 1994).

- Nitrogen oxides, for which road vehicles are the major source in Europe; they account for 63 per cent of EU emissions, while power stations account for just 20 per cent of emissions. The role of road traffic in the problem continues to grow as the numbers of vehicles on European roads grow.

- Volatile organic compounds (VOCs) are produced mainly by road vehicles, the chemical and petroleum industries, paints and glues, and the use of solvents in industrial processes. The United Nations defines VOCs as 'all organic compounds of anthroprogenic nature other than methane that are capable of producing photochemical oxidants by reaction with nitrogen oxides in sunlight'. This definition is so broad as to make it difficult to measure emissions and to identify trends in the production of VOCs.

- Ammonia (NH_3), a byproduct of animal waste and fertilizer use, and a problem mainly in regions using intensive agricultural techniques. Calculating emissions is difficult since they depend on a variety of different factors, such as the nitrogen content of animal feed and the conditions under which wastes are spread. Nevertheless, UN figures suggest that Europe produces about 800000 tonnes of NH_3 emissions every year (European Commission, 1995), hence it is now being taken more seriously by EU policymakers as an element in the broader problem of acidification. (This contrasts with the situation in the United States, where ammonia has so far drawn little attention in discussions about acid pollution.)

Debates about policy responses to acidification have been troubled consistently by the fact that different pollutants contribute at different levels to the overall problem of acidification from one region to another, depending on a variety of factors including the buffering capacity of soils, the distribution of emissions, local or regional climatic and weather conditions, and the neutralizing capacity of other chemicals. The Dobris Assessment concluded that sulphur was the dominant factor in central and eastern Europe while NO_x 'may be relatively more important' in western and southern Europe. Meanwhile, ammonia 'makes a significant contribution' in those countries with intensive cattle breeding programmes, such as Denmark, the Netherlands and parts of Britain (Stanners and Bourdeau, 1995, p. 36).

Early policy responses

Campaigns for a political response to urban air pollution in Europe date back to the 19th century, but it was not until the 1950s that local air pollution began to be addressed, and the common tactic was to build tall smokestacks on power stations with a view to dispersing the pollution to the winds. However, this had the effect of converting a local problem into an international problem. One of the consequences in Europe was that in parts of Sweden, downwind from the major industrial centres of Britain and Germany, the acidity of rain doubled between 1956 and 1965 (Lundholm, 1970). With air pollution becoming more than a local or a national issue, the need for an international political response became increasingly obvious. The result was a proposal submitted to the United Nations by Sweden in July 1968 for an international conference to discuss environmental problems; this led to the convening of the UN Conference on the Human Environment in Stockholm in June 1972 (for more details, see McCormick, 1995, chapter 5).

Two months earlier, the Organization for Economic Cooperation and Development (OECD) launched a four-year study in its 11 European member states, named the Co-operative Technical Programme to Measure the Long-Range Transport of Air Pollutants, or the LRTAP project. This looked into the causes and effects of sulphur emissions, of possible transport within Europe, and of possible deposition and adverse effects hundreds or even thousands of kilometres from the source. The results, published in 1977, provided convincing evidence of the chemistry and transport of acid pollution, and showed that precipitation in one country was being affected by emissions in others; the problem involved all European countries north of the Alps (OECD, 1977).

The beginnings of a significant political response can be dated to the 1975 Conference on Security and Cooperation in Europe (CSCE), held in Helsinki. Soviet leader Leonid Brezhnev challenged participants to reach agreement on three pressing issues: energy, transport and the environment. Only the latter was politically acceptable to all participants, and the Swedish and Norwegian governments took the opportunity to lobby for a focus on air pollution. The result was a decision to develop a programme for monitoring the long-range transport of air pollutants, starting with sulphur dioxide (CSCE Final Act, 1975). It was subsequently decided that since the OECD did not have the power to enforce its policy recommendations, and since the EEC at that time had only nine members (which did not include Norway or Sweden), responsibility for the programme would be vested with the UN Economic Commission for Europe (UNECE) (Wetstone and Rosencranz, 1983, p. 141). The UNECE had 34 European member states from both east and west, had an organizational structure already in place, and operated on the principle of trying to build consensus among its members. It accepted the project, and negotiations began on the development of an international convention on long-range transboundary air pollution.

Thanks mainly to an unwillingness by Britain and Germany to agree to legally binding controls, the Convention on Long-Range Transboundary Air Pollution (the UNECE Convention), signed in Geneva in November 1979 by 34 states and by the European Community, imposed little more than a general obligation on each signatory to 'endeavour to limit and, as far as possible, gradually reduce and prevent air pollution including long-range transboundary air pollution.' This was to be done with the use of the 'best available technology which is economically feasible in new and retrofitted plants'. The terms 'best available technology' and 'economically feasible' (the latter included at the insistence of West Germany) were subsequently given wide and loose interpretation.

Meanwhile, despite the reluctance of Britain and West Germany to acknowledge the need to take action to control acid pollution, the Community had begun to take steps to reduce SO_2 and NO_x emissions by limiting the sulphur content of gas oil and placing limits on NO_x emissions from vehicles. By 1980, this had produced a body of legislation which included a series of directives on the approximation of motor vehicle emissions (70/220, 72/306) and on the sulphur content of liquid fuels (75/716), and a directive limiting nitrogen oxide emissions from road vehicles (77/102).

Useful though these steps had been, they did not represent a strategic EC-wide response to air pollution generally, or to acid pollution specifically. As noted in Chapter 7, the Community was slower to respond to air pollution control than to water pollution control, and its earliest efforts in the former were motivated as much by concerns over trade distortions as by concerns over public health. The preamble to directives 70/220 and 75/716, for example, make no mention of environmental quality concerns, but argue instead that differences in national provisions 'are liable to hinder the establishment and proper functioning of the common market' and 'constitute a barrier to trade'.

The emphasis began to change in 1976 with a Commission proposal for a directive on SO_2 and suspended particulate matter (agreed in 1980 as 80/779). The preamble mentions Article 100 and concerns about trade, but also mentions Article 235 and the need to 'improve the quality of life and protect the environment . . . [and] to protect human health'. Although its goals and its timetable (member states were given until 1993 to comply) were modest, 80/779 was notable for the fact that – for the first time – it imposed uniform air quality standards across the EC. Its agreement was followed in 1981 by publication of the Third EAP, which – while still vague in its objectives – announced that the EC intended to 'gradually reduce total emissions by establishing minimum standards' and to reduce total emissions at large fixed sources with high stacks with a view to resolving the problems of acid pollution and transboundary air pollution.

The Germans increase the pressure

Concerned about the lack of a European consensus in favour of the UNECE Convention, the Swedish government decided to use the tenth anniversary of the 1972 Stockholm Conference to renew its calls for action. Participants agreed that sulphur and nitrogen compounds were the primary cause of acid deposition, and the conference helped encourage more states to ratify the convention. However, while political pressure exerted by the Scandinavians through the UNECE was an important element in Community calculations, a more immediate and influential impulse now came out of domestic developments in West Germany. A gap between the promises and the achievements of the federal government in environmental policy during the late 1970s led to growing concerns among West German environmental groups and the green movement, both enjoying new prominence in the aftermath of protests directed at the West German nuclear power programme. By exerting pressure for change at the level of the *Länder* (the German states), these groups were able to build support for reforms to federal law.

The federal government had acknowledged in the late 1960s that SO_2 was implicated in damage to plants and forests (Boehmer-Christiansen, 1989), but, with the attention of both government and environmental groups focused on the nuclear power issue during the 1970s, relatively little attention was paid to clean air issues (Boehmer-Christiansen and Skea, 1991, p. 187). As one of the biggest sources of the acidifying emissions affecting Scandinavia, West Germany faced substantial costs if European acid pollution controls were agreed; it needed to be convinced that there would be benefits also for West Germans. Attention was first drawn to the potential problem of forest damage in West Germany in 1978 as preparations were made for negotiations on the UNECE Convention, but the groundswell of political and public interest did not begin to develop until 1981, when media attention began to focus on an hypothesis developed by soil scientist Bernhard Ulrich about links between air pollution and forest death, or *Waldsterben*.

Forest damage was confirmed by government research during 1982, leading to new demands for a response from the southern *Länder* (notably Bavaria), which were more heavily forested – and produced less SO_2 – than the northern *Länder*. Leading the criticism was Franz-Josef Strauss, leader of the Bavarian-based Christian Social Union (CSU), which was then part of the opposition with the Christian Democrats (CDU). In an attempt to win public support, and to draw attention away from growing public criticism about the potential siting of US Pershing missiles in West Germany (notably from the increasingly vociferous green and peace movements), the troubled Social Democrat/Free Democrat coalition government of Helmut Schmidt agreed in June 1982 to respond to the problem of acid pollution with a Large Combustion Plant Regulation (GFAVo). The political implications were particularly important for the man who announced the change of policy, Hans-Dietrich Genscher, foreign minister and leader of the Free Democrats (FDP), whose party had the most to lose from growing support for the Greens. The rot had by then gone too far, however, and the FDP abandoned the Social Democrats in October, ushering in a new CDU/CSU/FDP coalition headed by Helmut Kohl.

Waldsterben was one of the primary issues in the March 1983 election that confirmed Kohl in power. Attempts to placate and keep at a distance its coalition partners in the CSU (a purely Bavarian party) encouraged Kohl to appoint members of the CSU to key positions in the new government, including the Interior Ministry. Their concerns about forest damage in Bavaria led to a tightening of the content of GFAVo, which finally became law in July 1983. It applied to all combustion plants of 50 megawatts or more, and set emission limits for seven major pollutants, including SO_2, NO_x, and carbon monoxide (CO). While the programme was generally considered a success, and *Waldsterben* had ceased to be a major public issue by 1985, the Schmidt government – just before its fall – had recognized the need for a multinational approach to acidification, mainly because more than half of net SO_2 deposition in West Germany was imported. Hence it had adopted a programme which included efforts through the UNECE and the European Community to encourage the adoption of West German standards internationally, and to encourage tighter vehicle emission standards at the European level. These goals were now adopted by the Kohl government (Boehmer-Christiansen and Skea, 1991, p. 193).

In June 1982, the Schmidt government had sent the EC Council of Ministers a request that the Community begin thinking along the same lines as the Germans in their approach to large combustion plants. The lobbying of interior minister Gerhart Baum was given impetus by the fact that the European

TABLE 8.1 *Key pieces of EU law on acidification*

70/220	Directive on road vehicle emissions. *Sets limits for emissions of carbon monoxide and unburned hydrocarbons from petrol-engined vehicles other than tractors and public works vehicles. Amended by 77/102 and 89/548.*
72/306	Directive on emissions from diesel-engined vehicles. *Sets limits on the opacity of emissions from diesel-engined vehicles except tractors and public works vehicles.*
75/716	Directive on the sulphur content of liquid fuels. *Harmonizes laws of member states relating to the sulphur content of specified liquid fuels.*
80/779	Directive on SO_2 and SPM concentrations. *Sets limits for ground level concentrations of sulphur dioxide and suspended particulates.*
84/360	Directive on emissions from industrial plants. *Framework directive that requires operation of specified industrial plants to be authorized in advance, with a view to preventing/reducing air pollution.*
85/203	Directive on NO_2 concentrations. *Sets limits on atmospheric concentrations of nitrogen dioxide.*
88/609	Directive on large combustion plants. *Requires staged reduction of emissions of SO_2, NO_x, and dust from plants with a rated thermal input greater than 50 MW.*
91/441	Directive on road vehicle emissions. *Includes all new model cars in emission limits for smaller cars set by 89/458, thereby requiring that catalytic converters be fitted to all new cars from 1992. Introduces limits for emissions of VOCs.*

Commissioner then responsible for the environment, Karl-Heinz Narjes, was also German (although Commissioners are prohibited from pursuing national interests, at least overtly). Baum lost his job with the fall of the Schmidt government in September, but his replacement Friedrich Zimmerman – a CSU politician sympathetic to Bavarian foresters – was even more supportive, and was also keen to undermine growing support for the Greens. The Commission published a draft directive in April 1983, its development encouraged by the fact that West Germany held the presidency of the European Council in the first half of 1983. The Germans went on to orchestrate a call at the June 1983 European Council in Stuttgart for 'immediate action' by the EC on acid rain to avoid an 'irreversible situation', and for EC measures aimed at 'rapid significant progress' towards acid pollution control.

The object of the draft directive was to address SO_2 and NO_x emissions by requiring authorization from relevant national authorities for the construction of new industrial plants (such as oil refineries and thermal power stations) or major alterations to existing plants. Before such authorization could be given, the authority had to be convinced that appropriate measures had been taken at the design stage to prevent or reduce air pollution. An early draft had required that emission limit values be fixed using 'state of the art' technology, but the Thatcher government – ever conscious of costs – succeeded in having this replaced by the phrase 'best available technology not entailing excessive costs' (Haigh 1992, 6.9–2), creating the ugly acronym BATNEEC. Member states were also encouraged to retrofit existing plants, and to exchange information on the prevention and reduction of air pollution. The directive on combating air pollution from industrial plants (84/360) went into force in 1984, and gave the member states until June 1987 to comply.

While the European Community was working on its own programme for the reduction of acid pollution, several of its member states continued to meet together to negotiate further reductions in SO_2, both informally and under the auspices of the UNECE Convention. In March 1984, ten countries (including EC members Denmark, France, the Netherlands and West Germany) met in Ottawa and committed themselves to a minimum 30 per cent reduction in SO_2 emissions by 1993, and were thereby dubbed the '30 per cent Club'. The same goal was formalized in a protocol to the UNECE Convention adopted in July 1985, and immediately signed by all members of the 30 per cent Club.

Since 84/360 was a framework directive, the assumption was that specific emission limits would be developed in a series of subsequent daughter directives; Britain had been sure to insist that agreement on these would be determined by unanimity rather than by a qualified majority vote, thereby allowing it to veto future proposals. The ink had barely dried on the industrial plants directive before a combination of mounting public concern, claims of improving scientific certainty (notably the conclusions of a Commission-sponsored symposium on acidification held in Karlsruhe in September 1983), and the possible trade distortions that might arise out of the German GFAVo encouraged the Commission to develop a daughter directive on large combustion plants (LCP) along the lines of the German legislation (for details on its development, see Boehmer-Christiansen and Skea, 1991, chapters 10–12, and Bennett, 1992, chapter 4). This it did, and published a draft in December 1983 that proposed setting emission standards for new plants (those built after January 1985), requiring reductions of emissions from those with a thermal capacity greater than 50 MW, and obliging every member state to draw up plans for a minimum 60 per cent reduction in SO_2 emissions and a minimum 40 per cent reduction in NO_x and particulate emissions by December 1995, from a 1980 baseline.

Discussions were now delayed as the Council and the Commission devoted their attention to a directive on vehicle emission reductions, and were complicated by a division of opinion on the issue.

• The Germans, the Dutch, and the Danish gave the draft LCP directive strong support. The Germans – as noted above – were driven most immediately by a combination of the growing influence of the Greens, and damage to German forests.

The most controversial aspects of West Germany's acid pollution problem were its nuclear power programme and the struggle to deal with vehicle emissions. West Germany was meeting about 30 per cent of its electricity needs with nuclear power, opposition to which was a major factor in support for the Greens, who won 27 seats in the 1983 Bundestag elections and 42 seats in the 1987 elections. Meanwhile, NO_x and hydrocarbons were central to the problem of *Waldsterben*, requiring a substantial cut in vehicle exhaust emissions. However, this meant taking on the powerful German car industry, and the independent German motorist. Autobahn speed limits arouse considerable passions in Germany, with many motorists regarding attempts to curb their impulses behind the wheel of a BMW as an attack on their civil rights. Despite the resistance, West Germany was more active than any other European nation (except perhaps Switzerland) in promoting regulations on car exhaust gases, and was able to cut NO_x emissions by 16 per cent between 1980 and 1992.

The Danes were among the earliest champions of emission reductions, encouraged mainly by the fact that they received 75 per cent of their sulphur deposition from their southern neighbours, and wanted to set an example. Denmark reduced the sulphur content of heavy and light fuel oils in order to cut emissions from local heating plants, domestic heating units and diesel-powered vehicles, which together accounted for about half its sulphur emissions, the remaining half coming from power stations. Legislative changes were given a new urgency with growing concerns about the extent of forest damage in Denmark; by 1993–94, more than one-third of its forests were damaged, a greater proportion than in any other EU member state.

- The French and the Belgians had the least to lose from emission control requirements because of their heavy reliance on nuclear power. Until 1984, France opposed pollution controls, but then switched sides and went so far as to commit itself to halving its SO_2 emissions by 1990. In the event, it went much further, achieving a two-thirds reduction by 1993, and cutting its NO_x emissions by 17 per cent. This seemed laudable on the surface, but came in large part as a result of investment in nuclear power. In 1980, nuclear generation met just 12 per cent of French electricity needs; by 1995, a network of nearly 60 reactors met more than 70 per cent of electricity needs, with hydroelectric stations another 14 per cent (Hewett, 1995, p. 155).

For its part, Belgium made heavy reductions in sulphur emissions during the 1980s, motivated mainly by a desire to send a strong message to neighbours such as France, Britain and Germany, from which it received more than half its sulphur deposition. Cumulatively, it had cut its SO_2 emissions by nearly two-thirds by 1993, and – despite the growth of road traffic – had also managed to cut NO_x emissions by one-fifth. To the concern of environmental groups, however, much of the SO_2 reduction resulted from the expansion of the Belgian nuclear power programme. Once almost entirely dependent on locally-mined coal, Belgium tripled its nuclear-generated electricity capacity between 1979 and 1989, and now meets 56 per cent of its electricity needs with nuclear power.

- The British, the Italians, the Greeks and the Irish were opposed to the directive (Hewett, 1995, p. 238). Britain was not only governed at the time by the anti-regulation Thatcher government, but, as the biggest producer of SO_2 in western Europe, faced the greatest potential costs in making the necessary reductions, and – since most of its emissions were blown offshore – the fewest potential benefits. The Thatcher government cast doubts on the veracity of the science, was suspicious about the link with West German domestic initiatives, and opposed Scandinavian attempts to encourage European states to commit themselves to specific reductions of 30 per cent or more in their SO_2 emissions. For their part, the Greek and Irish governments were concerned about the extent to which the directive would interfere with their economic development plans.

When the Executive Body of the UNECE Convention published its draft protocol committing signatories to 30 per cent reductions in SO_2 emissions in July 1985, Britain, Greece, and Ireland were the only EC member states which refused to sign.

The problem of the costs to poorer EC member states took on broader significance in January 1986 with the accession of Spain and Portugal. Since a unanimous vote was needed in the Council of Ministers to pass the directive, it was now agreed that it needed to be changed in order to move away from the idea of uniform emission reductions and to take account of differences among member states in levels of pollutive emissions, levels of industrial development, emission trends, and types of fuel available. The proposal was changed so as to impose different levels of emission reductions on the richer countries (using BATNEEC) and to exempt Greece, Ireland, Portugal and Luxembourg because they contributed so little to overall emissions. Reductions of 50 per cent would be required in Germany, France and some other states, of 40 per cent in Britain and Italy, of 10 per cent in Spain, and none at all in the exempted states.

Negotiations along these lines stumbled on during 1986 and 1987 with various and complex permutations proposed (see Boehmer-Christiansen and Skea, 1991, pp. 239–45). Poorer states such as Spain and Ireland continued to be concerned about the economic costs, and Italy balked at the implications given its reliance on high-sulphur coal. Some of the richer member states meanwhile objected to being given too little credit for previous efforts to reduce emissions, or objected to deadlines being set too far in the future. The problem was eased somewhat in 1986 and 1987 when the Dutch and Belgian presidencies of the Community proposed staged reductions. Matters came to a head in early 1988, when Germany once again took over the presidency of the EC. Not only would agreement win support for the Kohl government at home, but the presidency would be passing in July 1988 to Greece and in January 1989 to Spain, two poorer states with less incentive to orchestrate an agreement. The most critical factor, however, turned out to be domestic developments in Britain.

The British come around

As the world's first industrial state, Britain was also the first country in the world to begin feeling the effects of air pollution generated by the burning of fossil fuels, notably coal. The chemistry of acid pollution was outlined in the 1850s by Robert Angus Smith, a Scottish chemist undertaking research in and around Manchester, but it was not until the 1980s that a complete picture of the extent of the damage began to emerge. Research found that Britain's rain was commonly 100–150 times more acid than unpolluted rain, that Scottish lochs were as acidic as lakes in Norway and Sweden, that fish populations in many upland streams, rivers and lakes in Wales were declining, that air pollution was causing damage to trees, that the stonework on buildings was corroding, and that human health was being affected (UK Review Group on Acid Rain, 1984; Howells, 1983).

Despite its long history of industrialization and environmental activism, little in the way of an integrated approach to air pollution generally – or to acid pollution specifically – began to emerge in Britain until the mid-1980s. The government had acknowledged the plausibility of a link between acid pollution and SO_2 emissions as early as 1972, but took little action in response. At least three major factors explained the British position.

First, British pollution control policy was neither rational nor integrated. The Clean Air Acts of 1956 and 1968 had helped reduce smoke and dust pollution, and the Road Traffic Acts of 1972 and 1974 had imposed emission controls on road vehicles, but largely sidestepped the problem of industrial SO_2 and NO_x emissions. Meanwhile, the institutional structure of environmental policy-making was piecemeal and confused; the Department of the 'Environment' devoted barely 10 per cent of its time and resources to environmental issues (being essentially a department of local government), and Britain was to lack anything approaching an integrated pollution control agency until the creation in 1995 of a new Environment Agency. As late as 1984, the Royal Commission on Environmental Pollution was arguing that British pollution control policy suffered from inadequate resources, secretiveness, isolationism, a lack of forward planning and continuity, and a failure to keep abreast of pressing environmental problems (Royal Commission on Environmental Pollution, 1984).

Second, policy was made less by the government than by forces at the confluence of the relationship between two state-owned industries: the Central Electricity Generating Board (CEGB) and the National Coal Board (NCB). The CEGB was Britain's largest electricity producer (accounting for 80–90 per cent of production), the NCB's largest customer, and its 78 power stations (40 of them coal-fired) were the source of about 60 per cent of the UK's total SO_2 emissions (Fells, 1988, pp. 38–40). Despite a statutory responsibility for taking into consideration the environmental impact of its activities, the CEGB argued that the scientific evidence was inconclusive, and – against a background of the government cost-cutting that was a central tenet of Thatcherism – that the costs of retrofitting emission control equipment to power stations would be excessive. It also felt that SO_2 emissions would be addressed over the longer term by the gradual replacement of coal-fired stations by nuclear reactors.

Finally, perhaps the most telling influence on British air pollution policy in the early 1980s was the concern of the Thatcher government to plan for a widely expected strike by the powerful National Union of Mineworkers (NUM). Just as acid pollution was becoming a headline issue in Britain, the Thatcher administration was making preparations to take on the NUM. The cooperation of the NCB and the CEGB were central to those preparations: the NCB played a pivotal role in helping build coal stocks in anticipation of the strike, and the CEGB in maximizing the use of gas to generate electricity rather than coal, and – when the strike came in 1984–85 – in keeping power stations running as long as possible (Thatcher, 1993, pp. 358–9, 684). Under the circumstances, any talk of Britain making SO_2 reductions was unlikely. The Thatcher government won a political victory when the coal strike failed, but its immediate political concerns postponed any possibility of a concerted attempt to address the problem of SO_2 and NO_x emissions from power stations.

At about the time of the strike, the air pollution policies of the Thatcher administration were subjected to increasingly critical investigation by other quarters in government. The first indictment came from a 1984 report by the Environment Committee of the House of Commons, which concluded that acid pollution was a major problem, and enough was known about its causes and effects to justify action to reduce emissions (House of Commons Environment Committee, 1984). A second report – by the House of Lords European Communities Committee – examined the implications of European Community policy on Britain. It was more hesitant than the Commons report, but still acknowledged that acid pollution was a serious threat and that it would be 'foolish and dangerous' for no action to be taken to combat the problem (House of Lords Select Committee on the European Communities, 1984). The Thatcher administration ignored the conclusions, accepting only aCommons committee recommendation in favour of further monitoring and research.

Britain had signed the 1979 UNECE Convention, but worked against the inclusion of specific commitments, and made clear its opposition both to air quality standards and to percentage reductions. However, the stakes were raised when work was begun on what was to become the 1985 SO_2 protocol to the convention, requiring specific percentage reductions. At the same time, and thanks mainly to West German pressure, the European Community had begun developing the LCP directive. Despite its public statements, the Thatcher administration now began to show the first signs that it was wavering. In May 1984, Mrs Thatcher called a briefing session on government acid pollution policy, involving senior scientists and ministers. She may have been motivated less by concerns about acid pollution as a domestic issue, however, than by her campaign to win allies in the EC in support of Britain's attempts to reduce its budget contributions to the Community, an issue that was resolved at the EC summit in Fontainebleu in June 1984.

Thatcher also faced criticism from members of her own party. The Bow Group of centre-left Conservative members of parliament argued in mid-1984 that the Conservative party would 'reap electoral credit' if the government was to agree to cut SO_2 and NO_x emissions, and that Britain should join the 30 per cent Club. More significantly, the right-wing Centre for Policy Studies, founded by Thatcher herself in 1974, argued that the government position showed a 'lamentable' failure of imagination and judgement, and that the government should 'appropriate the green issue' (Bow Publications, 1984; Centre for Policy Studies, 1985). Meanwhile, criticism of the CEGB came from Scandinavian governments (notably Norway and Sweden), from the select committees of the Commons and the Lords, from government agencies such as the Nature Conservancy Council, and from the Department of the Environment itself which was privately critical of the Board's position.

In September 1986, following his return from a tour of Scandinavian acid pollution research facilities, conscious of the mounting criticism of the CEGB, and with the coal miner's union tamed, CEGB chairman Lord Marshall finally admitted that the CEGB was at least partly to blame for Britain's acid emissions, and proposed spending $600 million by 1997 on controlling emissions from two coal-fired power stations. Marshall's conversion was not yet absolute, however; while accepting that as much as a quarter of the cumulative total of acid rain that had fallen on Norway in the past 125 years came from Britain, he argued that even if all emissions ceased immediately, acid and sulphur would continue to flow out of Scandinavian soils for many years to come. Hence he believed that there was no great urgency in reducing emissions, but that a steady, continued reduction would allow stored acidity to be washed out of the soils (Pearce, 1986).

However, the CEGB was now being marginalized in policy decisions because the critical factor in British considerations was the desire of the Thatcher administration to privatize the electricity supply industry. When the details were announced in 1987, they ran counter to the desires of the CEGB and Lord Marshall (who ultimately resigned), and marked the end of the cosy relationship between the Board and the government. Since the sale might be complicated by any questions that remained about pollution control obligations on power stations, it was essential that these be resolved. Privatization was finally completed in 1990 when the CEGB was replaced by National Power (responsible for 70 per cent of existing CEGB power stations) and PowerGen (responsible for the rest); nuclear power stations later became the responsibility of a new publicly owned company, Nuclear Electric.

The decision on privatization came at a critical point in the negotiations then taking place in Brussels on the LCP directive, which had reached an impasse because of a British refusal to concede on bigger emissions reductions. In June 1988, a compromise was reached by which Britain agreed to SO_2 and NO_x emission reductions, but at levels lower than those sought by the European Commission and other EC member states: while France and West Germany committed themselves to 70 per cent SO_2 reductions and 40 per cent NO_x reductions by 2003 on 1980 levels, Britain committed itself only to 60 per cent and 30 per cent reductions respectively. These were the lowest reduction targets of any EC member state bar Greece, Ireland, Portugal and Spain (all but Spain were allowed to increase emissions). Under the terms of the 1994 SO_2 protocol to the UNECE Convention, however, Britain was later to commit itself to SO_2 reductions of 70 per cent by 2005, and 80 per cent by 2010. Ironically (considering all the fuss it had made), Britain was able to meet its SO_2 reduction targets with ease thanks to a switch from coal to gas in the electricity industry; it had reduced emissions by 1993 by 35 per cent, thus going well beyond the 20 per cent target set by the LCP directive.

The Thatcher government capitulated in large part because it had run out of negotiating space, finding itself painted into a corner by a combination of domestic policy aspirations (mainly electricity privatization) and the need to make concessions to its Community partners. There was also new evidence that Britain was importing much more sulphur from the continent than had earlier been believed. Research in the early 1980s suggested that only 11–15 per cent of the acidity in British rainfall came from continental sources; by the early 1990s, it was thought that as much as one-third of the sulphur falling on Britain came from the continent (Department of the Environment press release, 27 June 1996).

The influence of the Community on domestic pollution control policy in Britain was felt not only with the effects of the LCP directive, but in at least two other ways. First, the Environmental Protection Act passed in 1990 required that air and water pollution and waste be considered together, marking a significant shift towards the kind of integrated approach to pollution control that was to gain favour through-out the EC. The Act built on changes following in the wake of the creation in 1987 of Her Majesty's Inspectorate for Pollution (HMIP) and in 1989 of the National Rivers Authority (NRA). Operators were required to obtain authorizations for pollutive releases, to evaluate the impact of those releases, and to apply the BATNEEC principle to prevention and abatement. The decision on how best to achieve the reductions was left to the operators.

The integrationist goals of the Act were initially compromised by the division of responsibilities between HMIP and the NRA, and by the long tradition in Britain of devolving and decentralizing responsibility for implementation to local government (Carter and Lowe, 1995). Decentralization was maintained with the creation of an Air Pollution Control (APC) system which came into force in 1990–91, and allowed local authorities to issue authorizations for prescribed industrial processes. However, the shift towards integration was subsequently confirmed by the creation in 1995 of the Environment Agency, which replaced HMIP, the NRA, Waste Regulatory Authorities set up in 1990, and parts of the Department of the Environment. It could also be seen with steps taken during 1996 to integrate air quality monitoring sites run by 27 local authorities into a national network of more than 100 sites run by the Department of the Environment

(Department of the Environment press release, 25 March 1996).

The second effect of Community policy was to replace the accommodative and discretionary approach to pollution control long favoured in Britain with a steady shift towards the setting of specific goals and requirements long preferred by other EU member states. For example, the National Air Quality Strategy that was announced in August 1996 – which was driven more by concerns for human health than for the environment, and aimed mainly at addressing pollution from road vehicles – set air quality standards and objectives for benzene, butadiene, carbon monoxide, lead, ozone, nitrogen dioxide, sulphur dioxide and particulates, and proposed a ten-year target for the achievement of those objectives. As part of the plan, local authorities are obliged to regularly test the quality of air and to develop formal air quality improvement plans. Achieving the objectives may mean banning road vehicles from city centres, closing off heavily polluted roads, or allowing local authorities to require drivers to switch off their engines when their vehicles are stationary.

The large combustion plant directive

After nearly five years of negotiation, agreement was reached on the directive on large combustion plants (88/609) in June 1988, and it was adopted in November. It was one of the most important items of EU environmental legislation generally, a milestone in the EU response to acidification specifically, and one of the first pieces of EU environmental legislation adopted under the new Article 130s introduced by the Single European Act. The directive set emission limits for SO_2, NO_x, and dust for new plants, and required member states by July 1992 to draw up plans for the staged reduction of emissions from existing plants, and to limit emissions from new plants, with the overall goal of cutting SO_2 emissions across the EU as a whole by 58 per cent by 2003 (from a 1980 baseline), and NO_x emissions by 30 per cent by 1998. It was agreed that the SO_2 reductions would be achieved in three phases (23 per cent by 1993, 42 per cent by 1998, and 58 per cent by 2003), and that reduction targets would be different by member state; wealthier, more industrialized and more nuclear-reliant states such as Belgium, France and Germany would make the biggest reductions, while the three least industrialized states (Greece, Ireland and Portugal) were permitted increases in emissions (see Table 8.2).

It is always difficult to disaggregate the effects of regional, national and local action, but trends on SO_2 emissions in the EU have been positive. In 1980, the 12 member states of the EC produced more than 25 million tonnes of SO_2 among them. By 1993, they had cut those emissions by 47 per cent, more than twice the reduction intended under the terms of the LCP directive. Several countries (such as France and the Netherlands) cut emissions by two-thirds, although the greatest reductions (about 80 per cent) came in three countries (Austria, Sweden and Finland) which did not join the EU until 1995. The reductions were achieved by the use of low-sulphur coal and flue gas desulphurization technology, a switch from coal to gas, and the renewal of power plants. Only in the least industrialized member states were reductions modest, and in Portugal and Greece emissions actually rose (although in the former the increase was far smaller than allowed by the LCP directive). The figures for 1997 continued to show a positive trend: emissions for the EC-12 were down 67 per cent, well ahead of the reduction target for 1998 of 42 per cent (EMEP Web page, 2000).

The record with nitrogen oxides has not been so positive (although, to be fair, controls on emissions from road vehicles only took effect in 2000). For the EU-12 as a whole, emissions in 1997 were just under 9.8 million tonnes, a 19 per cent decrease on 1980 figures. Even more progressive states such as Denmark and the Netherlands had managed reductions only in the teens, while the EU's three poorer members (Spain, Portugal and Ireland) had all seen their emissions increase substantially. The EC-12 still had some way to go to meet their target of a 30 per cent decrease in emissions by 1998.

The major source of the NO_x problem is a combination of agricultural intensification, a growth in road traffic and an increase in the volume of goods transported by road. While the former problem has not been addressed in any methodical way

TABLE 8.2   Emission reductions under the 1988 Large Combustion Plant directive

Percentage reductions in emissions from 1980 baseline

	SO₂					NOₓ			
	1993 target	1993 actual	1997 actual	1998 target	2003 target	1993 target	1993 actual	1997 actual	1998 target
Belgium	40	63*	74	60	70	20	21*	28	40
Denmark	34	65	75	56	67	3	4	12	35
France	40	66	72	60	70	20	17	3	40
Germany	40	48	81	60	70	20	16*	46	40
Greece	+6	+28	+38	+6	+6	+94	0	+40	+94
Ireland	+25	28	27	+25	+25	+79	+71	+60	+79
Italy	27	58	70	39	63	2	+39	3	26
Luxembourg	40	58	71	50	60	20	**	9	40
Netherlands	40	65	73	60	70	20	2	19	40
Portugal	+102	+9	+18	+135	+79	+157	+48	+260	+178
Spain	0	34	45	24	37	+1	+32	10	24
UK	20	35	66	40	60	15	+2	28	30
EC-12	23	47	67	42	58	10	+12	19	30

* Figures for 1992; ** figure unavailable.

Sources: Target figures from European Commission, European Community Environment Legislation, Vol 2: Air (Office for Official Publications of the European Communities, 1992), pp. 214–15; 1993 emission figures from UN Economic Commission for Europe, Strategies and Policies for Air Pollution Abatement, ECE/EB.AIR/44, tables 1 and 2 (New York, Geneva: United Nations, 1995); 1997 emission figures calculated from EMEP Web page (2000).

– and has been exacerbated by the Common Agricultural Policy (which has encouraged overproduction) – the latter problems have been the subject of growing EU attention. About 70 per cent of the world's road vehicles are concentrated in North America and Europe. Car ownership continues to grow, bringing worsening problems with congestion, requiring the construction of new roads and highways and contributing to reductions in air quality, particularly in urban areas. EU legislation on vehicle emissions dates back to the 1970 directive (70/220) on the approximation of carbon monoxide and hydrocarbon emissions, since when subsequent laws have been directed at soot emissions from diesel engines (72/306), nitrogen oxides (77/102) and hydrocarbon evaporative emissions (91/441). The underlying motivation was originally economic: not just the removal of barriers to free trade within the Community, but also as a response to the economic pressures created by stringent emission standards introduced in the United States from the 1970s (Arp, 1993).

By European Commission calculations, accumulated EU legislation had – by 1996 – reduced emissions of carbon monoxide, hydrocarbons and nitrogen oxides by 90 per cent from a 1970 baseline. However, it also admitted that increases in the number of road vehicles and the number of kilometres travelled were likely counteracting the achievements (European Commission, 1996). With this problem in mind, the Commission hosted a series of meetings in 1992–95 with two advisory groups – the Motor Vehicle Emission Group (MVEG) and the Environmental Fuel Specifications Group (EFEG) – to look into the issue of vehicle emission standards for 2000. These led to the launch of the Auto-Oil programme discussed in Chapter 7, bringing together the automobile and oil industries with a view to developing a strategy on emission reductions. Commission research resulted in the conclusion that a reduction of VOC and NO_x emissions of 70 per cent on 1990 levels was needed, and the best way to proceed was to develop a package of measures, including emission standards, changes in fuel quality and improved inspection and maintenance, complemented by local and national measures including road pricing (making drivers pay to use roads), expanded public transport and the scrapping of old vehicles.

Towards a strategic approach to acidification

Despite the time and expense invested since the early 1980s in cutting SO_2 and NO_x emissions, acidification remains a problem in and downwind of the major industrialized areas of Europe. The work undertaken under the auspices both of the UNECE and of the European Community during the 1980s was source-led, meaning that it was focused on cutting emissions from the major sources of the pollutants involved in acidification. This created a phenomenon that has been described as 'tote-board diplomacy'; negotiations leading up to the UNECE Convention, to its protocols and to the LCP Directive were driven by attempts to encourage national governments to keep up with their neighbours by agreeing comparable or greater percentage reductions in emissions (Levy, 1993).

While these targets helped reduce emissions, not all European states were keeping up, either because they would not (for political and economic reasons) or because they could not (for technical and economic reasons). Concerned about the variable record, the Executive Board of the UNECE Convention in 1988 set up a Working Group on Abatement Strategies, charged with taking a new and broader-ranging look at the problem. Its report was presented in 1991, and came down in favour of a more flexible approach based on attempts to identify different levels of risk faced by different environments, viz. the concepts of critical loads and critical levels. The former is the level of exposure to a pollutant below which no harm would be done, and the latter is the level of concentrations of pollutants in the air above which harm might be done. So instead of encouraging percentage reductions in emissions, reductions would be based on the effects of pollutants on different environments.

To make this work, the states involved would need to map critical loads and critical levels within their borders, which would then be compared with pollutant deposition loads and levels. Policymakers would then have a more precise idea of the relationship between the biggest sources of pollution and the most sensitive environments, allowing them to focus on more tightly-defined emissions reductions in those states or regions causing the worst problems. The system is still under development, and critical loads for SO_2, NO_x, ozone and ammonia still need to be agreed, but preliminary results make it clear that the greatest problems in Europe are found in England, Germany, the Benelux states, northern Italy, Poland and the Czech Republic, and exceedance of critical loads is much less of a problem in Portugal, Spain, France, southern Italy, the Balkans and Greece.

While the first two protocols to the UNECE Convention were based on percentage reductions of emissions, when discussions began in 1989 on the development of a second sulphur protocol it was agreed that there should be an effects-based approach aimed at reducing the amount by which existing deposition loads exceeded critical loads to 60 per cent (otherwise known as '60 per cent gap closure'), and ultimately at reaching no exceedance of critical loads (or '100 per cent gap closure'). Although there would still be reductions in emissions using the same methods as before, these would not be based on simple percentage reductions, but rather on different percentage reductions for different states based on the extent to which critical loads were being exceeded in different parts of Europe. The sulphur protocol that was finally signed in 1994 by 27 countries and the European Union represented agreement that, by 2000, signatories would have achieved a 60 per cent gap closure. To reach this goal, it was calculated that European states would have to reduce their sulphur emissions by 2000 over a 1980 baseline by between as little as 38 per cent (Russia) and 50–55 per cent (Bulgaria, Spain) and as much as 80 per cent (Austria, Finland, France) or 90 per cent (Germany) (*Acid News* 4, October 1994, 10).

In 1996, the UNECE began work on a sixth protocol that would not only take the same critical loads approach, but would be based around multiple effects and multiple pollutants: it was aimed at dealing with acidification, air quality and tropospheric ozone by agreeing reductions of NO_x, ammonia and VOCs. The target date for completion was late 1997, but negotiations involved such a significantly different approach – and a different way of calculating the necessary reductions – that the target date was pushed back. In order to avoid duplication of effort as the European Union develops its own long-term plans to achieve a goal of no exceedance of critical loads, the UNECE and the European Commission agreed to work closely together on the drafting process.

Meanwhile, there were mounting concerns among its newer member states that the EU lacked a coordinated strategy on acidification. Sweden had done what it could during the 1970s and 1980s to exert pressure on its European neighbours through the UNECE, but – in relation to the EU, of which it was not yet a member – found itself on the outside looking in. Since it received about half its SO_2 deposition from the EU, this was obviously a source of some frustration. Upon joining the EU in January 1995, it was in a position to lobby for change from within, and almost immediately put a proposal to the Council of Ministers that the Commission study the efficacy of the EU programme.

In early 1996, the Commission began work on an acidification strategy, a draft of which was circulated to the member states in January 1997. It was based on the long-term target of ensuring no exceedance of critical loads for acid deposition (with an interim target of a 50 per cent gap closure), and was intended to complement the framework directive on integrated pollution prevention and control (IPPC) adopted in 1996 (96/61) (see Chapter 7). There were hopes that it would eventually cover all large combustion plants, industrial furnaces and production processes contributing to acidification, and require emission limits to be set for installations using best available technology, but taking into account geographical location and local environmental factors. Specifically, the main elements of the strategy were as follows (European Commission, 1997):

- The setting of national emission limits for SO_2, NO_x and ammonia, to be achieved by 2010.
- Ratification of the 1994 protocol to the UNECE Convention on sulphur emissions; this was achieved with the adoption of decision 98/686.
- The development of a directive aimed at imposing a 1 per cent limit on the sulphur content of heavy fuel oil.
- Limits on the sulphur content of marine fuels.
- The designation of the North Sea and Baltic Sea as SO_2 emission control zones. Negotiations on this were already taking place under the auspices of the Convention on Marine

Pollution (MARPOL), and the Commission proposed that ships in these seas would have to use fuels with a maximum sulphur content of 1.5 per cent.

• The strategy also outlined several economic instruments which might be used to help meet national emission ceilings, including differentiated tax rates on energy products.

Most importantly, one of the lynchpins of the strategy was to be a revision of the 1988 large combustion plant directive. The first draft published in April 1996 included suggestions for a further two-stage reduction in SO_2 and NO_x emissions by 2010, applying both to existing and new plants (the original directive applied only to existing plants), shifting the baseline for reductions from 1980 to 1990, setting exactly the same reduction targets for all member states except Greece, Ireland, Portugal and Spain, requiring energy efficiency standards for new plants with a view to reducing CO_2 emissions, and broadening controls to include gas turbines and clean coal technologies (European Commission, 1995). The shifting of the baseline to 1990 was immediately criticized by several member states – including Denmark, the Netherlands and Sweden – which argued that they would be penalized for having made major reductions in the 1980s. However, their concerns paled by comparison to the furore that was unleashed in May 1997 when the Commission published revised emission reduction targets that were seven times greater for Belgium.

As this book went to press, several additional new initiatives were underway that would have an impact on acid pollution in the EU. The goals of the 1996 framework directive on ambient air quality assessment and management (96/62) included the development of daughter directives setting limit and alert values for 12 pollutants, including SO_2, NO_x and suspended particulates, and the Auto-Oil programme discussed in Chapter 7 promised to have a substantial impact on emissions of SO_2 and NO_x. In June 1999, the Commission proposed two directives aimed at addressing acidification, eutrophication of lakes and rivers, and the formation of tropospheric ozone by setting emission reduction targets to be met by 2010: 78 per cent for SO_2, 60 per cent for VOCs, 55 per cent for NO_x, and 21 per cent for ammonia. The costs were put at 7.5 billion euros annually, but the benefits to health care were put at 17–32 billion euros annually (*European Policy Analyst*, 3rd quarter 1999, p. 62). There were also several proposals under consideration to further limit vehicle emissions, notably through directives on emissions from light commercial vehicles, off-road mobile machinery, aircraft and diesel engines, and a proposal aimed at controlling VOC emissions from refueling operations at service stations.

Chapter 9

Nature and Natural Resources

Policies on the protection of nature are a core element in the national environmental regimes of EU member states, most of which have developed programmes aimed at protecting wildlife and at managing natural habitats such as highlands, moors, grasslands, wetlands, rivers, lakes and coastal areas for their ecological value and for recreation. These matters have not been high on the environmental agenda of the EU, however, mainly because – unlike chemicals, waste, air and water quality, or acidification – there has been no immediate or obvious relationship between protecting nature and building the single market. This has not stopped the Commission from couching the justification for its proposals for laws on the protection of birds and natural habitats in economic terms; until recently, however, the lack of a clear link with the economic goals of European integration has discouraged the EU from developing a broad-ranging approach to the management of wildlife, which still remains largely in the hands of the member states.

By contrast, policy on the management of natural resources has very much been part of the agenda of economic integration. However, while the EU has built a substantial body of policies and laws in such areas as agriculture and fisheries, natural resource issues have rarely been addressed or characterized by the EU as part of its body of environmental interests. The conservation of fisheries has been part of the Common Fisheries Policy and has been aimed at managing catches so as to ensure equitable access to supplies, rather than at ensuring the welfare of marine ecosystems as a factor in the maintenance of fisheries. Agriculture has only been an element in environmental policy to the extent that concerns have been raised about the extent to which the Common Agricultural Policy has encouraged practices incompatible with a chemical-free environment. The EU's activities in forestry have focused on two very precise areas – the protection of forests from pollution and from fires – responsibility for the management of forests being left squarely with the member states. Finally, energy policy has been directed at questions of supply rather than at the environmental implications of energy use. Policy in all these areas is addressed by the related DG and the related set of ministers, rather than by the Environment DG and environmental ministers, somewhat undermining the goal of respecting the integrative principle.

The result has been a rather haphazard and unsatisfactory approach to the management of nature and natural resources, with laws addressing only selected elements of the overall picture. There are signs that the situation is about to change, however, with greater attention now being paid to the need to develop a strategic approach to the management of wildlife and habitats, and to integrate biodiversity policy with policies on agriculture, fisheries, forestry, energy, transport and tourism. Furthermore, there is discussion of the need to integrate approaches to fisheries management with protection of the aquatic environment; to develop a European forestry strategy with a view to conserving forest biodiversity, increasing the production of wood as a source of energy, and extending forests as a sink for carbon dioxide emissions; and to promote energy efficiency and the use of renewable sources of energy as part of the EU response to dealing with climate change (see Chapter 10). As these initiatives progress, important omissions from the EU environmental policy agenda are slowly being addressed.

Biodiversity

One of the consequences of the spread of industry, the intensification of agriculture and the extension of human settlements has been pressure on natural habitats: change to ecosystems, the destruction of woodlands and wetlands, and a growth in the threats posed to animals, plants and natural areas. Natural selection and extinction are both features of the evolutionary process, but human activity has added new breadth and depth to the threats posed to wildlife. Just how serious those threats have become is difficult to say, however, because science has been unable to agree on the number of species on earth, or on the extent to which they are threatened. About 13 000 species of mammals and birds have been identified, as well as 10 550 reptiles and amphibians and about 25 000 flowering plants, but estimates of the total number of species range as high as 5 to 15 million, and debates rage about how many are threatened by human activity.

Western Europe is home to relatively few species, in part because of its temperate climate, and in part because of the legacy of several centuries of man-made change to the natural environment. They continue to face considerable pressure from human activity, the problems ranging from the general to the specific: the loss of wetlands to land reclamation, pollution, drainage, recreational use and forest plantation; the fragmentation of habitats through man-made changes to the landscape; the loss of sand dunes to urbanization, recreational use and forest plantation; the replacement of natural and semi-natural woodlands with managed forests based around exotic species; the loss of meadows and other semi-natural agricultural habitats; the intensification and specialization of agriculture and forestry; and the threats posed by forest fires, hunting, fishing and collecting (EEA, 1998, chapter 8). In addition, concerns have been voiced in recent years about the possible long-term effects on species distribution of climate change.

Biological diversity, or biodiversity, was defined by the 1992 Convention on Biological Diversity as 'the variability among all living organisms from all sources, including . . . terrestrial, marine and other aquatic ecosystems and ecological complexes of which they are part', and refers not only to variety among species, but also to genetic variation within and between species, and to variety among ecosystems (quoted in EEA, 1998, p. 145). There was no mention of the problems faced by nature in the First EAP, only passing mention in the Second EAP, and policy developments since then have revolved mainly around two key pieces of legislation – the 1979 birds directive designed to protect wild birds and their habitats, and the 1992 habitats directive designed to protect wildlife and natural habitats.

Early European initiatives were controversial, since the Council and the member states questioned the legal basis for EU action on the grounds that it was moving away from the economic goals of the treaties and the principles upon which initial

Community environmental policy had been based (Johnson and Corcelle, 1995, p. 298). DGXI subsequently went to pains to argue that nature conservation was an integral part of land use policy, could be compatible with agriculture and other economic activities, and could also stimulate the creation of new jobs (see, for example, the editorial by environment commissioner Ritt Bjerregaard, *Natura 2000 Newsletter*, 1 May 1996). Its arguments have tended to fall on deaf ears, however, and the prompting for much of the EU biodiversity policy that has developed since then has come from a combination of pressure from the European Parliament, and the requirements of international law.

The 1979 birds directive (79/409), which was adopted in April 1979, grew out of Commission research indicating a reduction in the number and populations of migratory bird species stemming from the use of chemicals in agriculture, from hunting, and from habitat destruction caused by pollution, agricultural intensification and development. Recitals to the directive referred to the Community objectives of improving living conditions, promoting harmonious development of economic activities and continuous and balanced expansion, but were otherwise vague on the economic justification. The directive was aimed at promoting the protection of migratory birds naturally occurring in their wild state in the EU, and their eggs, nests and habitats; these species were listed in two annexes. For the 'particularly vulnerable species' listed in Annex I, member states are expected to take strong measures, including the creation of special protected areas (SPAs), particularly wetlands, and to prohibit the hunting or capture of these birds. The original list of 74 species was expanded to 144 by directive 85/411, and by 1996 stood at 182. Meanwhile, Annex II species – of which there are 72 in all – are less immediately threatened, and can be hunted within certain limits; for example, the use of snares, explosives and certain automatic and semi-automatic weapons is prohibited.

The birds directive was followed up by laws on a select group of species. Regulation 348/81 banned the import of parts and products from whales and other cetaceans, including leather articles treated with cetacean oil. Directive 83/129 – which was generated mainly as a result of pressure from the European Parliament – led to a ban on the import of seal pup skins and related products, such as shoes and clothes (except for those resulting from traditional hunting techniques used by Inuit people), and regulation 2496/89 banned the import of raw and worked ivory from African elephants. Given levels of public support for all three ideas, none of these laws was particularly controversial.

During the early 1980s, the Community also became party to – or implemented the terms of – several key pieces of international law on wildlife and nature, beginning with the 1979 Berne Convention on European Wildlife and Habitats. The biggest body of EU law on biodiversity has been driven by the terms of the Convention on International Trade in Endangered Species of Fauna and Flora (CITES), which was opened for signature in Washington DC in 1973 and came into force in January 1975. The convention set up a system of permits and certification aimed at controlling or prohibiting trade in endangered species of wildlife. The Community implemented the terms of the treaty by regulation 3626/82, which allowed member states to take even stricter measures than those outlined under CITES. Given that the Community was one of the three largest markets in the world for trade in wildlife – along with the United States and Japan – the regulation had a substantial impact on the reduction of trade.

Following the model of CITES, protected species were listed under three appendices to the regulation: I listed those species threatened with extinction which were or might be affected by trade, II listed those species which might become threatened unless trade was regulated, and III listed all species regulated by any party to the convention, and for which the cooperation of other parties was needed. The regulation was amended 21 times before being repealed by regulation 338/97, which adapted controls to the new circumstances of the single market and harmonized the implementation of the terms of CITES across the member states. This had in turn been amended eight times by the end of 1999. Most of the amendments to both laws extended the list in light of changes to the convention, and there are now more than 820 species listed under Appendix I, nearly 29 000 under Appendix II, and nearly 230 under Appendix III.

Because there was no standard EU-wide classification or inventory of threatened habitats and species in the 1980s, it was difficult to be sure about the extent of the biodiversity problem in the EU. Furthermore, protected areas came in a confusing array of categories developed by a combination of national and international law. For example, there were 59 biosphere reserves (areas recognized within the UNESCO Man and the Biosphere programme), seven World Heritage sites (with national and universal cultural and natural value, as defined under the 1975 World Heritage Convention), 135 sites designated under the 1974 Helsinki Convention and the 1976 Barcelona Convention, and 1157 sites designated under the birds directive. There were also nearly 960 protected areas that came under five categories developed by the International Union for Conservation of Nature and Natural Resources (EEA, 1995, pp. 112–13). In addition, member states had their own definitions of 'protected area', with some intended to restrict or ban all human activity other than recreation and research, while others were populated and exploited for economic gain by farmers and foresters.

The Commission responded in 1988 by broadening its view of the biodiversity problem and proposing a new directive on the protection of natural and semi-natural habitats, suggesting that a comprehensive network of protected areas be set up aimed at ensuring the maintenance of threatened species and habitat types. The proposal was adopted in May 1992 as directive 92/43, which was aimed at protecting selected habitats for their own sake rather than because they were home to valuable species. It identified species and habitat types of special Community interest, giving them 'favourable conservation status' if the natural range of the species and the area covered by the habitat was stable or growing. By 1996, Annexes listed 200 animal species, 434 plant species and 253 habitat types, ranging from estuaries and mudflats to alpine rivers, heaths, grasslands, bogs, caves and forests.

The directive provided for the creation of a network of habitats of Community significance under the label Natura 2000. Member states were asked to carry out an assessment of the listed habitat and species types within their borders, and then submit a list – including sites protected under the birds directive – to the Commission by June 1995. From these lists, a grand list of Sites of Community Importance (SCIs) was then to be developed by the Commission, which was to judge the sites according to such characteristics as their relative value at the national level, their importance as part of a migration route, and their overall value in terms of the six biogeographical zones covered by the EU: boreal, continental, Atlantic, alpine, macronesian and Mediterranean. Member states were then given six years from June 1998 to designate these sites as Special Areas of Conservation (SACs), to set up the necessary conservation measures, including management plans, and to take all the steps necessary to avoid the deterioration of the habitats or disturbance of the species. New sites are to be added to the Natura 2000 network as and when needed. By 1999, all 15 member states had developed lists of proposed special protected areas covering as much as 23 per cent of land area in Denmark, 13–14 per cent in Austria and Belgium, and less than 5 per cent in France, Germany, Greece, Ireland, Italy, Portugal and the UK (EEA, 1999, appendices p. 27).

In addition to these legislative arrangements, EU policy on biodiversity also includes several funds set up to promote environmental management, including the protection of biotopes. These date back to 1982 and 1983 and the decision by the European Parliament to fund several small-scale projects, mostly of an exploratory nature. The idea was taken a stage further in 1984 with the creation under regulation 1872/84 of Actions by the Community relating to the Environment (ACE), which set aside funding to support – among other things – activities under the auspices of the birds directive. Both Parliament and the Commission lobbied to broaden the scope of funding beyond birds to other species and their habitats, but without success. ACE ran for three years and was then extended to 1991, providing a total of 30 million ecus.

Meanwhile, habitat protection in the Mediterranean and northern European maritime regions was included in the objectives of the MEDSPA (1986–91) and NORSPA (1989–91) programmes. The former supported projects in the Mediterranean area, with an emphasis on water resources, the prevention of water pollution and waste disposal; the latter focused on the coastal areas and waters of Northern Europe, emphasizing the conservation of marine life and the integrated management of biotopes. More funding came out of the LEADER programme, set up in 1991 to improve the development potential of rural areas; it funded several projects to restore species diversity through the protection and introduction of indigenous species that diversify agricultural production in marginal areas.

TABLE 9.1   *Key pieces of EU law on biodiversity and GMOs*

79/409	Directive on the conservation of wild birds. *Establishes general duty on member states to protect all species of wild birds found in Europe, and their habitats.*
348/81	Regulation on import of whale products. *Establishes common rules for imports of whales and other cetacean products.*
3626/82	Regulation on the 1973 endangered species convention. *Approves terms of the Convention on International Trade in Endangered Species of Wild Fauna and Flora (CITES) (Washington DC, 1973).*
83/129	Directive on imports of seal pup skins. *Prohibits importation of skins of certain seal pups and derived products.*
1872/84	Regulation on environmental funding. *Establishes COE environmental fund for clean technologies and protection of sensitive areas.*
2496/89	Regulation on imports of ivory. *Prohibits import of raw and worked ivory from African elephants.*
90/219	Directive on genetically modified micro-organisms. *Establishes measures to protect human health and the environment from dangers arising from contained use of GMOs.*
90/220	Directive on deliberate release of GMOs. *Harmonizes protection measures taken by member states in the event of the deliberate release of GMOs into the environment.*
3907/91	Regulation on nature conservation. *Establishes rules for action by the Community relating to nature conservation (ACNAT).*
92/43	Directive on natural habitats and fauna and flora. *Establishes classification system for habitat types and species; contributed to implementation of Convention on Biological Diversity (Rio de Janeiro, 1992).*
1973/92	Regulation establishing LIFE. *Establishes a financial instrument for the environment (LIFE).*
338/97	Regulation on 1973 convention on trade in endangered species. *Brings EU into compliance with the objectives of CITES.*

To support projects under the habitats directive, a new fund for nature – Actions by the Community for Nature (ACNAT) – was created in 1991 under regulation 3907/91, but was almost immediately superceded by LIFE (Financial Instrument for the Environment), a much more ambitious and broad-based fund aimed specifically at the environment and designed to set aside 400 million ecus between 1992 and 1995 in support of the Fifth EAP. It was renewed in 1996 with the creation of LIFE II, which set aside 450 million ecus between 1996 and 1999, nearly half of which was earmarked for nature protection projects related to the birds and habitats directives. In 1999, funding was made available for the first time under LIFE II to eastern European countries, with seven projects being funded in Romania. LIFE III was under discussion as this book went to press.

The most recent initiative in the area of nature protection has been a proposal from the European Commission for a strategy on biodiversity. This was prompted by the Convention on Biological Diversity, opened for signature at the Rio Earth Summit in 1992, which the Community ratified in December 1993, the same month that it came into force. The objectives behind the convention are the conservation of biodiversity, the sustainable use of species and habitats, and a fair and equitable division of the benefits arising from the use of genetic resources. Since it encourages signatories to develop national strategies for the conservation and sustainable use of biological diversity, the Council of Ministers in December 1995 agreed the need to develop a Community strategy aimed at filling in the gaps in existing policy and complementing the plans of the member states. The resulting Commission proposal used the birds and habitat directives and the proposed framework water directive (see Chapter 7) as foundations, and argued the need for a series of action plans designed to integrate biodiversity policy within policies and programmes for which the EU has competence, such as agriculture, fisheries, forestry, energy, transport and tourism (European Commission, 1998a).

Genetically-modified organisms

The late 1990s saw the emergence of a public debate about the use of genetically-modified organisms and micro-organisms

(GMOs). Most of the debate centered on concerns about the effects of genetic engineering on human health, but as public concerns grew, so more reference was made to the effects of GMOs on biodiversity. Whether or not it was an environmental issue, most of the EU's initiatives on the matter – which date back to 1990 – came out of DGXI, which by 1997 found itself in the middle of an increasingly vocal debate about GMOs, and being pulled in several different directions (*European Voice*, 26 November–2 December 1998, p. 14). On one side was the EU's 50 billion euro biotechnology industry (fronted by multinationals such as Monsanto) and the Commissioners for trade and industry. On the other side were organizations representing consumer and environmental interests, several of the EU's largest food retailers (which refused to use genetically-modified ingredients in their 'own-brand' products), the Commissioners for consumer affairs and the environment, and the governments of selected member states, notably Austria, Belgium, Finland, France, Luxembourg, the Netherlands and Sweden. (In 1997, Austria and Luxembourg banned the sale and cultivation of GM crops, including those approved for EU-wide cultivation, prompting a call for legal action by the Commission.) In the middle was public opinion, which was confused – but vaguelly disturbed – about the GM issue.

Genetic modification (or engineering) is a process by which individual genes can be copied and transferred from one organism to another to alter the genetic makeup of the recipient organism with a view to transferring or deleting specific characteristics. This can produce, for example, bacteria, fungi, viruses, plants, insects, fish or mammals whose genetic material has been altered in order to increase resistance to disease, increase yield, or provide some other physical property. Theoretically, a gene from one species can be implanted into any other, and genetic engineering can provide benefits in terms of food production. For example, it could help reduce the loss of food supplies from disease, viruses and pests, control weeds, improve the nutritional value of foods, make foods last longer, and make crops resistant to drought and frost. It has so far been used mainly in the food industry, in pharmaceuticals, and in the production of new energy sources.

Despite its benefits, there are concerns that genetic engineering can have a negative impact on the environment by creating modified organisms that compete with unmodified organisms and species, displace natural populations and alter ecological cycles and interactions, or by transferring new genetic traits to other species and upsetting the natural ecological balance. While the impact of the introduction of GMOs is uncertain, the EU has so far taken a precautionary approach to the issue, setting the ball rolling in 1988 with a Commission proposal for the development of a coherent programme of risk assessment, looking at the routine and accidental release of GMOs. As with dangerous chemicals, the emphasis has been on setting up a system of notification so that relevant national authorities can keep themselves informed about where GMOs are being used.

The first two directives – 90/219 on the contained use of GMOs, and 90/220 on the release into the environment of GMOs – were adopted in April 1990. The former covers all activities relating to GMOs and their routine release as wastes or in airborne emissions, and their accidental release, while the latter requires environmental evaluation and approval for the deliberate release of GMOs. In 1997, the issue became a matter of wider public debate when the Commission adopted a proposal for a uniform approach to the labelling of genetically-modified products. EU law means that marketing consent for the release of GMO products takes at least one to two years; as of 1999, none had been approved unanimously (EEA, 1999, p. 11). The EU record stands in notable contrast to that of the United States, where genetic modification has been a part of commercial agriculture for some years. European public opinion is in favour of a moratorium on the approval and marketing of GM crops in order to allow more time for research into their long-term effects. However, since most GM produce consumed in the EU is imported from the United States, a moratorium would court the danger of a transatlantic trade war, and would not comply with World Trade Organization rules.

During 1998–99, a struggle broke out between the Commission, the Council and Parliament over plans to update 90/220. The Commission proposed an amendment designed to make the procedure for approving GM crops simpler and more open to public scrutiny. However, several governments argued that it was too lax in assessing the possible health risks of GM products, while the biotechnology industry argued that the regulations were still too complicated, and that final approval should be granted by an independent regulatory agency rather than the Council, because the latter was prone to making political rather than scientific judgements. *European Voice* described the Commission's views on the GM issue as schizophrenic, arguing that

> it does not appear to be able to make up its mind whether the biotechnology industry is an exciting new sector which will generate hundreds of thousands of new jobs and help Europe lead the world in *the* technology of the 21st century, or whether consumers should be protected from the as-yet-unknown long-term effects of eating plants which have been designed in laboratories. (*European Voice*, 26 November–2 December 1998, p. 14; 25–31 March 1999, p. 21)

It might equally have commented that the Commission has not yet decided whether the GM issue is primarily one of protecting public health or the environment, or both.

Meanwhile, the EU had become involved in negotiations taking place under the auspices of the Convention on Biological Diversity to develop a biosafety protocol to ensure safe management of the transfer, handling and use of GMOs. The protocol was to have included a PIC procedure and rules on liability and redress, labelling, and standards for assessing the potential impact of releasing GMOs, and was due to have been signed in February 1999. However, disagreements broke out between the so-called Miami Group (the United States, Canada, Australia, Argentina, Chile and Uruguay), the EU, and representatives of Southern states (the 'Like-Minded Group'). The latter wanted a strong protocol, and accused the EU of being influenced by the Miami Group, which wanted trade in genetically engineered food to be governed by international trade rules rather than being tied to an environmental convention. Greenpeace accused the EU of opting for a weak protocol because the EU market for genetically engineered foods was declining in the face of consumer concerns, and the agro-biotech industry would be 'desperate' to exploit the South as an alternative market (Greenpeace International Web page, 1999).

Fisheries

Fish are a valuable natural resource, and yet – reflecting the rather confused definition of the parameters of 'environmental' policy in the EU – the management and conservation of fish stocks are rarely included in discussions about EU environmental policy. At least part of the problem stems from confusion about the meaning of the term 'conservation', a problem well-illustrated by the argument made by Coffey (1996). She suggests that fisheries conservation involves managing the harvesting of renewable resources, and maintaining stocks at levels which permit their rational and sustainable exploitation. However, she suggests that *nature* conservation 'involves the protection of species and habitats and wider goals such as the maintenance of biological diversity', thus implying that the term 'conservation' has two different meanings. In truth, it does not, and it has historically been used more consistently in relation to the idea of managing resources for exploitation rather than protecting such resources. As noted in Chapter 3, the terms 'conservation', 'sustainable development' and 'sustainable exploitation' are all interchangeable, and thus EU policies on fisheries conservation are just as much a part of the environmental *acquis* as are those on the management of air and water quality. Nonetheless, fisheries policy is mentioned by Johnson and Corcelle (1995) only in relation to water quality; fisheries policy is mentioned only briefly in *Europe's Environment: The Second Assessment* (EEA, 1998, pp. 221–5); and EU legislation and policy on fisheries management is listed on the Europa Web site not under the work of the Environment DG, but under that of the Fisheries DG.

The Treaty of Rome made provision for a Common Fisheries Policy (CFP), but it was not until the 1970s that this finally began to take shape, prompted by the decision by coastal states to extend their fishing zones from 12 miles to 200 miles in the face of dwindling stocks and falling catches, and by the accession to the Community of three new fishing nations, Britain, Denmark and Ireland. Attempts to resolve competing claims to fishing grounds and to develop an equitable management plan for Community fisheries were bitter and controversial, but they finally resulted in the adoption of regulations 2057/82 and

170/83 establishing a system for conserving fisheries resources in Community waters, and by the agreement of the CFP in 1983, which was modified in 1992. Its goals were driven by the precautionary principle, and were aimed at resolving conflicts over territorial fishing rights and preventing overfishing by setting catch quotas. Even though fishing employs just 0.2 per cent of the EU workforce, and accounts for less than 1 per cent of the economies of most member states, the fishing industry is a key part of life in coastal communities all around the EU, and so has important economic implications for some of Europe's poorer regions.

Conservation is at the heart of the CFP, and is promoted in three main ways. First, the CFP has opened all the waters within the EU's 200-mile limit to all EU fishing boats, but gives member states the right to restrict access to fishing grounds within 12 miles of their shores. One of the problems with this arrangement was that it was difficult to police, so, since 1995, all EU fishing boats have had to be licensed, and the Commission has been given greater powers to monitor fishing activities using satellites and its own (few) inspectors on the ground, and to monitor every stage in the fishing process from catching to landing to sales.

Second, the CFP prevents overfishing by imposing quotas (Total Allowable Catches, or TACs) on the take of Atlantic and North Sea fish. Stock levels are assessed annually, and the TACs are fixed at the end of each year by the Council of Ministers on the basis of scientific advice, including that from national experts in the Commission's own Scientific, Technical and Economic Committee for Fisheries. Limits are placed on the catch of particular species in specific areas, and are divided up as quotas among the member states, which can then allocate them locally or exchange them with other member states. The CFP also prevents overfishing by regulating fishing areas and equipment. For example, limits have been set on the mesh size of fishing nets, and minimum weights have been established for catch sizes so as to prevent catches of young fish.

Third, the CFP guides negotiations with other countries on access to waters outside those controlled by member states, and on the conservation of fisheries. The EU has so far reached more than two dozen agreements with non-member states, and takes part in the work of – and has signed agreements developed by – several international fisheries organizations, including the Northwest Atlantic Fisheries Organization (NAFO), the International Baltic Sea Fishery Commission (IBSFC), and the North Atlantic Salmon Conservation Organization (NASCO). International treaties signed by the Community include the following:

- Protocol to the International Convention for the Conservation of Atlantic Tunas (Rio de Janeiro, 1966).
- Convention on Future Multilateral Cooperation in the Northwest Atlantic Fisheries (Ottawa, 1978).
- Convention for the Conservation of Salmon in the North Atlantic Ocean (Reykjavik, 1982).
- Convention on Fishing and Conservation of the Living Resources in the Baltic Sea and the Belts (Gdansk, 1982).

At the core of the CFP was regulation 170/83, which established a 20-year Community system for the conservation and management of fishery resources. Following a mid-term review, it was replaced in 1992 when regulation 3760/92 was adopted with the goal of introducing alternative fisheries management measures to integrate conservation and aquaculture, including the commercial rearing of fish, the establishment of zones where fishing was restricted or prohibited, the placing of limits on the time that vessels could spend at sea, and the introduction of technical measures relating to fishing gear. Criticism continued to be levelled at EU policy, however, with concerns about conservation policies being ineffective, about weaknesses in monitoring arrangements, and about failures to integrate fisheries policy with broader environmental objectives.

In 1997, ministers from North Sea states and representatives from the EU met in Bergen, Norway, and – quoting the precautionary principle – agreed to an 'ecosystem approach' to managing the marine environment, based on protecting processes in ecosystems critical to the maintenance of productivity, taking into account food-web interactions, and protecting the chemical, physical and biological environment necessary to the well-being of ecosystems. In July 1999, the Commission – quoting the integrative principle – sent a communication to the Council and the EP in which it argued that interactions between fisheries and marine ecosystems should be integrated into the CFP, in co-ordination with nature protection policies (Commission, 1999).

TABLE 9.2   *Key pieces of EU law on fisheries, agriculture, forestry and energy*

2057/82	Regulation on fishing activities. *Establishes control measures for fishing by vessels of member states.*
170/83	Regulation on the conservation of fisheries. *Establishes Community system for the conservation and management of fishery resources.*
797/85	Regulation on efficiency of agricultural structures. *Introduces concept of environmentally sensitive farming into the Common Agricultural Policy.*
3528/86	Regulation on the protection of forests from air pollution. *Helps member states take periodic inventories of damage to forests from air pollution, and establish a network of observatories.*
3529/86	Regulation on the protection of forests from fire. *Introduces measures to prevent and monitor forest fires.*
1615/89	Regulation on forest information. *Establishes the European Forestry Information and Communication System.*
91/565	Decision on CO_2 emissions and energy efficiency. *Establishes Specific Actions for Vigorous Energy Efficiency (SAVE), to limit CO_2 emissions by improving energy efficiency.*
2092/91	Regulation on organic agriculture. *Sets up harmonized framework for labelling, production and control of organic agricultural products.*
2078/92	Regulation on agricultural production methods. *Requires member states to establish aid schemes to encourage agricultural production methods compatible with the protection of the environment and the maintenance of the countryside.*
3760/92	Regulation on fisheries and aquaculture. *Establishes Community system for management of exploitation of living aquatic resources so as to promote sustainable development.*
93/500	Decision on renewable energy. *Promotes renewable energy sources in the EC (ALTENER).*
98/352	Decision on renewable energy. *Establishes ALTENER II.*

There is clearly more work to be done before a workable policy on the conservation of fisheries can emerge.

Agriculture

The Common Agricultural Policy has been one of the most controversial elements of European integration since its inception under the terms of the Treaty of Rome in 1958. It had five objectives: to increase agricultural productivity, to ensure a 'fair standard of living' for the agricultural community, to stabilize markets, to assure the availability of supplies, and to ensure that supplies reached consumers at reasonable prices (Grant, 1997, pp. 64–5). Increases in productivity were related to the promotion of technical progress, which was to include in practice the use of chemicals, fertilizers, biotechnology and intensive methods of agriculture. The use of such methods has helped make the EU a world leader in the development and manufacture of agrochemicals (although, as noted above, it lags behind the United States in biotechnology), but it has also helped ensure that European agriculture has brought substantial and usually negative change to the European environment; Grant (1997, pp. 200–2) lists five areas in which the impact of modern agriculture has given rise to concern:

1 Water pollution arising from runoff from agricultural land, which can lead to the aesthetic deterioration of rivers, can damage marine life and can introduce pesticides and nitrates into drinking water.
2 The effects on landscape of changes wrought by attempts to improve the 'efficiency' of farming, such as making fields bigger by removing hedges and woodland, or constructing farm buildings that intrude on the landscape.
3 Damage to soil brought on by intensive agriculture. In particular, mismanagement of farmland can lead to soil erosion, reducing the productive capacity of land and leading to the siltation of rivers and lakes.
4 Air pollution created by burning straw or wood, or by spreading manure or animal slurry and creating offensive smells.
5 Threats to biodiversity caused by the use of pesticides and fertilizers, the loss of mixed farming systems, the 'reclama-

tion' of wetlands, and the alteration of habitat as farming has intensified.

Attempts have been made to promote environmentally-sensitive agriculture (for example, with regulations 797/85 and 2078/92), but the EU is far from agreeing an agri-environmental policy that is acceptable to farmers and environmentalists, and this is unlikely to happen without wholesale reforms to the Common Agricultural Policy. In only two relatively narrow areas has EU law so far had much impact on the relationship between agriculture and the environment: the control of pesticides (discussed in Chapter 6), and the promotion of organic agriculture. Under regulation 2092/91, the Community introduced a framework for the labelling, production and control of organic farming, and has since developed this goal with nearly two dozen amendments to that regulation. Strict requirements are set out before agricultural products can be marketed in the EU as organic and, in particular, restrictions are imposed on the range of products that can be used as fertilizers and pesticides. Organic farming is still very much a minority affair, accounting for barely 2 per cent of the agricultural land of the EU, but the rate of conversion to organic farming is accelerating and demand for organic produce is growing, suggesting that this will likely be an important area for future policy developments.

Forestry

One sector which has so far played only a peripheral role in the development of EU environmental policy – but which nevertheless is a substantial part of the natural resource issue – is the forestry and forest-based products industry, including woodworking, pulp and paper, and printing and publishing. It brings together everything from a few large multinationals to hundreds of thousands of small and medium enterprises, accounts for about 10 per cent of the manufacturing output of the EU by value, and directly employs about 2.2 million people. Furthermore, the EU is the biggest trader and the second biggest consumer of forest products in the world (European Commission, 1998b). From an economic and social perspective, forests are a critical factor in EU calculations on the management of natural resources. They are also important from an environmental perspective, given their role in the welfare of biodiversity. All the more surprising, then, that the welfare and management of forests should so far have played a peripheral role in EU environmental planning.

Forests cover about one-third of the land area of Europe, the proportion having grown over the last 200 years as a result of afforestation programmes and better forest management. The most heavily forested regions are found in Sweden, Finland, southern Germany, Austria and southwest France, while Denmark and Spain have seen the most rapid growth in forest cover in recent decades. Unfortunately, quality has not always accompanied quantity, and the spread of forests has been driven more by commercial needs than by concerns about biodiversity. Rather than preserving or promoting natural woodland, modern forestry has meant intensification, increasing uniformity, the widespread use of exotic tree species, and the fragmentation of natural habitats. The result is that less than one-third of Western Europe's total forest area is natural or semi-natural, and the area of natural and semi-natural deciduous and coniferous forest continues to decline. To make matters worse, forest is under attack from pests, pollution and – particularly in the Mediterranean region – from forest fires (EEA, 1998, p. 161).

There is no EU forestry policy, although several attempts have been made to develop a strategic approach to forestry issues. In 1981, the Commission submitted a proposal for a Community forestry policy, but while the idea was supported by the European Parliament, it was turned down by the Council of Ministers. The Commission tried again in 1983 and in 1988, and while the Council still refused to adopt a formal strategy and action plan, it did adopt the regulations set out in the 1988 proposal. The Commission strategy included goals such as encouraging the contribution of forestry to the development of rural life, ensuring the supply of renewable raw materials (the EU is a major importer of timber and wood products) and contributing to environmental improvement (Johnson and Corcelle, 1995, pp. 432–3).

In January 1997, Parliament sent a renewed request to the Commission to develop a European forestry strategy, couching it in terms of the need to manage forests so as to conserve forest biodiversity, to increase the production of wood as a source of energy, to extend forests as a sink for carbon dioxide emissions (see Chapter 10), and to contribute towards EU rural development programmes. The Commission duly responded with a communication to the Council and the EP, emphasizing that it had no intention of adopting competence for EU forestry policy, but that it was interested solely in promoting 'better coordination and complementarity' between EU and member state policies.

Recent developments in the field of EU forestry policy have revolved around the information-gathering and advisory systems set up in the late 1980s. These included the European Forestry Information and Communication System (Efics) set up in 1989 under regulation 1615/89, and designed to improve the quality of information on national forest inventories, particularly through the use of remote sensing and Geographical Information Systems. Also in 1989, a Standing Forestry Committee was formed to bring together representatives of the Commission and the member states, with the goal of providing expertise and advice to the Commission. In addition, in 1997–98 consultative committees for forests, forestry and forestry-based industries were formed to bring together professionals from these three areas to advise the Commission.

Useful though these broad-based responses may be, in terms of more specific regulatory developments EU forestry policy has so far focused on just two rather narrow areas: the protection of forests from pollution and from fires. In the first case, policy dates from the adoption of regulation 3528/86 which established a scheme to protect forests from air pollution and to encourage member states to undertake a periodic assessment of the health of forests, to set up networks of observation points, and develop pilot projects and field experiments to improve understanding of air pollution in forests and its effects. Ten million ecus was set aside for the period 1987–92 to help member states. Additional funding was made available under regulation 1613/89, and the programme was extended for another five years by regulation 2157/92 which combined the observation network with a more intensive system of forestry surveillance.

The programme to protect forests from fire was prompted mainly by events in the Mediterranean states where forest fires are a common summertime occurrence; it has been estimated that in the five southern states alone (Portugal, Spain, France, Italy and Greece), there are 26 000 fires every year, an average of 18 are burning at any one time, and anywhere up to 500 000 hectares of forest are lost every year (Johnson and Corcelle, p. 436). The EU legislative response dates from the adoption of regulation 3529/86, which encouraged member states to reinforce protective measures with preventative measures, including the use of forest clearing equipment, fire breaks, observation posts and information campaigns. A budget of 20 million ecus was set aside for the period 1987–92, the budget was increased by regulation 1614/89, and the programme was renewed for five years by regulation 2158/92 (amended by 804/94). The Cohesion Fund also provides assistance for the rehabilitation of forests destroyed by fire.

The protection of Europe's forests from air pollution and fire is clearly a priority, but EU policy still has some way to go if forest management is to be integrated into the broader scheme of EU environmental policy. As the principle of sustainable development works its way more fully into European priorities, as the pressure mounts to exploit forests for renewable energy and as part of the EU response to climate change, and as more attention is paid to rural development – especially in eastern European states as they join the EU – the need to develop a broad-ranging EU forestry strategy will push forestry issues further up the environmental agenda.

Energy

The EU energy programme is remarkable less for its attempts to address the link between energy use and environmental problems than for the paucity of such attempts. As with water, energy policy is partly a matter of supply, but it is also partly a matter of the implications of energy use for the environment. Clean water and energy both need to be available in sufficient quantities and at low enough prices to keep consumers and industry content, but attention also needs to be paid to the environmental dimensions: energy generation and consumption has implications both for air and water quality, and the dependence of industrialized countries on fossil fuels is the cause of most of their worst environmental problems: the pollution of water through oil spills and runoff, the production of the bulk of the SO_2, NO_x, hydrocarbons and suspended particulates involved in air pollution generally and in acidification specifically, and the production of the CO_2 implicated in climate change.

Despite this, the link between energy production and environmental problems has rarely been made in Commission policy-making or in the deliberations of the Energy Council, where the focus has been much more on issues such as competition in the energy market. This is made abundantly clear in the only full-length study of EU energy policy to date (Matláry, 1997), which makes only passing mention of the environment, and is ultimately an analysis of energy market deregulation and of efforts to secure commercial energy supplies. The bias is also made clear in the mission statement of the Energy and Transport DG (Europa Web page, 2000), whose objectives are (1) to address the problem of external dependency, given that the EU depends on imports for nearly half its energy needs, a proportion which is expected to grow to 70 per cent by 2020; and (2) to integrate European energy markets, and increase competition in the interests of lowering the costs of energy. A third and minor objective is to ensure the 'compatibility' of energy and environmental policy, although most of the initiatives in this area come out of the Environment DG rather than the Energy and Transport DG.

Whatever its objectives, energy policy has occupied a relatively lowly place on the EU agenda, just as it has on the agendas of most of the member states. It attracted attention as the single market programme began to pick up speed in the mid-1980s, but energy policy initiatives brought the Commission, the member states and interest groups into conflict with one another, and after 1992 the Commission became much less active in this area (Matláry, 1997, p. 1). The low level of interest is ironic given that two of the original European Communities – coal and steel, and Euratom – dealt with two key sources of energy. It is explained in part by the very different levels at which different sources contribute to overall energy needs in different member states, thereby complicating attempts to develop common policies. Overall, European energy needs in 1997 were met mainly by natural gas (34 per cent), oil (27 per cent), electricity (26 per cent), and renewables such as geothermal and solar power (7 per cent). However, the contribution of each of these sources – and levels of self-sufficiency – varied substantially:

- while Britain and Denmark are almost totally self-sufficient in oil and gas, France, Germany and Italy must import 95–98 per cent of their oil, while several other countries – including Belgium, Finland, Ireland, Portugal, Spain and Sweden – must import nearly all their oil and natural gas needs;
- while Britain, Germany and Greece meet 80–90 per cent of their coal needs domestically, Denmark, Italy, the Netherlands and Portugal must cover all their needs with imports;
- while nuclear power plays a significant role in France (78 per cent of electricity needs), Belgium (60 per cent), Sweden (46 per cent), and Britain, Finland, Germany and Spain (all about 28–30 per cent), seven countries – Austria, Denmark, Greece, Ireland, Italy, Luxembourg and Portugal – have no nuclear generating capacity at all;
- while hydro and wind power play a significant role in Austria (66 per cent of electricity needs), Sweden (46 per cent), Portugal (38 per cent), and Finland, Italy and Spain (17–19 per cent), they provide less than 2 per cent of electricity needs in Belgium, Britain and the Netherlands (all figures from European Commission, 2000).

The link between energy issues and environmental policy was made in a number of EU publications in the first half of the 1990s, but in the form of recommendations rather than of substantive policy developments. The Fifth EAP emphasized the importance of long-term energy strategies to ensure that environmental stress from energy supply and use was reduced to sustainable levels, particularly given the growth in transport. Guidelines were drawn up in a 1994 green paper on energy policy (European Commission, 1994) which stressed that a Community energy policy offered the best possibilities for the development of integrated resource planning. A 1996 green paper on renewable sources of energy (see below) was couched mainly in terms of the need to reduce dependency on energy imports, to promote job creation and to underpin regional development; the only reference to the environment came in the discussion about the contribution that renewables could make to reductions in CO_2 emissions (Commission, 1996). In all the initiatives that have come out of the EU on energy, the link with environmental issues has been the subject of small bodies of law in just two areas: increasing energy efficiency, and promoting the use of renewables.

The energy efficiency programme (which should be distinguished from attempts made by the Community to reduce energy consumption) dates from 1978 and the adoption of directive 78/170 setting minimum performance requirements for heat generators for space heating and hot water. In 1989, a Community programme was established for improving the efficiency of electricity use, and in 1991 the Community set up the SAVE programme (Specific Actions for Vigorous Energy Efficiency) (directive 91/565) under which 35 million ecus was set aside for 1991–95 to help encourage member states to introduce national programmes for greater energy efficiency. Member states were to submit information to the Commission annually, explaining what they were doing and which bodies were responsible. The programme for energy consumption of household appliances was meanwhile expanded to cover heat generators (82/885), hot-water boilers (92/42), and refrigerators and freezers (94/2). Industry was opposed to mandatory standards, so in 1997 the Commission switched to voluntary agreements; in cooperation with the European Association of Consumer Electronics Manufacturers (EACEM), voluntary agreements were developed to reduce energy consumption by washing machines, and by televisions and video recorders in standby mode, to be phased in from 2000.

Directive 93/76 built on the SAVE programme but offered mainly general principles and few specific suggestions, other than including energy certification for buildings, billing consumers on the basis of actual consumption of heating and hot water and promoting thermal insulation of new buildings. There were proposals that the SAVE programme should include regular energy inspections for cars, and an estimate that the programme would account for a quarter of CO_2 reductions, but the subsidiarity principle was raised and the content pared down (Skjaerseth, 1994, p. 31; Haigh, 1996, p. 175). SAVE was replaced in 1996 by SAVE II, under which 45 million ecus of spending was set aside over a period of five years.

The second energy/environmental area in which the EU has been active has been the promotion of renewable sources of energy, such as hydro, solar and wind power. The Commission has argued that greater use of renewables could improve the security of energy supply, reduce fuel imports, create new jobs, and contribute towards the reduction of the CO_2 emissions implicated in climate change. The promotion of renewables was behind the ALTENER programme (Programme for the Promotion of Renewable Energy Sources in the Community) (directive 93/500), which set aside 40 million ecus over five years (1993–97) with the objective of helping increase the renewable share of energy supply to 8 per cent in 2005, of tripling the production of electricity from renewables, and of meeting 5 per cent of road vehicle fuel needs with biofuels (alcohol, ethanol and other fuels made from plant material). By decision 98/352, the programme was extended as ALTENER II, to run from 1998 to 2002.

In late 1996, the Commission published a green paper drawing attention to the importance of renewables in energy supply, and proposing a doubling in their share of primary energy to 12 per cent by 2010. It suggested that this should be done by increasing the use of photovoltaic systems on buildings, creating large wind farms, and developing biomass installations for combined heat and power plants (European Commission, 1996). Predictably, the proposal was criticized by the electricity industry as being 'more than ambitious' and requiring 'very large economic sacrifices'. For the European Parliament the proposal was too modest, and it argued in favour of a 15 per cent target.

These case studies of EU approaches to biodiversity, fisheries, agriculture, forestry and energy emphasize the lack of universal or global understanding of the parameters of environmental policy within the EU institutions. As noted in Chapter 2, the precautionary and integrative principles have become two of the lynchpins of the European approach to environmental management issues, and yet the management of natural resources has tended to be treated as an issue quite separate from most of the other elements of EU environmental policy, such as air and water pollution and the management of waste. This stands as further illustration that while the EU has a variety of *policies* in particular areas that come under the general rubric of 'the environment', it is still some way from being able to claim to have an environmental *policy*.

Chapter 10

Ozone, Climate Change and the International Dimension

The role of the member states of the EU in international political and economic debates has taken on a new significance since the Single European Act, as they have coordinated their interests in a growing number of policy areas. This has allowed the 15 member states to speak collectively rather than individually in negotiations on regional, international and global matters, thereby redefining the global role played by western Europe. The power of the EU is most obvious in matters with an economic dimension, given that it accounts for 28 per cent of global gross national product (World Bank, 1997), more than 36 per cent of global imports and exports (International Monetary Fund, 1998, pp. 2–5), and nearly 15 per cent of global commercial energy consumption. Statistics such as these – combined with the growing authority won by the Commission to negotiate on behalf of the member states – have drawn the EU increasingly into international debates and agreements on the environment.

This chapter looks at two cases in which there has been a close relationship between environmental policy developments at the European and international levels. Each reflects different aspects of the handicaps and opportunities inherent in the policy-making structure of the EU, in the policy relationships between the member states and the EU, and in those among the member states. In the first case – negotiations on reductions in substances that deplete the ozone layer – international agreement was reached relatively quickly, the EU (after early reluctance) played a key role in brokering that agreement, a body of appropriate EU laws was quickly adopted, and the global production of ozone-depleting substances by the mid-1990s had declined by 80–90 per cent from their peak values (EEA, 1998, p. 60). The policy response was helped by the relatively strong scientific evidence of a link between cause and effect, the avail-ability of alternatives to ozone-depleting substances, and the narrow dimensions of the source of the problem: the control of ozone-depleting substances was a matter for a discrete group of industries in a limited number of countries, none of which offered significant opposition.

The second case – negotiations on reductions in the gases implicated in global warming – has proved much more difficult and controversial. The EU set out with a modest agenda in 1988–92, but took an increasingly aggressive stance and devel-oped a determination to play a leading role in achieving inter-national agreement on emission reductions. However, it found itself handicapped by disagreements among its member states, unable to reach agreement on how to meet its emissions reduc-tion targets, and unable to exert pressure for significant change on other countries, notably the United States. Not only do ques-tions still remain about the science of climate change, but the policies proposed by the Commission in response have implica-tions for major industries and for everyone who consumes commercial energy. The most controversial proposal – for a carbon energy tax – has raised troubling questions about sover-eignty and about the competence of the EU.

The two issues stand in notable contrast to one another; in the first, accord among EU member states helped promote a quick and effective response. In the second, the debate over the response involved many more countries and several powerful industrial lobbies, and – while the EU has been a key actor in negotiations – it has been unable to use its economic power to help build a political consensus in favour of action.

The EU as an international actor

The primary actors in the agreement and implementation of international law are states, although other actors – such as cor-porations and international organizations – are increasingly recognized as the subjects of such law. The EU is not a state in the sense that it has sovereignty over its citizens, but it is much more than a conventional international organization; not only can it develop and adopt legislation which is directly binding on its member states, but it can also negotiate with third parties on behalf of its member states, and enter into binding agreements with those parties. Its powers in this regard have been particularly evident in the field of environmental policy where – beginning with two 1975 decisions approving the terms of the Paris Convention on the Prevention of Marine Pollution from Land-Based Sources – the Community has been signatory to 30 international environmental treaties (see Table 10.1), and – by the end of 1999 – had adopted 96 regulations and decisions approving the terms of those treaties.

While the EU can no longer be ignored by non-member states or international organizations with which it has dealings, its powers and status vary from one issue to the next, and it suffers from what Hill (1993) has called a 'capability-expectations gap', meaning that it is not always able to use its economic power to deliver hard results. The international role of the EU is least ambiguous in areas relating to trade and commercial relations, since Articles 110–16 of the Treaty of Rome (now Articles 131–35) outlined a Common Commercial Policy for the Community. Article 113 authorized the Commission to conduct negotiations with third parties, and it subsequently became the primary representative of Community interests in negotiations under the General Agreement on Tariffs and Trade, now the World Trade Organization.

Article 228 of the Treaty of Rome (now Article 300) went further by giving the Commission the power to make recommendations to the Council in the case of concluding agreements with third parties generally, and allowing the Council to authorize the Commission to open and conduct the necessary negotiations. The extent of Commission competence was unclear, however, as was the matter of whether the internal competence of the Community could give rise to external competence as well, but it was assumed that the Community could only enter into international agreements with third parties on policy issues or areas for which specific provisions had been made in the treaties. The matter was addressed by the Court of Justice in 1971 in Case 22/70 (*Commission v. Council (AETR)*).

The immediate issue in the case was a dispute between the Commission and the Council over an international agreement on road transport. The Commission claimed that it had competence, because the power to develop a common transport policy necessarily included the right to reach agreements with third parties. The Council disagreed, arguing that Article 228 only allowed the Commission to reach such agreements on issues for which the treaty made such provisions. The Court sided with the Commission, arguing that treaty-making powers were not restricted to the policy areas covered by Articles 113 and 228, and that there were implied powers for the Commission to conclude treaties with third parties in areas which may flow from 'other provisions of the Treaty and from measures adopted, within the framework of those provisions, by the Community institutions'. In other words, the Court concluded that whenever the Community adopted common rules in a particular area, the member states no longer had the right – individually or collectively – to enter into agreements with third parties that affected those rules: 'as and when those rules come into being, the Community alone is in a position to assume and carry out contractual obligations with third countries affecting the whole sphere of application of the Community legal system'.

In policy areas within which the EU has a large measure of competence, or even sole competence, it is possible for it to sign an international agreement without the member states also signing; such areas include the Common Agricultural Policy, the Common Commercial Policy, competition, and common policies on fisheries and air transport. In such cases, the EU has only one vote. Conversely, in policy areas where the EU has little or no competence – including criminal justice, education and taxation – the member states alone have the power to sign international treaties, in which case they have 15 independent votes. However, there are political and practical difficulties in defining the boundaries between domestic and external policy, and between economic and non-economic policy. The result is that it is usually unclear where competence for negotiations with third parties lies, hence the member states and the EU often take part together, competence is shared, the EU has the power to cast a vote in addition to those of the member states, and the result is what are called 'mixed agreements': those where the subject matter falls within the competence both of the EU and the member states, and which are signed both by the EU and by the member states (Smith, 1997).

While the role of the EU in international negotiations on commercial policy is clear, and on common foreign and security policy is emerging, in the case of environmental policy it still

TABLE 10.1 *Environmental treaties signed by the European Community*

Year	City	Subject	Year adopted by EC
1974	Paris	Prevention of marine pollution	1975
1976	Barcelona	Protection of Mediterranean from pollution	1977
1976	Bonn	Protection of Rhine from chemical pollution	1977
1978	Ottawa	Cooperation on northwest Atlantic fisheries	1978
1979	Geneva	Long-range transboundary air pollution	1981
1980	London	Cooperation on northeast Atlantic fisheries	1981
1980	Canberra	Antarctic marine living resources	1981
1979	Berne	European wildlife and habitats	1982
1979	Bonn	Migratory species of wild animals	1982
1982	Reykjavik	Salmon in the north Atlantic ocean	1982
1973	Washington	Trade in endangered species	1982
1982	Gdansk	Fishing and living resources in the Baltic Sea	1983
1969	Bonn	Pollution of the North Sea by oil	1984
1983	Geneva	International agreement on tropical timber	1985
1966	Rio de Janeiro	Conservation of Atlantic tuna	1986
1985	Vienna	Protection of the ozone layer	1988

TABLE 10.1 *Continued*

Year	City	Subject	Year adopted by EC
1987	Regensburg	Management of water resources in the Danube basin	1990
1990	Magdeburg	International commission for protection of the Elbe	1991
1989	Basel	Transboundary movements of hazardous wastes	1993
1990	Lisbon	Accidental pollution of northeast Atlantic	1993
1992	Rio de Janeiro	Biological diversity	1993
1992	New York	Climate change	1994
1974	Helsinki	Protection of Baltic marine environment	1994
1992	Helsinki	Transboundary watercourses and international lakes	1995
1991	Salzburg	Protection of the Alps	1996
1994	Sofia	Protection and sustainable use of the Danube	1997
1994	Paris	Combatting desertification	1998
1992	Paris	Protection of northeast Atlantic marine environment	1998
1992	Helsinki	Transboundary effects of industrial accidents	1998
1996	Wroclaw	International commission for protection of the Oder	1999

tends to be both *ad hoc* and inconsistent. It is a treaty obligation under Article 174(1) that the EU should promote 'measures at international level to deal with regional or worldwide environmental problems' and under Article 174(4) that, within its sphere of competence, it should 'cooperate with third countries and with the competent international organizations ... [and such] cooperation may be the subject of agreements between the Community and the third parties concerned, which shall be negotiated and concluded in accordance with Article 228 [now 300]'. As noted in Chapter 4, the European Council also agreed in Dublin in 1990 that the Community should play a leading role in promoting international action on the environment. It is unclear, however, where the responsibilities of the member states and the EU begin and end, so negotiations on the environment have been left in something of a twilight world.

Until recently, where the EC/EU has become a party to an international environmental agreement, it has not usually been the primary participant in negotiations, but has signed only after the member states have reached a common position and have all signed in their own right. This was true, for example, of the 1979 Convention on Long-Range Transboundary Air Pollution discussed in Chapter 8, where the reluctance of Britain and West Germany to acknowledge the extent of the problem of acid pollution was a far greater factor in the final content of the convention than any kind of consensus that had emerged among the Community member states.

On other occasions, the member states have been unable to reach unanimity among themselves, causing legal problems both within the EU and in EU relations with third parties. A prime example came in 1985 at a meeting of signatories to the convention on trade in endangered species (CITES) (see Chapter 9). The view of the Commission was that the issue came under exclusive Community competence since trade in endangered species was a commercial policy matter, and that in the absence of a common EC position, the member states were not entitled to act unilaterally. Six member states disagreed, arguing that the particular species under discussion were not yet part of the appendices to the convention, and thus were not within EC competence. In the event, all ten Community member states decided to abstain from voting (Haigh, 1992).

By contrast, in the cases of the ozone layer and climate change conventions, the member states reached common positions before final negotiations began, and the Commission was thus able to lead such negotiations on behalf of the member states. These examples were illustrative of a growing trend among EU member states to work as a group on international environmental issues, and to bring their considerable economic power to bear on negotiations.

The ozone layer: the problem

Stratospheric ozone forms between about 15–50 km (9–30 miles) above the surface of the earth when oxygen molecules are split by ultraviolet radiation from the sun and then bond with other oxygen molecules to form ozone (O_3). The ozone layer is essential to human health, helping screen out harmful ultraviolet radiation (UV-B), excessive amounts of which can cause sunburn, eye disorders such as cataracts, infectious skin disease, skin cancer, skin aging and depression of the immune system. It can also kill micro-organisms and cells in animals and plants, decrease photosynthesis, damage seed quality, reduce crop yields, and limit the production of phytoplankton in aquatic ecosystems, affecting the early development stages of fish, shrimp and other marine species (UNEP, 1995). UV-B radiation can also contribute to the formation of tropospheric (ground-level) ozone, which is harmful to human health. Ground-level ozone is a byproduct of interactions involving various pollutants generated by industrial processes, notably volatile organic hydrocarbons and nitrogen oxides.

One of the earliest international environmental issues to capture public attention emerged in the early 1970s when scientists warned that exhaust gases from high-flying supersonic transport planes (SSTs) such as Concorde could damage the ozone layer. While this issue died a relatively rapid death, evidence gathered in the late 1970s and early 1980s revealed that the ozone layer was being threatened from another quarter, viz. interactions between ozone and chemicals reaching the stratosphere as a byproduct of human activity (Nance, 1991). Notable among these ozone-depleting substances (ODS) were chlorofluorocarbons (CFCs), hydrochlorofluorocarbons (HCFCs), halons, nitrogen oxides and methyl bromide (a toxic gas used mainly as a pesticide).

CFCs are synthetic, inert, non-toxic, non-flammable, chlorine-based compounds once widely used as aerosol propellants, refrigerants, coolants, sterilizers, solvents, and as blowing agents in foam production. Invented in the United States by DuPont and General Motors in 1928, the number of uses of CFCs expanded quickly enough for global production to double roughly every five years until 1970, by which time the USA was producing about half the world total, and DuPont alone about half the US total (Parson, 1993, p. 29). While they were initially thought to be benign, research by the 1970s was suggesting that they were broken down in the stratosphere by ultraviolet radiation, releasing chlorine which went on to destroy ozone. Contrary to descriptions in the media in the 1980s which spoke of a 'hole' in the ozone layer, the destruction in fact led to a thinning of the ozone layer, notably over the polar icecaps where ozone levels were estimated to have dropped by as much as 40 per cent in the 1970s and 1980s. Meanwhile, levels over northern urban areas and over parts of South America and Australasia were found to have dropped by about 2–3 per cent, and by as much as 10 per cent over Australia during the southern summer. Over Europe, ozone concentrations fell by about 7 per cent between 1979 and 1993 (EEA, 1995, p. 53). At the same time, the amount of UV-B reaching the earth's surface was increasing.

By 1998, international policy measures had resulted in reductions of global annual production of ODS of as much as 80–90 per cent, and the complete phasing out in industrialized countries of all ODS except HCFCs and methyl bromide. However, it is still too early to see the results in the form of increased ozone concentrations and reduced amounts of UV-B radiation reaching the surface of the earth. The stability of CFCs and halons ensures that they will remain intact for decades, continuing to break down ozone long after they first infiltrated the stratosphere. Ozone depletion is expected to peak by 2010, and recovery is not expected until the middle of the century, assuming full compliance with the terms of international agreements aimed at reducing the production and consumption of ODS.

The ozone layer: the policy response

The European response to the problem of ozone depletion must be seen in the context of international responses to the problem, which focused around the signature in March 1985 of the framework Vienna Convention for the Protection of the Ozone Layer, the agreement of the 1987 Montreal protocol to the convention, and subsequent meetings of signatories. The Vienna convention in turn must be seen in the context of policy developments dating back to the early 1970s, when research into the SST issue in the United States first drew attention to the potential threat posed by human activity to the ozone layer (for details, see Morrisette, 1989).

In the face of opposition from industry, the United States began taking action to limit the release of CFCs in 1977, and adopted a ban on the use of CFCs in most non-essential aerosols in 1978. It also exerted pressure on the European Community – by then the biggest producer and exporter of CFCs, accounting for 38 per cent of world production – to follow suit. In the face of Anglo-French resistance, the EC responded with a rather tame 1978 resolution calling on member states to cooperate on research, on manufacturers to identify alternatives to CFCs, and on users to reduce emissions. This was followed with a 1980 decision (80/372) requiring member states to ensure no increases in the CFC production capacity of domestic industries, and to cut the use of selected CFCs in aerosol cans by 30 per cent by 1981, from 1976 levels. However, this was little more than a symbolic gesture designed, argues Jachtenfuchs (1990), to demonstrate willingness to the United States that the EC was prepared to take action on the issue. The decision did not freeze the production of CFCs, but rather the production capacity (which was larger), and the 30 per cent reduction had anyway already been achieved.

Meanwhile, the UN Environment Programme (UNEP) had become involved in the issue, beginning with its sponsorship of a meeting in Washington DC in 1977 at which delegates from 33 countries and the EC heard the results of the latest research. Prompted mainly by pressure from Norway and Sweden, UNEP began work in 1981 on an international agreement on the ozone layer, and negotiations began in Vienna in 1982; the Community was represented both by the Commission and by delegates from the member states. Political support for action had, however, entered something of a trough; the Reagan administration in the United States had halted research into CFCs, and the Community was unwilling to consider reductions in CFC production or use. In 1982 it adopted a second decision (82/795), but this did little more than confirm the measures outlined in the 1980 decision, extending them to other sectors using CFCs, such as refrigeration and solvents.

Jachtenfuchs (1990) suggests that, by the beginning of 1985, negotiations on the ozone layer issue were dominated by the question of how the EC would participate, and that they were being used by the Commission as a tool to win greater powers over environmental policy. In the event, the Environment Council authorized the Commission to participate on behalf of the Community. When the Vienna Convention was signed in March 1985 both by the Community and by 22 countries, this represented the first occasion on which the EC had been allowed to become party to a 'mixed' international agreement in which both the Community and its member states were represented.

Because of the lack of a scientific consensus on the problem, the Vienna convention involved no obligations on its signatories beyond monitoring and research, instead leaving the development of specific control measures for later protocols. Political and public pressure for such measures grew following the publication in the journal *Nature* in June 1985 of the results of research by a British Antarctic Survey team concluding that the ozone layer over the Antarctic had been depleted by 30 per cent. Discussions now began on a protocol to the convention that would give it more substance. These saw the emergence of two groups: a US/Canadian-led coalition of countries known as the Toronto Group, which was in favour of a global ban on the use of CFCs as aerosol propellants, but supported no limit on other uses of CFCs, and an EC-led coalition with France and Britain at its core which argued that banning aerosol use would not address the problem of non-aerosol use, and that the only effective response was a blanket production capacity limit of the kind outlined in the 1980 and 1982 Community decisions.

The balance of political opinion had meanwhile begun to shift in the United States, where changes in the leadership of the Environmental Protection Agency led to the adoption in late 1986 of an EC proposal for an immediate freeze in CFC production, but extended this by calling for steps leading to a 95 per cent reduction (Parson, 1993, pp. 38–41). Majority public opinion in the United States was in favour of action, but neither government nor industry was willing to adopt a unilateral phase-out for fear that this would provide European CFC producers with an even larger market share than they already enjoyed. For their part, the French, British and German governments were loathe to agree to more ambitious goals, being keen to protect the interests of their national CFC industries, which were the largest producers in the Community; these included ICI in Britain, Atochem in France and Hoechst in Germany. However, the positions of European industry were changing, as revealed by the support given in 1988 by the European industry council CEFIC and by ICI to a CFC phase-out (Parson, 1993, p. 46). By mid-1987, the weight of scientific opinion had helped move the EC from agreement on a freeze, to agreement on a 20 per cent reduction, to agreement on a 50 per cent reduction (Morrisette, 1989).

Meanwhile, a diplomatic wrangle had emerged over the question of the role of the Commission in negotiations (Jachtenfuchs, 1990). As noted above, the Environment Council had authorized the Commission to negotiate on behalf of the Community, but without the ability to modify the Community position without referring back to the Council. The United States was opposed to the idea of the Community being represented by the Commission on the grounds that it could calculate CFC production for the Community as a whole, allowing reductions in one member state to be compensated by increases in another (an ironic position to take, given its support for a very similar approach to dealing with climate change – see below). The USA insisted that the protocol to the Vienna convention be signed by each member state separately, but the Community delegation refused. In the end, it was decided that the protocol would be signed by the Commission and by each of the member states.

The Protocol on Substances that Deplete the Ozone Layer was signed in Montreal in September 1987, and came into force on 1 January 1989. It required that industrialized countries freeze and then reduce production of five kinds of CFC by 50 per cent by 1999, calculated from a 1986 baseline. It was immediately criticized by several countries and by environmental groups for not going far enough, and a meeting of signatories to the convention in Helsinki in May 1989 saw the 12 EC member states joining a large group of countries pushing for a complete CFC phase-out by 2000. New scientific evidence had by then begun to emerge about the depletion of the ozone layer in the northern hemisphere, and a meeting of parties to the convention in London in 1990 led to further amendments, speeding up the timetable for the reduction and consumption of CFCs and halons, and adding to the list of controlled substances ten further kinds of CFCs, as well as carbon tetrachloride and methyl chloroform. The parties met again in 1992 and agreed to bring forward the dates for the end of production and consumption of CFCs, carbon tetrachloride, methyl chloroform and halons.

Haigh (1992) raises the interesting question of what might have happened had the member states of the Community individually entered negotiations on the ozone layer issue. While noting that the United States deserved credit for creating the pressure that led to negotiations, he suggests that a protocol along the lines suggested by the Toronto Group – a ban on the use of CFCs as aerosol propellants only – would presumably have been adopted in 1985, to which several Community member states would likely have become parties. Not only would several countries not have signed, however, but the protocol would have needed a complete revision following confirmation of the ozone hole discovery. 'In the event,' argues Haigh,

> the EC not only ensured that the Protocol had a better form but also delivered intact a bloc of twelve industrialised countries central to any successful action . . . The result was an ideal situation whereby several countries contributed solutions to a global issue and learned from one another during the process.

When it came to developing European legislation implementing the terms of the 1987 protocol, the European Parliament, the Economic and Social Committee, and several environmental NGOs pushed for more aggressive goals, the latter going so far as to threaten to organize a boycott of CFC-producing industries that would not support greater reductions; notable among these were Atochem and ICI (Jachtenfuchs, 1990). The Com-

TABLE 10.2 *Key pieces of EU law on the ozone layer and climate change*

80/372	Decision on chlorofluorocarbons (CFCs). *Requires reductions in use of CFCs in aerosol cans.*
82/795	Decision on CFCs. *Consolidates precautionary measures on CFCs in the environment.*
88/540	Decision on the 1985 ozone layer convention. *Approves terms of the Convention for the Protection of the Ozone Layer (Vienna, 1985).*
3322/88	Regulation on substances that deplete the ozone layer. *Implements terms of 1987 Montreal protocol to the 1985 ozone layer convention.*
89/419	Decision on protection of the ozone layer. *Allocates import quotas for CFCs.*
594/91	Regulation on substances that deplete the ozone layer. *Establishes regulations on trade in and production of CFCs.*
93/389	Decision on greenhouse gases. *Establishes national programmes for monitoring and limiting carbon dioxide and other greenhouse gas emissions.*
2047/93	Regulation on trade in ozone-depleting chemicals. *Permits trade in ozone-depleting chemicals with certain states that were not parties to the 1987 Montreal Protocol to the ozone layer convention.*
94/69	Decision on 1992 climate change convention. *Approves terms of the UN Framework Convention on Climate Change (New York, 1992).*
94/826	Decision on CFCs. *Allocates import quotas for selected CFCs, halons, carbon tetrachloride and other substances posing a threat to the ozone layer.*
3093/94	Regulation on substances that deplete the ozone layer. *Places controls on the production, import, export, supply, use and recovery of ozone-depleting chemicals, including CFCs, halons, HBFCs and HCFCs.*

mission, however, argued that the Community should implement the terms of an agreement that had been difficult enough in itself to reach, rather than going beyond those terms. Measures implementing the terms of the Montreal protocol were finally instituted under regulation 3322/88, which required a freeze on the production and consumption of CFCs and halons at 1986 levels, a reduction by 50 per cent from 1988, and an 80 per cent reduction from 1993. Responsibility for production cuts was placed on the producers of controlled substances rather than on the member states. Consumption was to be cut not by reducing demand, but by setting limits on the quantities of controlled substances that producers could sell within the Community, and by setting quotas for imports into the EC of controlled substances.

Regulation 3322/88 was repealed three years later by 594/91, which introduced amendments to the Montreal protocol agreed at meetings of the parties in 1989/90, even going beyond the terms of those amendments. CFC production and consumption was to be phased out in the Community by 1 July 1997 (instead of the 1 January 2000 target set in the amendments to the protocol), although CFCs could still be produced for use in developing countries (until 2010), and recycled material could still be used. Under regulation 3952/92, the phase-out date was set at 1 January 1996. This was repealed in turn by regulation 3093/94 on the production, trade, use and recovery of ODS. In 1997, the Commission developed a proposal for a revision of 3093/94 that would place a complete ban on CFC use from 2000, on methyl bromide from 2001, and on the use of HCFCs in refrigeration and air-conditioning equipment from 2008. However, manufacturers and users opposed tighter restrictions on HCFCs, arguing that applying production controls in the EU would give the advantage to producers in countries lacking such controls. Meanwhile, the ban on methyl bromide was opposed by several southern EU member states on the grounds that there were no proven alternatives.

A compromise was worked out in which the ban on methyl bromide was delayed to 2005, with southern member states allowed to meet slower phase-out targets. A phase-out was also agreed for HCFC production, which was to be frozen between 2000 and 2008, and phased out gradually, with a complete ban in 2025. The proposal was adopted by the Commission in 1998, and described by environment commissioner Ritt Bjerregaard as 'the European Union's final step in eliminating all ODS' (European Commission press release, 1 July 1998). In addition to the arrangements for HCFCs, its key elements included a plan to phase out the use, production and supply of methyl bromide by 2005 (using more ambitious interim targets than those set out by the Montreal protocol), progressive bans on the use of HCFCs in refrigeration, foams and solvents, and an immediate ban on sales of CFCs and on sales and use of halons.

Global production and emissions of ozone-depleting substances have fallen sharply since the late 1980s; for example, production of CFC-11 by major manufacturers in industrialized countries grew from 290 000 tonnes in 1980 to 382 000 tonnes in 1987, but was down to just 33 000 tonnes in 1995. Overall, global production of CFCs in 1995 was only 10–20 per cent of its peak value (EEA, 1998, p. 66). Unfortunately, the presence of CFCs in the atmosphere ensures that the ozone layer will not fully recover until at least 2033, and perhaps as late as 2050. Hence ultra-violet radiation levels are expected to continue to grow, as will their associated effects on human health. The EEA concludes that if measures currently in force are fully implemented, additional cases of skin cancer caused by ozone depletion should peak at 78 per million per year in about 2055. Increases in UV radiation are likely to be largest in the western parts of the EU because of relative ozone depletion levels (EEA, 1999, appendices p. 7).

Climate change: the problem

The question of climate change – otherwise known as global warming, or the greenhouse effect – has proved controversial, with opinion divided on just how serious a problem it may be (assuming it is a problem at all), on the response that should be adopted, and on how the burden of that response should be shared among different countries. The political, scientific and economic issues involved have been far more complex than those relating to the ozone layer, hence agreement on how to address the issue has proved more difficult to reach, and the EU has found itself involved in much more difficult negotiations on policy.

The greenhouse effect is a natural phenomenon: life on earth is made possible by the fact that solar radiation is trapped by gases in the atmosphere. Some of the radiation is reflected back into space, but much remains within the atmosphere creating the conditions that make it possible for life to exist. Concerns have arisen, however, from the theory that the build-up of gases produced by industrial activity may be trapping more heat in the atmosphere, perhaps leading to an increase in average global temperatures, with a variety of potentially negative effects.

There are several so-called 'greenhouse gases', the most prominent being CFCs, methane and carbon dioxide (CO_2). The production of CFCs has been addressed by the action taken to protect the ozone layer, but it will be several decades before they finally dissipate, and they have by far the most potent warming effect of all greenhouse gases. Meanwhile, methane is produced by bacterial activity in bogs, swamps, rice paddies, and in the stomachs of cattle and other livestock, by forest fires, and by the release of natural gas. The volume in the atmosphere has more than doubled in the last 300 years as a result of human activity – mainly the intensification of agriculture – and continues to increase at a rate of about 1 per cent per year. At the same time, however, methane is relatively easy to control because it has a life of just ten years in the atmosphere, and a 10–20 per cent cut in production would be enough to halt the increase in the proportion of methane in the atmosphere. Such a cut could be achieved by improving feed and nutrition for cattle and sheep.

The real problem lies with CO_2, which accounts for nearly two-thirds of greenhouse gas emissions in the EU, and which has been the focus of most of the political attention to date. CO_2 is one of the byproducts of burning fossil fuels; with the increase in the consumption of fossil fuels since the mid-19th century, more CO_2 has been emitted into the atmosphere. The problem has been exacerbated by the removal of forest cover, because trees are a natural 'sink' for CO_2 (that is, they absorb CO_2). The cumulative effect is that there is now 150 per cent more CO_2 in the atmosphere than there was before the industrial age. As CO_2 and other greenhouse gases build up in the atmosphere, more solar radiation is trapped, leading to the possibility that global mean air temperatures may be increasing – they have already increased by 0.6°C (1°F) since 1850, but there is no consensus regarding the link with CO_2; the increase may just be part of a natural process of climate change.

The UN Intergovernmental Panel on Climate Change (IPCC) suggests that the amount of CO_2 in the atmosphere may double in the next 90–100 years, that emissions reductions of 50–70 per cent are needed simply to stabilize current concentrations of greenhouse gases in the atmosphere, and that – without action on emissions – the world might become warmer by a factor of 3°C (5°F) by 2050, up from the current global average of 14°C (57°F). However, while there is little question that such temperature increases are possible, there is little agreement on whether such warming will actually happen, or on why it will happen, or on its possible effects. The essential problem is that very little is really understood about global climate, or about how all the factors interact with one another to influence climate.

Most notably, climatologists still have many questions regarding the role of clouds, the formation of which is unpredictable, and which may increase as a result of global warming, perhaps offsetting some of its effects by reflecting more radiation back into space. Different kinds of clouds have different reflective capacities; for example, tropical storm clouds are so thick that they trap three times as much heat as northern temperate clouds, and also reflect sunlight back into space. Furthermore, little is understood about the ability of oceans – another natural sink for CO_2 – to absorb CO_2 or heat, or about their effects on climate and weather.

If global warming is indeed occurring, there are several possible effects:

- Warming may be greater in higher latitudes than on the equator, so the evapo-transpiration cycle might speed up leading to a loss of soil moisture in those areas where most of the world's crops are grown; wheat yields might fall, rice could become sterile, and the reproductive capacity of trees might be affected. On the other hand, a warmer climate could encourage plant growth, which would increase the absorption of CO_2.
- Since liquids expand when heated and contract when cooled, global warming could cause the volume of the oceans to increase. Meanwhile, the polar icecaps could begin to melt. The combination of these two effects could raise sea levels, causing damage to coastal areas.
- Given that the temperature difference between the poles and the equator drives most of the world's weather, global

warming could bring about a change of weather patterns (and, indeed, may already have done so). It could also change the direction and speed of ocean currents, which could cause changes in the ecology of fisheries.

Climate change: the policy response

The theory of the greenhouse effect has been understood since the 1890s, but it has only been since the mid-1980s that it has become a significant international policy concern (for more details, see Jäger and O'Riordan, 1996). Records of atmospheric concentrations of CO_2 began to be kept in the United States in 1958, and by the late 1970s it had become clear that levels were rising. At the same time, research suggested that CO_2 was not the only culprit, but that methane, nitrous oxide and CFCs were also implicated. The findings of computer models were enough to prompt the convening in 1979 of the first UN-sponsored World Climate Conference in Geneva, but it was attended mainly by scientists and attracted little political attention.

In 1988, the UN convened the IPCC to assess scientific evidence to date, to discuss potential environmental impacts and to develop policy responses. It concluded that human activities were leading to an increase in atmospheric concentrations of greenhouse gases, and that there was an enhanced greenhouse effect at work. It also made several predictions regarding global temperature changes and regional climate changes that could occur. By the time the second World Climate Conference was held in Geneva in 1990, policymakers had begun to pay more attention to the problem, and the United Nations drew up a Framework Convention on Climate Change which was signed by more than 150 countries and the European Community at the 1992 Earth Summit in Rio de Janeiro. Under the terms of the convention, industrialized countries undertook to stabilize their CO_2 emissions at 1990 levels by 2000, promised to set reduction targets by 1997, and mostly accepted the scientific case for action.

The need for a Community policy on climate change was first raised in a Commission research policy statement in 1985, and was the subject of a European Parliament resolution in 1986, but

it was not mentioned in the Fourth Environmental Action Programme (1987–92). By 1988, the Commission was taking more
interest in the issue, and argued that the best medium-term
response was to improve energy efficiency and to promote the
use of renewable energy. In June 1990, the European Council
meeting in Dublin made a call for the adoption of strategies and
targets to reduce greenhouse gas emissions, and a joint meeting
of environmental and energy ministers in October agreed that
CO_2 emissions should be stabilized at 1990 levels by the year
2000. However, it was acknowledged that not all member states
could be expected to make the same percentage reductions; those
with 'relatively low energy requirements . . . may need targets
and strategies which can accommodate that development, while
improving the energy efficiency of their economic activities'. In
other words, there would be lower expectations on less industrialized countries such as Portugal and Greece.

The Commission (and particularly environment commissioner Carlo Ripa di Meana) had by then decided that the Community should take a leading role in international discussions
on climate change leading up to the 1992 Earth Summit, a position that was helped by the policies adopted by several member
states to reduce greenhouse gas emissions at the national level
(Wagner, 1997, p. 312). Exemplifying the extent to which
the environment cuts across different policy areas, the DGs
responsible for external relations, economic analysis, the internal market, agriculture, transport, development aid, the
environment, research, energy and tax were all brought into
inter-service discussions on the issue, with the lead being taken
by DGXI, DGXVII (energy) and DGXXI (tax) (Skjaerseth,
1994, p. 27). A draft Communication was developed, suggesting that CO_2 emissions might need to be cut by 10–20 per cent,
that energy efficiency alone was unlikely to achieve a result like
this, and that economic and fiscal incentives might be the best
approach (Haigh, 1996, pp. 162–3).

Discussions initially revolved around the allocation of different CO_2 reduction targets for different member states, but this
idea was eventually abandoned and replaced in 1992 by a three-
part 'climate package':

1 Promotion of greater energy efficiency through the SAVE
   programme created in 1991, and promotion of renewable

energy through the ALTENER programme created in 1993 (see Chapter 9).

2   Adoption of a 'monitoring mechanism' (decision 93/389) under which the member states were to develop and implement national programmes for CO_2 reductions. They were also to provide the Commission with information on these programmes, on current CO_2 emissions, and on the expected economic impact of the measures adopted. The Commission was then to circulate this information to other member states, and to assess the national programmes in order to determine whether or not they were sufficient to meet EU commitments.

3   A carbon energy tax. Without question the most controversial of the Commission proposals, the carbon tax – suggested by the Commission in a communication to the Council in June 1992 – was based on the idea of imposing taxes both on CO_2 emissions and on the energy content of fuels. It was prompted by concerns that Denmark, Germany and the Netherlands were considering introducing their own taxes, and by a growth in interest in market-based methods of achieving environmental policy goals (Collier, 1996). The tax would be levied on all fossil fuels, the Commission suggesting that rates be introduced progressively from a base rate equivalent of $3 per barrel of oil in 1993, rising by $1 per barrel each year to a maximum equivalent to $10 per barrel in 2000. It estimated that the tax would raise the price of natural gas by 14 per cent and of petrol by 6 per cent if the costs were passed on to the consumer (Johnson and Corcelle, 1995, p. 176). Among the most ardent opponents of the idea were industry-oriented DGs (such as those responsible for industry and the internal market), the business lobby, and even Persian Gulf oil producers (Skjaerseth, 1994, pp. 28–31).

Running alongside the debate over the tax was what Haigh (1996, p. 167) describes as a 'curious side-show' in the process leading up to ratification of the UN climate change convention. Germany, the Netherlands and the three Scandinavian member states were the most active champions of the carbon tax, even going so far as to link their support for ratification of the UN convention to adoption of the tax. However, Britain refused to stand down, implying that it would not be concerned if the Community did not ratify the convention, and that Britain would ratify on its own. This concerned countries such as Spain, which planned to offset its own CO_2 increases with reductions made by more industrialized member states. In the event, a compromise was agreed by which the decision on the tax was left to Ecofin, while emphasis was placed on the possibility of national taxes that might be equivalent to the proposed European tax. In December 1994, the Council of Ministers agreed to drop the idea of a carbon tax, instead agreeing to allow member states to develop their own taxes; only six so far have done so – Austria, Belgium, Denmark, Finland, the Netherlands and Sweden. Debate on a European energy tax was revived in the late 1990s, however, with Spain offering the greatest resistance to the idea. (For more details on the carbon tax issue, see Zito, 2000, chapter 4.)

Because the EU is responsible for 14.8 per cent of the world's annual commercial energy consumption, and is the source of about 13 per cent of the world's annual CO_2 production, it is clearly deeply involved in the climate change issue. Furthermore, climate change policy should be a perfect example of the merits of collective action – everyone who uses fossil fuel contributes to the problem to some extent, and everyone feels the effects to some extent. Individual states can act, but no single state acting alone will be able to have much of an impact on addressing the overall problem, and it will impose economic handicaps on itself if it tries. However, while the EU response to climate change began with a series of ambitious – perhaps overambitious – proposals aimed at putting the EU at the forefront of international efforts, its policy goals were steadily watered down as a result of a combination of political and economic pressures (for further discussion, see Wagner, 1997, pp. 324–33). These included the following:

- Uncertainty over the links between cause and effect, and over predicting the likely sectoral and regional impact of climate change.
- The difficulty of allocating emission-abatement measures equitably among the member states, a challenge which has been complicated by different levels of economic develop-

ment, different per capita CO_2 emissions, and different energy structures and needs.

- Concerns about loss of sovereignty, which have led some member states to raise the issue of subsidiarity and to criticize the potential increase in the powers of the Commission that might come from an EU climate change policy. Much of the opposition to the carbon tax, for example, was based on the argument that such a tax would impose a handicap on European industries, and that it should not be imposed unless it was adopted as well by other OECD states. Concurrently, there was the criticism (notably from the UK) that taxation was the responsibility of the member states, and that a carbon tax would provide the Commission with an independent source of income, thereby increasing its powers.

- The opposition of powerful industries, notably the chemical and petroleum lobbies which have been concerned not only about the likely impact on their profits, but also about the likely impact on the EU international trade position if it was to take unilateral action (Fish and South, 1994, p. 32).

- The failure of other industrialized countries (notably the United States) to commit themselves to significant reductions in greenhouse gas emissions. The Earth Summit resulted in an agreement by most of these states to voluntarily reduce their emissions to 1990 levels by 2000, but it quickly became clear that they were not delivering. Without a sense that all major producing countries were sharing the burden of the costs of emission reductions, no progress was likely to be made.

These problems resulted in the EU member states adopting national plans and targets considerably at variance with each other. At one end of the scale were Denmark, Germany and the Netherlands, which adopted targets that were more ambitious than those of the EU as a whole, and aimed at CO_2 reductions of 20–25 per cent. In the middle were states such as Britain and France, which made their targets conditional upon those set by other states, and aimed for stabilization of emissions. Finally, Greece, Luxembourg and Portugal had no national policies at all (Skjaerseth, 1994, pp. 34–5). By the mid-1990s, the prognosis for emission reductions was not good: it was estimated that instead of a projected 11 per cent reduction in CO_2 emissions by 2000, there was more likely to be a reduction of 3–4 per cent at best (Grubb, 1995, pp. 172–3). The EEA subsequently revealed that CO_2 emissions from the EU as a whole fell by less than 1 per cent in the period 1990–96 (see Table 10.3), and not always as a result of deliberate emissions reduction policies; low economic growth had played a role in some countries, and economic restructuring had been a key factor in eastern Germany (EEA, 1999, appendices, pp. 4–5).

Against this background of a lack of political consensus, it was all the more surprising that a meeting of the Environment Council in March 1997 should reach agreement on a 15 per cent reduction in emissions of CO_2, nitrous oxide and methane by 2010, using 1990 as a base, and weighted according to their global warming potential. With the credibility of the EU on the global stage at the forefront of their minds, the ministers devoted the meeting almost exclusively to this one issue, progress on which had been blocked by a French insistence that targets be differentiated according to the per capita emissions of each member state. Despite opposition from industry, the ministers agreed a 'burden-sharing' arrangement under which different reduction targets were set for different states: France, with its large nuclear power industry, was assuaged by having to meet no targets at all; Austria, Denmark, Germany and Luxembourg accepted reduction targets of 25–30 per cent; Belgium, Italy, the Netherlands and Britain accepted 7–10 per cent targets; and Greece, Ireland, Portugal, Spain and Sweden were to be allowed increases of between 5 and 40 per cent. Confirmation depended upon the outcome of the third meeting of parties to the climate change convention, to be held in Kyoto, Japan, in December 1997. (The first and second had been held in Berlin and Geneva in 1995 and 1996.)

The Kyoto meeting was intended to give more substance to the climate change convention by producing a protocol committing industrialized countries to a reduction in emissions of a package of six greenhouse gases by the period 2008–12. In the event, it achieved much less, the waters being muddied by a dispute between the EU and the United States over the best way to proceed. The EU proposal for a blanket 15 per cent cut by all industrialized countries by 2010 was met with opposition from oil-exporting states and from industries that depended on fossil fuels. Most importantly, though, it was opposed by the

TABLE 10.3 CO2 emissions in the EU, 1990–96

	1990		1996		% change in total emissions 1990–96
	Total emissions (million tonnes)	Per capita emissions (tonnes per person)	Total emissions (million tonnes)	Per capita emissions (tonnes per person)	
Luxembourg	13.0	32.5	7.0	17.5	−46
Germany	1014.0	12.3	910.0	11.1	−10
UK	615.0	10.6	593.0	10.2	−4
Austria	62.0	7.6	62.0	7.6	0
Italy	442.0	7.7	448.0	7.8	+1
France	392.0	6.7	399.0	6.8	+2
Greece	85.0	8.1	92.0	8.8	+8
Portugal	47.0	4.8	51.0	5.2	+8
Spain	226.0	5.7	248.0	6.2	+10
Belgium	116.0	11.4	129.0	12.6	+11
Finland	59.0	11.6	66.0	12.9	+11
Ireland	31.0	8.6	35.0	9.7	+13
Netherlands	161.0	10.3	185.0	11.8	+14
Sweden	55.0	6.3	63.0	7.2	+14
Denmark	52.0	10.0	60.0	11.5	+15
Total	3372.0	9.0	3348.0	9.0	−0.7

Source: Calculated from figures in EEA, Environment in the European Union at the Turn of the Century (Copenhagen: EEA, 1999), appendices, p. 4.

United States, which announced in October that it would not stabilize emissions until 2012 at the earliest, or make cuts before 2017. Furthermore, even these modest goals were dependent upon developing countries agreeing to make reductions.

Faced with opposition from a Republican-dominated Congress and a powerful fossil fuel lobby, the US delegation went to Kyoto with minimalist goals in mind. Its undertaking to stabilize emissions was conditional upon other industrialized countries accepting emissions targets, on credit being given to countries which had planted trees to absorb CO_2, and on the adoption of a system of emissions trading under which polluting countries could buy the rights to higher emissions from countries that had reduced their emissions. The EU was opposed to such measures, environment Commissioner Ritt Bjerregaard accusing the United States of wanting to 'buy the right to pollute' from countries in industrial decline. However, the EU argument was undermined by the fact that it had already agreed the burden-sharing scheme (a cousin of emissions trading) among its member states.

Meanwhile, further complications were added by the position of developing states. CO_2 emissions were growing rapidly in several of the more industrialized states such as China, Brazil, India, Indonesia, Mexico and South Korea, whose governments pointed out that the EU, Japan and North America were making the biggest contributions to the problem (being responsible for 44 per cent of global CO_2 emissions among them), and argued that obligations to cut their CO_2 emissions would amount to handicaps on their domestic industrial plans.

In the event, the Kyoto conference agreed only modest goals. The EU continued to propose the most ambitious targets, calling for reductions in emissions of the three major greenhouse gases of 7.5 per cent by 2003 and 15 per cent by 2010, on 1990 levels. Russia proposed an overall cut of 3 per cent by 2010, with every country setting its own national goal. For its part, the United States would only support a return to 1990 levels by 2008–12. The final agreement set different goals for different countries with different time limits for different gases, aimed at an overall 5 per cent cut in greenhouse gas emissions by 2008–12, using 1990 as a base. Japan agreed to a 6 per cent reduction, the United States to 7 per cent, and the EU to 8 per cent (see Table 10.4), with demonstrable progress to be made by 2005.

TABLE 10.4 CO_2 *emissions reductions in the EU*

	Actual % change 1990–96	% reductions agreed pre-Kyoto	% reductions agreed post-Kyoto
Luxembourg	–46	–30	–28
Germany	–10	–25	–21
Denmark	+15	–25	–21
Austria	0	–25	–13
UK	–4	–10	–12.5
Belgium	+11	–10	–7.5
Italy	+1	–7	–6.5
Netherlands	+14	–10	–6
France	+2	0	0
Finland	+11	0	0
Sweden	+14	+5	+4
Ireland	+13	+15	+13
Spain	+10	+17	+15
Greece	+8	+30	+25
Portugal	+8	+40	+27
Total	–0.7	–15	–8*

* Equivalent to 550–600 million tonnes, or the total emissions of Britain.
Source: DGXI, *Second Communication from the European Community Under the UN Framework Convention on Climate Change*, 26 June 1998, p. 29.

Meanwhile, more than 130 developing countries were exempted, despite the fact that China and India were already responsible for 18 per cent of global CO_2 emissions in 1995, and are expected to become the biggest producers of CO_2 by the middle of the 21st century.

Article 4 of the Kyoto protocol – which became known as the 'EU bubble' – allowed the EU and its member states to meet their targets jointly through a differentiated commitment among the member states. The overall EU target having now been reduced from 15 per cent to 8 per cent, member states had to go back to the drawing-board in deciding how responsibilities should be shared. Several member states which had agreed large reductions before Kyoto now took the opportunity to renegotiate their commitments on more favourable terms, and final agreement was only reach after an ill-tempered, all-night Environment Council meeting in June 1998. Among the other key elements in the protocol were the 'flexible mechanisms' (or flex-mex for short), which included the emissions trading system, an allowance for developed countries to meet some of their reductions through cooperative projects with developing countries, and agreement that activities that absorbed carbon (such as planting trees) could be offset against emission targets.

One of the most notable aspects of the Kyoto discussions was the extent to which key elements were based on ideas introduced into the discussions by the United States. Seven years after it had agreed its stabilization goals, and after Carlo Ripa de Meana had pledged European leadership on the issue, the EU watched as discussions were driven by the US delegation, casting an eye on its powerful domestic oil and automobile industries. The result was confirmation that divisions among its member states had handicapped the EU which – instead of exerting its political and economic power at Kyoto – now moderated its stance in light of the ideas introduced by the United States. Nonetheless, in June 1998 the Environment Council reached final agreement on the contribution of each of the member states towards the Kyoto goal of an overall 8 per cent cut in emissions, although this was dependent upon agreement being reached on the specific actions needed at the EU level. The Commission subsequently published a strategy based on voluntary agreements with firms in the energy, transport, agriculture and industrial sectors. Options included the promotion of renewable energy and energy efficiency, greater fuel efficiency for passenger cars, and an afforestation programme. As this book went to press, a green paper was also under development on the idea of emissions trading.

Further meetings of the signatories to the climate change convention took place in Bonn and in Buenos Aires in 1998. Bonn was a chance for preparatory talks prior to Buenos Aires, at which it was hoped by the EU that details would be agreed on emission reduction policies to put into effect the goals agreed at Kyoto. Little in the way of a consensus was achieved at Bonn, however, and the discussions at Buenos Aires produced only a two-year plan of action, setting up a timetable for agreement on the means of achieving greenhouse gas emission reductions. Disagreements between the USA and the EU continued, with the former continuing to demand that emissions limits be imposed on developing countries, and the latter wanting limits placed on the ability of any one nation to buy emission credits.

According to the EEA (1999, appendices, p. 5), total EU greenhouse gas emissions are projected to rise by 6 per cent by 2010 from a 1990 baseline. Thanks to a shift from solid to gaseous fuels, the increase in CO_2 emissions will be much smaller than the increase in total energy consumption, but the change is a long way from the 8 per cent decrease in emissions discussed at Kyoto, and very far from the 50–70 per cent reductions that the UN estimates are needed simply to stabilize atmospheric greenhouse gas concentrations. The main problem will be the growing number of vehicles on European roads – while industrial CO_2 emissions are projected to fall by 15 per cent by 2010, transport emissions are projected to grow by 40 per cent.

The cases of negotiations on the ozone layer and climate change suggest that European integration has provided both advantages and disadvantages in approaches to the resolution of international environmental problems. In cases where there is political and economic agreement among the member states, they can use their collective power and influence to lobby for more ambitious international goals than might have been the case were they to approach a problem from 15 different national perspectives. However, in cases where there is disagreement among the member states, they are apt to fail to bring effective pressure to bear on other parties. A handicap they continue to experience relates to the ambiguities concerning the powers of the EU in international negotiations relative to those of the member states.

Conclusions

There is little question that the EU institutions have been both active and productive in addressing the issue of environmental management, and that they have been a fertile source of the laws, green papers, white papers, strategies and action programmes needed to support the goal of improving the quality of the environment surrounding more than 270 million people. At the end of the day, however, one fundamental question remains: what difference has all this activity made? Is the European Union a cleaner, healthier and safer place in which to live as a consequence of all the laws and policies generated by the EU, and have the actions of the governments of the member states been supported or handicapped by those laws and policies? Unfortunately, it is impossible to answer this question with precision, because it is difficult – and in some cases impossible – to disaggregate the effects of EU policy from those of actions taken by local and national government in the EU, or from broader and less quantifiable changes in the economic and social climate.

There is clear evidence that EU law has strengthened national law in those countries that lacked significant environmental policies before they joined the EU, such as Greece and Portugal. There is also clear evidence that the requirements of future membership of the EU is obliging central and eastern European states to expand and tighten their national environmental policies. Finally, there is evidence that the requirements of EU law _ and the pressure to develop European policies – have led to productive action across the member states in selected policy areas, such as acidification, climate change, waste management, and air and water quality. At the same time, however, there has been less progress in other areas, suggesting the need for more attention on the part of member states and the EU as a whole.

The most authoritative source of information on the state of the European environment is the series of triennial reports now being published by the European Environment Agency (EEA). These look at trends across Europe – not just in the European Union – and focus on effects rather than causes; in other words, they look at the results of policies rather than at the links between particular policies and particular problems. All that can be surmised from these reports, then, is the trends that have emerged as a result of a combination of the policies pursued by local government national government and the institutions of the European Union. We cannot even be sure that all these trends are a result of the deliberate actions of government in the field of environmental management; much of the improvement in air and water quality in central and eastern Europe, for example, has come as a result of the closure of inefficient industries rather than as a result of the application of tighter quality control regulations.

In its 1999 report, the EEA concluded that there had been 'some progress, but a poor picture overall', that there were uncertainties arising from a lack of data and future socioeconomic developments, that it was difficult to understand clearly the direction in which the EU was heading, and that the state of the EU's environment remained 'a serious concern' (EEA, 1999, pp. 7, 9). In general, the EEA concluded, Europe's water and air was cleaner, there was more public awareness of the threats posed by chemicals to food and water, fish stocks were better managed, the EU was quieter (thanks to the laws adopted on noise pollution), and differences in environmental standards posed less of a handicap than before to trade among the member states. By individual sectors, however, the record was mixed, with progress in one area often being offset by worsening problems in another:

- *Hazardous substances.* Chemical risk has been reduced, and emissions and concentrations of some persistent organic pollutants and heavy metals are falling, but for 75 per cent of the large volume chemicals on the market, there has been too little analysis of their toxic effects. Following a 30–50 per cent increase in the output of the chemical industry, emissions of chemicals and hazardous substances are expected to increase, particularly in more industrialized regions. The phasing out of leaded petrol – driven by the requirements of EU law – more than halved emissions of lead between 1990 and 1996, and emissions and concentrations of lead, dioxins and PCBs are expected to continue to fall, but those of mercury, cadmium and copper are expected to increase. Meanwhile, the use of chemical pesticides has fallen steadily in the EU, but thanks to accumulation in ecosystems it will be some time before they cease to have a negative environmental effect.

- *Waste.* The EU is generating and transporting more solid waste, and EU waste prevention measures have not so far been reflected in a significant change in the amount of waste generated, particularly from households. Municipal waste production per capita grew by 3 per cent between 1990 and 1995, and was expected to be up by 9 per cent (over 1990 levels) by 2000, standing in stark contrast to the target of a 21 per cent *reduction.* Europeans – particularly those in northern and central member states – have been recycling more of their glass and paper, but the overall rates for the EU have not had much impact on these two sources of waste.

- *Air quality.* There have been substantial reductions in most member states in emissions of several key air pollutants, including sulphur dioxide, nitrogen oxides, volatile organic compounds, and lead. However, while levels of these pollutants have declined, and emissions from stationary sources (such as factories and power stations) have fallen, many European cities still have dirty air because of heavy (and growing) concentrations of road vehicles. The volume of road traffic is expected to almost double by 2010 (from 1990 levels), helping keep concentrations of particulate matter, nitrogen dioxide and ozone above their guide values, and possibly cancelling out the benefits of vehicle emission controls.

- *Water quality.* There has been a significant decrease in the number of heavily polluted rivers in the EU thanks to reductions in point source discharges, and discharges of organic matter have fallen by 50–80 per cent since the mid-1980s. However, nutrient input from agriculture is still high, nitrate concentrations in rivers and lakes have remained about the same since 1980, and in intensively farmed regions of the EU they are expected to remain a problem unless further action is taken. Overall, the quality of lakes and rivers in the EU is expected to improve, mainly due to developments in urban waste water treatment.

- *Acidification.* This is one area in which there has been clear progress, much of it the result of the requirements of EU law, and the situation is only expected to improve with time. Emissions of all the major pollutants implicated in acidification have fallen: sulphur dioxide emissions were expected to be down by 70 per cent by 2010 compared to 1990 levels, nitrogen oxide emissions were expected to be down 45 per cent, and ammonia emissions down 18 per cent. The number of ecosystems experiencing levels of acid deposition above their critical loads is expected to be reduced by 80 per cent by 2010 over 1990 levels.

- *Biodiversity.* Land use and changes in land use have combined with pollution and the introduction of alien species to pose a threat to the EU's biodiversity, and these problems are expected to remain a factor for years to come. Intensive agriculture continues to exert pressure on natural habitats, helping threaten 45 per cent of Europe's reptiles and 42 per cent of its mammals with extinction, introducing nitrogen and phosphorus into surface waters, and emitting acidifying ammonia into the atmosphere. There are also fears that climate change will have an impact on species distribution, particularly in arctic and mountainous regions, and in southern Europe.

- *Energy consumption.* Energy consumption in the EU continues to grow, particularly in the transport sector. Using 1985 as a baseline with an index of 100, energy use by freight transport was up to 132 in 1995 (and is projected to be nearly 200 by 2010), while energy use by passenger transport was 141 in 1995 (and is projected to be nearly 170 by 2010). Tourism is also projected to contribute substantially to energy use: from a baseline of 100 in 1985, it was up to 145 in 1995, and could be as high as 220 in 2010. The EEA notes that EU economies have been less energy intensive in recent years, but that there is a growing demand for energy in absolute terms, with increased personal mobility jeopardising the EU's ability to achieve many of its environmental policy targets, notably action on climate change.

- *The ozone layer.* There have been sharp falls in emissions of ozone-depleting substances in the EU, moving even faster than the rate required by international agreements; CFC production fell by 90 per cent between 1990 and 1995 alone. The ozone layer over Western Europe continues to become thinner, though, contributing to an increase in rates of skin cancer. The EEA concludes that the ozone layer will not begin to recover until the mid-2030s, and will not fully recover until at least 2050.

- *Climate change.* Emissions of greenhouse gases have also fallen, but only slightly; in the case of carbon dioxide, they fell by just 1 per cent between 1990 and 1996. The EU agreed at Kyoto to reduce greenhouse gas emissions by 8 per cent by 2008–12 from 1990 levels, but emissions are in fact projected to rise by 6 per cent by 2010 (over 1990 levels), and atmospheric concentrations of nitrous oxide, carbon dioxide and methane are projected to rise by as much as 20 per cent, 45 per cent and 80 per cent respectively by 2050. The main source of the increase will be road traffic; while industrial CO_2 emissions are expected to fall by 15 per cent by 2010, and little change is expected in the heat and power producing industries, emissions from transport are expected to grow by 40 per cent.

- *Noise pollution.* Despite all the efforts of the EU in this area, the EEA estimates that about one-third of the inhabitants of the EU live in dwellings with significant exposure to noise from road and air traffic. The problems are expected to worsen as growing levels of road transport increase the demand for new and bigger roads, which will become more congested and noisier, and as the volume of air traffic increases in tandem with the tourist industry.

As the EU expands into central and eastern Europe, the challenge of meeting environmental targets will inevitably become more difficult and more expensive. The EEA is confident that emissions of key air and water pollutants will decrease in the accession countries, but with their expanding economies, countries like Poland, Hungary and the Czech Republic will see levels of consumption and production growing much faster than those in the existing 15 member states. Their agricultural systems will become more intensive, their transportation systems will expand, consumer demand and waste production will grow, the number of vehicles on their roads will grow, and demands for all the materials, substances and opportunities that accompanied industrial expansion in the west will expand. They will have the advantage of being able to be more proactive in dealing with environmental issues than was the case in the west, they will hopefully be able to learn from the mistakes of the west, and they will be obliged from the beginning to work to achieve standards that were only agreed among western EU member states after they had travelled some distance along the road of integration. Nonetheless, there will be much greater pressures on the environment and natural resources, and the challenge of addressing environmental problems in eastern Europe will be that much greater.

The logic of the regional approach

Against this background of mixed progress and potentially substantial future problems, then, what is there to be said for the regional approach to environmental issues as exemplified by the record of the European Union? By no means is there political or public consensus that membership of the EU has been beneficial to the member states, although opinion varies from one country to another, and from one issue to another. Eurobarometer polls find that support for European integration tends to be highest in the poorer member states such as Ireland, Greece and Portugal, while scepticism is greater in newer or wealthier member states such as Denmark, Sweden, Austria and Britain.

In regard to environmental policy, however, there is strong support across all member states for EU activities. When interviewees are asked which issues they feel are priorities for the EU, there is majority support (65–90 per cent) for EU action on issues such as unemployment and poverty, protecting consumers, a common defence policy, a common foreign policy, social policy, and the environment. In 1995, 69 per cent of respondents agreed that decisions on the environment should be taken at the EU level rather than at the national level (European Commission, 1995c). The autumn 1998 Eurobarometer poll found that 66 per cent of respondents favoured joint EU decision-making on the environment over national-level decision-making (ranking it seventh out of 18 policy areas), and that 86 per cent of respondents saw protecting the environment as a priority for the EU (European Commission, 1999b).

Unfortunately, Eurobarometer polls do not ask respondents *why* they feel that the environment is an issue better dealt with at the EU level. If they did, the following reasons may be among their arguments:

1   Environmental problems do not respect national borders, and – in order to be resolved – must often be addressed by multiple administrations and governments working together. This is particularly true of air and water pollution, and of the management of shared resources such as rivers, coastal waters, fisheries and migratory species.

2   Individual countries working alone may be reluctant to take action on the environment for fear of placing themselves at an economic disadvantage by having to bear the cost of action alone. Multiple countries working together may be less resistant to taking action because they are involved in a joint endeavour with shared costs and benefits. The importance of burden-sharing was exemplified by the EU response to acidification; as noted in Chapter 8, after several years of lonely opposition the Thatcher government found itself encouraged to take action in the late 1980s by – among other things – the logic of sharing the costs which were divided up among the member states very broadly on the basis of the size of their respective economies. So, while poorer states such as Greece, Ireland and Portugal were allowed to increase their emissions of sulphur dioxide and nitrogen oxides as their economies grew, richer industrialized member states agreed to reductions ranging between 2 and 40 per cent.

3   As a result of the 'leader–laggard' dynamic discussed in Chapter 3, governments with a progressive approach to environmental problems can set a pace which may encourage those with a less progressive approach to take action, when otherwise they might not. The case of the EU offers many examples of states with a more aggressive approach to environmental management (such as Germany or the Scandinavian states) increasing the political pressure on those more reluctant to take action (such as Britain or the Mediterranean states).

4   While there are normally few sanctions or tools that can be used by one country or group of countries effectively to encourage another country or group of countries to take action on the environment, regional integration provides

compelling economic reasons for joint action. Not least of these is the pressure to build free trade or the single market by harmonizing laws. The rationale behind most of the early action taken by the European Community on environmental problems was that different environmental standards posed a real or potential barrier to the construction of the common market. Thus it was in the economic interests of all the members of the Community to reach a consensus on action.

5   A shift of resources, investment and research can help poorer countries deal with the problems imposed by the burden of tightening environmental controls. Structural assistance creates channels for the movement of funds from richer to poorer states, helping the latter offset some of the costs of the investments they must make in upgrading pollutive industries or building pollution controls into new plant. At the same time, the new opportunities offered to their industries and services by the single market provide profits that they can use to offset the costs of environmental controls. Thus Greece, Spain and Portugal were encouraged to develop national environmental policies when they joined the EU, and eastern European states are being encouraged to tighten their environmental laws even before they join.

6   Regional integration encourages member states to realize how many environmental problems they either share or have in common, and how they can benefit from – or contribute to – a culture of cooperation on such problems.

7   Countries acting alone may be reluctant to share data, information and ideas for fear of losing economic advantage, while countries acting in concert can help maximize the efficiency of their actions by sharing such data. The exchange of information has been a requirement of individual pieces of European law, such as the 1984 directive on air pollution from industrial plants which requires that member states exchange information on their experience in reducing pollution and on the procedures and equipment used. It has also been the subject of its own laws, such as directive 90/313 requiring member states to make information on the environment publicly available.

While there are many benefits to regional cooperation on environmental matters, the effect of free trade on environmental standards is not without its problems. As well as the common concerns about loss of sovereignty and national independence, and about the creation of a new level of 'big' government, there are also problems related more specifically to the impact of actions in areas such as environmental management:

1 The removal of non-tariff barriers to trade – or the increased competition produced by the single market – results in the loss of national protection for industry, and the demands of progressive governments can lead to the imposition of new rules in poorer states. The effect can be to impose new costs on marginal industries which may compel them to close, with a resulting loss of jobs and damage to local economies.

2 While 'leader' states can compel a tightening of laws in 'laggard' states, the laggards can also compel a loosening of laws in leader states by arguing that environmental controls in the latter are unnecessary, or are a disguised barrier to imports, or that more scientific research is needed.

3 The removal of trade barriers can encourage industry to move to those regions of a free trade area that have the loosest laws on environmental management, particularly if different member states are allowed derogations from the law, or are given more modest targets in terms of air or water quality. This can lead to the development of 'pollution havens' and provide poorer states or regions with a competitive advantage.

On balance, however, the regional approach to the resolution of environmental problems offers many advantages over isolated national approaches. In the midst of all the debates and controversies about the nature and consequences of regional integration, there are selected policy issues where it is clear that a joint approach makes better sense; preeminent among those issues is the question of managing the human environment.

Appendix: Treaty Provisions

This appendix quotes the key provisions of the treaties relating to environmental policy, and is particularly designed to show the changes of emphasis brought by the Single European Act, Maastricht and Amsterdam.

1   1957 Treaty of Rome – EEC

There was no mention of the environment in the Treaty of Rome, and such environmental laws and policies as were developed before the Single European Act were based mainly on a combination of Articles 100 and 235.

Article 2

The Community shall have as its task, by establishing a common market and progressively approximating the economic policies of Member States, to promote throughout the Community a harmonious development of economic activities, a continuous and balanced expansion, an increase in stability, an accelerated raising of the standard of living and closer relations between the States belonging to it.

Article 30

Quantitative restrictions on imports and all measures having equivalent effect shall, without prejudice to the following provisions, be prohibited between Member States.

Article 36

1   The provisions of Articles 30 to 34 shall not preclude prohibitions or restrictions on imports, exports or goods in transit justified on grounds of public morality, public policy or public security; the protection of health and life of humans, animals or plants; the protection of national treasures possessing artistic, historic or archeological value; or the protection of industrial and commercial property. Such prohibitions or restrictions shall not, however, constitute a means of arbitrary discrimination or a disguised restriction on trade between Member States.

Article 100

The Council shall, acting unanimously on a proposal from the Commission, issue directives for the approximation of such provisions laid down by law, regulation or administrative action in Member States as directly affect the establishment or functioning of the common market.

Article 235

If action by the Community should prove necessary to attain, in the course of the operation of the common market, one of the objectives of the Community and this Treaty has not provided the necessary powers, the Council shall, acting unanimously on a proposal from the Commission and after consulting the Assembly, take the appropriate measures.

2   1957 Treaty of Rome – Euratom

The Euratom treaty made provision for action aimed at protecting workers and the public from the effects of ionizing radiation, radioactivity and the disposal of radioactive waste.

Article 2

In order to perform its task, the Community shall, as provided in this Treaty:

(a) promote research and ensure the dissemination of technical information;
(b) establish uniform safety standards to protect the health of workers and of the general public and ensure that they are applied;

Article 30

Basic standards shall be laid down within the Community for the protection of the health of workers and the general public against the dangers arising from ionising radiation.

The expression 'basic standards' means:

(a) maximum permissible doses compatible with adequate safety;
(b) maximum permissible levels of exposure and contamination;
(c) the fundamental principles governing the health surveillance of workers.

Article 35

Each Member State shall establish the facilities necessary to carry out continuous monitoring of the level of radioactivity in the air, water and soil and to ensure compliance with the basic standards.

The Commission shall have the right of access to such facilities; it may verify their operation and efficiency.

Article 37

Each Member State shall provide the Commission with such general data relating to any plan for the disposal of radioactive waste in whatever form as will make it possible to determine whether the implementation of such plan is liable to result in the radioactive contamination of the water, soil or airspace of another Member State.

The Commission shall deliver its opinion within six months, after consulting the group of experts referred to in Article 31.

3   1987 Single European Act

The Single European Act brought changes which had a significant impact on approaches to environmental policy. Most notably, a new Article 100a made more explicit the links between environmental protection and the functioning of the common market, and a new Title VII (Articles 130r–130t) confirmed that the environment was now a central policy concern of the Community, set out the goals of Community environmental policy, and the underlying principles in the formulation of that policy.

Article 100a (now 95)

1   By way of derogation from Article 100 and save where otherwise provided in this Treaty, the following provisions shall apply for the achievement of the objectives set out in Article 8a. The Council shall, acting by qualified majority on a proposal from the Commission in cooperation with the European Parliament and after consulting the Economic and Social Committee, adopt the measures for the approximation of the provisions laid down by law, regulation or administrative action in Member States which have as their object the establishment and functioning of the internal market.

2   Paragraph 1 shall not apply to fiscal provisions, to those relating to the free movement of persons nor to those relating to the rights and interests of employed persons.

3 The Commission, in its proposals envisaged in paragraph 1 concerning health, safety, environmental protection and consumer protection, will take as a base a high level of protection.

4 If, after the adoption of a harmonisation measure by the Council acting by a qualified majority, a Member State deems it necessary to apply national provisions on grounds of major needs referred to in Article 36, or relating to protection of the environment or the working environment, it shall notify the Commission of these provisions.

The Commission shall confirm the provisions involved after having verified that they are not a means of arbitrary discrimination or a disguised restriction on trade between Member States.

By way of derogation from the procedure laid down in Articles 169 and 170, the Commission or any Member State may bring the matter directly before the Court of Justice if it considers that another Member State is making improper use of the powers provided for in this Article.

5 The harmonisation measures referred to above shall, in appropriate cases, include a safeguard clause authorising the Member States to take, for one or more of the non-economic reasons referred to in Article 36, provisional measures subject to a Community control procedure.

Title VII Environment

Article 130r (now 174)

1 Action by the Community relating to the environment will have the following objectives:

- to preserve, protect and improve the quality of the environment;
- to contribute towards protecting human health;
- to ensure a prudent and rational utilisation of natural resources.

2 Action by the Community relating to the environment shall be based on the principles that preventive action should be taken, that environmental damage should as a priority be rectified at source, and that the polluter should pay. Environmental protection requirements shall be a component of the Community's other policies.

3 In preparing its action relating to the environment, the Community shall take account of:

- available scientific and technical data;
- environmental conditions in the various regions of the Community;
- the potential benefits and costs of action or of lack of action;
- the economic and social development of the Community as a whole and the balanced development of its regions.

4 The Community shall take action relating to the environment to the extent to which the objectives referred to in paragraph 1 can be attained better at Community level than at the level of the individual Member States. Without prejudice to certain measures of a Community nature, the Member States shall finance and implement the other measures.

5 Within their respective spheres of competence, the Community and the Member States shall cooperate with third countries and with the relevant international organisations. The arrangements for Community cooperation may be the subject of agreements between the Community and the third parties concerned, which shall be negotiated and concluded in accordance with Article 228.

The previous paragraph shall be without prejudice to Member States' competence to negotiate in international bodies and to conclude international agreements.

Article 130s (now 175)

The Council, acting unanimously on a proposal from the Commission and after consulting the European Parliament and the Economic and Social Committee, shall decide what action is to be taken by the Community.

The Council shall, under the conditions laid down in the preceding subparagraph, define those matters on which decisions are to be taken by a qualified majority.

Article 130t (now 176)

The protective measures adopted in common pursuant to Article 130s shall not prevent any Member State from maintaining or introducing more stringent protective measures compatible with this Treaty.

4   1992 Treaty on European Union

The Maastricht treaty confirmed that the environment was an area of shared competence between the EU and the member states, and defined sustainable growth as one of the fundamental goals of European integration.

Article 2

The Community shall have as its task, by establishing a common market and an economic and monetary union and by implementing the common policies or activities referred to in Articles 3 and 3a, to promote throughout the Community a harmonious and balanced development of economic activities, sustainable and non-inflationary growth respecting the environment, a high degree of convergence of economic performance, a high level of employment and of social protection, the raising of the standard of living and quality of life, and economic cohesion and solidarity among Member States.

Article 3

For the purposes set out in Article 2, the activities of the Community shall include, as provided in this Treaty and in accordance with the timetable set out therein:

(a) the elimination, as between Member States, of customs duties and quantitative restrictions on the import and export of goods, and of all other measures having equivalent effect; . . .

(c) an internal market characterised by the abolition, as between Member States, of obstacles to the free movement of goods, persons, services and capital; . . .

(k) a policy in the sphere of the environment; . . .

(o) a contribution to the attainment of a high level of health protection; . . .

(s) a contribution to the strengthening of consumer protection;

(t) measures in the spheres of energy, civil protection and tourism.

Article 3b (now 5)

The Community shall act within the limits of the powers conferred upon it by this Treaty and of the objectives assigned to it therein.

In areas which do not fall within its exclusive competence, the Community shall take action, in accordance with the principle of subsidiarity, only if and in so far as the objectives of the proposed action cannot be sufficiently achieved by the Member States and can therefore, by reason of the scale or effects of the proposed action, be better achieved by the Community.

Any action by the Community shall not go beyond what is necessary to achieve the objectives of this Treaty.

Title XVI Environment

Article 130r (now 174)

1   Community policy on the environment shall contribute to pursuit of the following objectives:

- preserving, protecting and improving the quality of the environment;
- protecting human health;
- prudent and rational utilisation of natural resources;
- promoting measures at international level to deal with regional or worldwide environmental problems.

2   Community policy on the environment shall aim at a high level of protection taking into account the diversity of situations in the various regions of the Community. It shall be based on the precautionary principle and on the principles that preventive action should be taken, that environmental damage should as a priority be rectified at source and that the polluter should pay. Environmental protection requirements must be integrated into the definition and implementation of other Community policies.

In this context, harmonisation measures answering these requirements shall include, where appropriate, a safeguard clause allowing Member States to take provisional measures, for non-economic environmental reasons, subject to a Community inspection procedure.

3   In preparing its policy on the environment, the Community shall take account of:

- available scientific and technical data;
- environmental conditions in the various regions of the Community;
- the potential benefits and costs of action or lack of action;
- the economic and social development of the Community as a whole and the balanced development of its regions.

4   Within their respective spheres of competence, the Community and the Member States shall cooperate with third countries and with the competent international organisations. The arrangements for Community cooperation may be the subject of agreements between the Community and the third parties concerned, which shall be negotiated and concluded in accordance with Article 228.

The previous subparagraph shall be without prejudice to Member States' competence to negotiate in international bodies and to conclude international agreements.

Article 130s (now 175)

1 The Council, acting in accordance with the procedure referred to in Article 189c [the codecision procedure] and after consulting the Economic and Social Committee, shall decide what action is to be taken by the Community in order to achieve the objectives referred to in Article 130r.

2 By way of derogation from the decision-making procedure provided for in paragraph 1 and without prejudice to Article 100a, the Council, acting unanimously on a proposal from the Commission and after consulting the European Parliament and the Economic and Social Committee, shall adopt:

- provisions primarily of a fiscal nature;
- measures concerning town and country planning, land use with the exception of waste management and measures of a general nature, and management of water resources;
- measures significantly affecting a Member State's choice between different energy sources and the general structure of its energy supply.

The Council may, under the conditions laid down in the preceding subparagraph, define those matters referred to in this paragraph on which decisions are to be taken by a qualified majority.

3 In other areas, general action programmes setting out priority objectives to be attained shall be adopted by the Council, acting in accordance with the procedure referred to in Article 189b and after consulting the Economic and Social Committee.

The Council, acting under the terms of paragraph 1 or paragraph 2 according to the case, shall adopt the measures necessary for the implementation of these programmes.

4 Without prejudice to certain measures of a Community nature, the Member States shall finance and implement the environment policy.

5 Without prejudice to the principle that the polluter shall pay, if a measure based on the provisions of paragraph 1 involves costs deemed disproportionate for the public authorities of a Member State, the Council shall, in the act of adopting that measure, lay down appropriate provisions in the form of:

- temporary derogations, and/or financial support from the Cohesion Fund to be set up no later than 31 December 1993 pursuant to Article 130d.

Article 130t (now 176)

The protective measures adopted pursuant to Article 130s shall not prevent any Member State from maintaining or introducing more stringent protective measures. Such measures must be compatible with this Treaty. They shall be notified to the Commission.

5   1997 Treaty of Amsterdam

The main effect of changes under Amsterdam was to attach a new emphasis to the goal of promoting sustainable development. Under the preamble, the seventh recital was changed, with the italicized phrase added:

> DETERMINED to promote economic and social progress for their peoples, *taking into account the principle of sustainable development and* within the context of the accomplishment of the internal market and of reinforced cohesion and environmental protection, and to implement policies ensuring that advances in economic integration are accompanied by parallel progress in other fields.

Article 2 was changed to read as follows:

> The Community shall have as its task, by establishing a common market and an economic and monetary union and by implementing the common policies or activities referred to in Articles 3 and 3a, to promote throughout the Community a harmonious, balanced and sustainable development of economic activities, a high level of employment and of social protection, equality between men and women, sustainable and non-inflationary growth, a high degree of competitiveness and convergence of economic performance, a high level of protection and improvement of the quality of the environment, the raising of the standard of living and quality of life, and economic and social cohesion and solidarity among Member States.

Article 3c (now 6)

> Environmental protection requirements must be integrated into the definition and implementation of the Community policies and activities referred to in Article 3, in particular with a view to promoting sustainable development.

Article 130r(2) (now 174(2)) was changed to read as follows:

> 2   Community policy on the environment shall aim at a high level of protection taking into account the diversity of situations in the various regions of the Community. It shall be based on the precautionary prin-

ciple and on the principles that preventive action should be taken, that environmental damage should as a priority be rectified at source and that the polluter should pay.

In this context, harmonization measures answering environmental protection requirements shall include, where appropriate, a safeguard clause allowing Member States to take provisional measures, for non-economic environmental reasons, subject to a Community inspection procedure.

Paragraphs 1, 2 and 3 of Article 130s (now 175) were changed to require the Council to consult with the Committee of the Regions (in addition to the Economic and Social Committee and Parliament).

Bibliography

Arp, Henning (1992) 'The European Parliament in European Community Environmental Policy', Working paper EPU 92/13 (Florence: European University Institute).

—(1993) 'Technical Regulation and Politics: The Interplay between Economic Interests and Environmental Policy Goals in EC Car Emission Legislation', in J. D. Liefferink, P. D. Lowe and A. P. J. Mol (eds), *European Integration and Environmental Policy* (London: Belhaven Press).

Baldwin, Robert (1995) *Rules and Government* (Oxford: Clarendon Press).

Barrett, Mark and Rodri Protheroe (1994) *Sulphur Emissions from Large Point Sources in Europe* (Colchester: Pollen Consultancy).

Bennett, Graham (1992) *Dilemmas: Coping With Environmental Problems* (London: Earthscan).

Bering, Charles C. (1996) 'Garbage Trucks and Closed Borders: The "Proximity Principle" in Europe and the United States', *International Environmental Affairs*, vol. 8, no. 3, pp. 191–211.

Boehmer-Christiansen, Sonja (1989) *The Politics of Environment and Acid Rain: Forests Versus Fossil Fuels*, SPRU Occasional Paper 29, Brighton.

—and Jim Skea (1991) *Acid Politics: Environmental and Energy Policies in Britain and Germany* (London: Belhaven).

Bongaerts, Jan (1999) 'Carbon Dioxide Emissions and Cars: An Environmental Agreement at EU Level', *European Environmental Law Review*, vol. 8, no. 4 (April), pp. 101–04.

Bow Publications (1984) *A Role for Britain in the Acid Rainstorm* (London: Bow Publications).

Carter, Neil and Philip Lowe (1995) 'The Establishment of a Cross-Sector Environment Agency', in T. S. Gray (ed.), *UK Environmental Policy in the 1990s* (Basingstoke: Macmillan).

Center for Chemical Process Safety (1994) *Guidelines for Evaluating the Characteristics of Vapor Cloud Explosions, Flash Fires, and BLEVEs* (New York: American Institute of Chemical Engineers).

Centre for Policy Studies (1985) *Greening the Tories, New Policies on the Environment* (London: Centre for Policy Studies).

Cini, Michelle (1996) *The European Commission: Leadership, Organisation and Culture in the EU Administration* (Manchester: Manchester University Press).

Cobb, Roger W. and Charles D. Elder (1983) *Participation in American Politics* (Baltimore: Johns Hopkins University Press).

Coffey, Clare (1996) 'Introduction to the Common Fisheries Policy: An Environmental Perspective', *International Environmental Affairs*, vol. 8, no. 4, pp. 287–307.

Collier, Ute (1996) 'The European Union's Climate Change Policy: Limiting Emissions or Limiting Powers?', *Journal of European Public Policy*, vol. 3, no. 1, pp. 122–38.

— (1997) 'Sustainability, Subsidiarty and Deregulation: New Directions in EU Environmental Policy', *Environmental Politics*, vol. 6, no. 2, pp. 1–23.

Collins, Ken (1995) 'Plans and Prospects for the European Parliament in Shaping Future Environmental Policy', *European Environmental Law Review*, vol. 4, no. 3 (March), pp. 74–7.

— and David Earnshaw (1993) 'The Implementation and Enforcement of European Community Environment Legislation', in D. Judge (ed.), *A Green Dimension for the European Community: Political Issues and Processes* (London: Frank Cass).

Coss, Simon (1999) 'How the EU Works: Directing the Course of Directives', *European Dialogue*, issue 3 (May–June), <http://europa.eu.int/comm/dg10/eur_dial/current.html#art3>.

Court of Auditors (1992) 'Special Report No. 3/92 Concerning the Environment, Together with the Commission's Replies', *Official Journal* 92/C245/vol. 35.

Donnelley, Martin and Ella Ritchie (1997) 'The College of Commissioners and their *Cabinets*', in Geoffrey Edwards and David Spence (eds), *The European Commission*, 2nd edn (London: Cartermill).

Europa Homepage (1998) *Water Quality in the European Union*, <http://www.europa.eu.int/water/water-framework/index_en.html>.

European Commission (1989a) Statement on the broad lines of Commission policy, presented by the president of the Commission to the European Parliament, Strasbourg, 17 January, in *Bulletin of the European Communities*, Supplement 1/89.

— (1989b) *Communication from the Commission to the Council and the European Parliament: A Community Strategy for Waste Management*, Brussels, 18.09.1989, SEC(89)934 final.

— (1994) *Green Paper on Energy Policy*, COM (94) 659.

— (1995a) Report from the Commission on the state of implementation of ambient air quality directives, Brussels, 26.7.95, COM(95) 372 final.

— (1995b) Staff Working Paper on Acidification, SEC 95, 2057.

— (1995c) *Europeans and the Environment* (Brussels: DGXI Documentation Centre).

— (1996a) *The Commission's Programme for 1996*, Supplement to the *Bulletin of the European Union*, COM(95) 512 final.

—(1996b) *Implementing Community Environmental Law*, COM(96)500, Brussels (December).

—(1996c) *Future Strategy for the Control of Atmospheric Emissions from Road Transport, Taking into Account the Results from the Auto Oil Programme*, unpublished Commission background document, April 1996.

—(1996d) *Green Paper on Renewable Sources of Energy*, COM (96) 576.

—(1997a) *Communication from the Commission to the Council and the European Parliament Concerning the Application of Directives 75/439/EEC, 75/442/EEC, 78/319/EEC and 86/278/EEC on Waste Management*, Brussels, 27.02.1997, COM (97) 23.

—(1997b) 'Enlarging the Environment', *Newsletter on Environmental Approximation*, issue 3 (May), <http://europa.eu.int/comm/dg11/news/enlarg/news3.htm>.

—(1998a) *Fifteenth Annual Report on Monitoring the Application of Community Law – 1997*, in Official Journal of the European Communities, C250, vol. 41 (10 August).

—(1998b) *Communication on a European Community Biodiversity Strategy*, COM (98) 42.

—(1998c) *Communication from the Commission to the Council and the European Parliament on a Forestry Strategy for the European Union*, COM (98) 649.

—(1999a) *Communication on Fisheries Management and Nature Conservation in the Marine Environment*, COM (99) 363.

—(1999b) *Eurobarometer Report No. 50* (Brussels: European Commission).

European Environment Agency (1995) *Environment in the European Union 1995* (Luxembourg: Office of Official Publications of the European Communities).

—(1997) *Air Pollution in Europe 1997, EEA Environmental Monograph No. 4* (Copenhagen: European Environment Agency).

—(1998) *Europe's Environment: The Second Assessment* (Luxembourg: Office for Official Publications of the European Communities).

—(1999) *Environment in the European Union at the Turn of the Century* (Copenhagen: EEA).

European Parliament (1996) *Report from the Committee on the Environment, Public Health and Consumer Protection on the Commission Communication to the Council and the European Parliament on European Community Water Policy*, COM(96) 59 final, Brussels: Official Journal of the European Communities, C series no. 347.

Fells, Ian (1988) 'The Trials of Privatising Electricity', *New Scientist*, 11 February.

Fish, Arthur L. and David W. South (1994) 'Industrialized Countries and Greenhouse Gas Emissions', *International Environmental Affairs*, vol. 6, no. 1, pp. 14–44.

Freestone, David (1991) 'European Community Environmental Law and Policy', *Journal of Law and Society*, vol. 18, no. 1, Spring, pp. 135–54.

Garner, Robert (1996) *Environmental Politics* (London: Prentice Hall).

Golub, Jonathan (ed.) (1998a) *New Instruments for Environmental Policy in the EU* (London: Routledge).

—(1996b) 'State Power and Institutional Influence in European Integration: Lessons from the Packaging Waste Directive', *Journal of Common Market Studies*, vol. 34, no. 3, pp. 314–39.

Grant, Wyn (1997) *The Common Agricultural Policy* (Basingstoke: Macmillan).

Grubb, Michael (1995) 'Climate Change Policies in Europe: National Plans, EU Policies and the International Context', *International Journal of Environment and Pollution*, vol. 5, nos. 2/3, pp. 164–79.

Haas, Peter M. (1993) 'Protecting the Baltic and North Seas', in R. O. Keohane *et al.* (eds), *Institutions for the Earth: Sources of Effective International Environmental Protection* (Cambridge, MA: MIT Press).

Haigh, Nigel (1992a) *Manual of Environmental Policy: The EC and Britain* (Harlow: Longman).

—(1992b) 'The European Community and International Environmental Policy', in Andrew Hurrell and Benedict Kingsbury (eds), *The International Politics of the Environment* (Oxford: Clarendon Press).

—(1996a) Background paper to the Joint Public Hearing 'Effective Environmental Protection – Challenges for the Implementation of EC Law', Brussels (30 May).

—(1996b) 'Climate Change Policies and Politics in the European Community', in Tim O'Riordan and Jill Jäger (eds), *Politics of Climate Change: A European Perspective* (London: Routledge).

—and David Baldock (1989) *Environmental Policy and 1992* (London: Department of the Environment).

—and Chris Lanigan (1995) 'Impact of the European Union on UK Environmental Policy Making', in Tim S. Gray (ed.), *UK Environmental Policy in the 1990s* (London: Macmillan).

Hanf, Kenneth and Alf-Inge Jansen (1998) *Governance and Environment in Western Europe: Politics, Policy and Administration* (Harlow: Longman).

Hartley, T. C. (1988) *The Foundations of European Community Law*, 2nd edn (Oxford: Clarendon Press).

Hayes-Renshaw, Fiona, C. Lequesne and P. Mayor-Lopez (1989) 'The Permanent Representations of the Member States of the European Communities', *Journal of Common Market Studies*, vol. 2, pp. 119–37.

—and Helen Wallace (1997) *The Council of Ministers* (New York: St Martin's Press).

Hewett, Jonathan (ed.) (1995) *European Environmental Almanac* (London: Earthscan).

Hill, Christopher (1993) 'The Capability–Expectations Gap, or Conceptualising Europe's International Role', *Journal of Common Market Studies*, vol. 31, no. 3, pp. 305–28.

Howells, W. R. (1983) 'The Effects of Acid Precipitation and Land Use on Water Quality and Ecology in Wales and the Implications for the Authority', Report for the Welsh Water Authority, Powys, 27 April.

House of Commons Environment Committee (1984) *Fourth Report: Acid Rain* (London: HMSO).

House of Lords (1984) House of Lords Select Committee on the European Communities *22nd Report: Air Pollution* (London: HMSO).

—(1992) House of Lords Select Committee on the European Communities, Session 1991–92, HL 53 (1992), 9th Report, *Implementation and Enforcement of Environmental Legislation*, vol. 1 (March), Report HL 53-I.

Hogwood, Brian W. and Lewis A. Gunn (1984) *Policy Analysis for the Real World* (Oxford: Oxford University Press).

International Monetary Fund (1998) *Direction of Trade Statistics* (Washington DC: IMF).

Jachtenfuchs, Markus (1990) 'The European Community and the Protection of the Ozone Layer', *Journal of Common Market Studies*, vol. XXVIII, no. 3, pp. 261–77.

Jäger, Jill and Tim O'Riordan (1996) 'The History of Climate Change Science and Politics', in Tim O'Riordan and Jill Jäger (eds), *Politics of Climate Change: A European Perspective* (London: Routledge).

Jans, Jan (1996a) 'The Development of EC Environmental Law', in Gerd Winter (ed.), *European Environmental Law: A Comparative Perspective* (Aldershot: Dartmouth Publishing Co.).

—(1996b) 'Objectives and Principles of EC Environmental Law', in Gerd Winter (ed.), *European Environmental Law: A Comparative Perspective* (Aldershot: Dartmouth Publishing Co.).

—(1996c) 'The Competences of EC Environmental Law', in Gerd Winter (ed.), *European Environmental Law: A Comparative Perspective* (Aldershot: Dartmouth Publishing Co.).

Johnson, Stanley P. and Guy Corcelle (1995) *The Environmental Policy of the European Communities*, 2nd edn (London: Kluwer Law International).

Johnston, Mary Troy (1994) *The European Council: Gatekeeper of the European Community* (Boulder, CO: Westview).

Judge, David (1993) ' "Predestined to Save the Earth": The Environment Committee of the European Parliament', in David Judge (ed.), *A Green Dimension for the European Community: Political Issues and Processes* (London: Frank Cass).

Keohane, Robert O., Peter M. Haas and Marc A. Levy (1993) 'The Effectiveness of International Environmental Institutions', in

R. O. Keohane *et al.* (eds), *Institutions for the Earth: Sources of Effective International Environmental Protection* (Cambridge, MA: MIT Press).

Koppen, Ida J. (1993) 'The Role of the European Court of Justice', in Duncan Liefferink, Philip Lowe and Arthur Mol (eds), *European Integration and Environmental Policy* (London: Belhaven).

—(1997) 'The EU Regulation of Waste: Free Circulation or Self-Sufficiency?', in Randall Baker (ed.), *Environmental Law and Policy in the European Union and the United States* (Westport, CT: Praeger).

Krämer, Ludwig (1995) *EC Treaty and Environmental Law*, 2nd edn (London: Sweet & Maxwell).

—(1996) 'The Elaboration of EC Environmental Legislation', in Gerd Winter (ed.), *European Environmental Law: A Comparative Perspective* (Aldershot: Dartmouth Publishing Co.).

Lefevere, Jürgen G. J. (1997) 'The New Air Directive on Air Quality Assessment and Management', *European Environmental Law Review*, vol. 6, no. 7 (July), pp. 210–14.

Levy, Marc A. (1993) 'European Acid Rain: The Power of Tote-Board Diplomacy', in Peter M. Haas, Robert O. Keohane and Mark A. Levy (eds), *Institutions for the Earth* (Cambridge, MA: MIT Press).

Lister, Charles (1996) *European Union Environmental Law: A Guide for Industry* (Chichester: John Wiley).

Lodge, Juliet (ed.) (1989) *The European Community and the Challenge of the Future* (London: Pinter).

Long, Tony (1998) 'The Environmental Lobby', in Philip Lowe and Stephen Ward (eds), *British Environmental Policy and Europe: Politics and Policy in Transition* (London: Routledge).

Lundholm, B. (1970) 'Interactions between Oceans and Terrestrial Systems', in S. F. Singer (ed.), *Global Effects of Environmental Pollution* (Dordrecht: Reidel).

Macrory, Richard (1992) 'The Enforcement of Community Environmental Laws: Some Critical Issues', *Common Market Law Review*, vol. 29, pp. 347–69.

—(1996) 'The Scope of Environmental Law', in Gerd Winter (ed.), *European Environmental Law: A Comparative Perspective* (Aldershot: Dartmouth Publishing Co.).

Matláry, Janne Haaland (1997) *Energy Policy in the European Union* (Basingstoke: Macmillan).

Mazey, Sonia and Jeremy Richardson (1993) 'Environmental Groups and the EC: Challenges and Opportunities', in David Judge (ed.), *A Green Dimension for the European Community* (London: Frank Cass).

—and — (1997) 'The Commission and the Lobby', in Geoffrey Edwards and David Spence (eds), *The European Commission*, 2nd edn (London: Cartermill).

McCormick, John (1995) *The Global Environmental Movement*, 2nd edn (London: John Wiley).

—(1997) *Acid Earth: The Politics of Acid Pollution*, 3rd edn (London: Earthscan).

Meadows, Donella H., Dennis L. Meadows, Jorgen Randers and William H. Behrens III (1972) *The Limits to Growth* (New York, N.Y.: New American Library).

Middlemas, Keith (1995) *Orchestrating Europe: The Informal Politics of the European Union, 1973–1995* (London: Fontana Press).

Montgomery, Mark (1995) 'Reassessing the Waste Trade Crisis: What Do We Really Know?', *Journal of Environment and Development*, vol. 4, no. 1 (Winter), pp. 1–28.

Morrisette, Peter M. (1989) 'The Evolution of Policy Responses to Stratospheric Ozone Depletion', *Natural Resources Journal*, No. 29, pp. 793–820.

Motard, Sylvie (1996) 'The European Parliament's Role in the Elaboration of the European Union's Environmental Policy in the Context of the Intergovernmental Conference', *European Environmental Law Review*, vol. 5, no. 3 (March), pp. 79–83.

Nance, John J. (1991) *What Goes Up: The Global Assault on Our Atmosphere* (New York, N.Y.: Morrow).

Organization for Economic Cooperation and Development, Environmental Directorate (1977) *The OECD Programme on Long Range Transport of Air Pollutants: Summary Report* (Paris: OECD).

Organization for Economic Cooperation and Development (1997a) *Environmental Data Compendium 1997* (Paris: OECD).

—(1997b) *Transfrontier Movements of Hazardous Wastes, 1992–93* (Paris: OECD).

Parson, Edward A. (1993) 'Protecting the Ozone Layer', in Peter M. Haas, Robert O. Keohane and Mark A. Levy (eds), *Institutions for the Earth: Sources of Effective International Environmental Protection* (Cambridge, MA: MIT Press).

Pearce, Fred (1986) 'Unravelling a Century of Acid Pollution', in *New Scientist*, 25 September.

Porter, Gareth and Janet Welsh Brown (1991) *Global Environmental Politics* (Boulder, CO: Westview Press).

Rehbinder, Eckard and Richard Stewart (eds) (1985) *Environmental Protection Policy, Vol. 2 – Integration Through Law: Europe and the American Federal Experience* (Firenze: European University Institute).

—and —(1988) *European Protection Policy: Legal Integration in the United States and the European Community* (New York: De Gruyter).

Richardson, Jeremy (1994) 'EU Water Policy: Uncertain Agendas, Shifting Networks and Complex Coalitions', *Environmental Politics*, vol. 3, no. 4, pp. 139–67.

—(1996) 'Eroding EU Policies: Implementation Gaps, Cheating and Re-steering', in Jeremy Richardson (ed.), *European Union: Power and Policy-Making* (London: Routledge).

Rosenbaum, Walter (1998) *Environmental Politics and Policy* (Washington, D.C.: CQ Press).

Royal Commission on Environmental Pollution (1984) *Annual Report 1984* (London: HMSO).

Rucht, Dieter (1993) ' "Think globally, act locally"? Needs, Forms and Problems of Cross-national Cooperation among Environmental Groups', in J. Duncan Liefferink, Philip Lowe and Arthur Mol (eds), *European Integration and Environmental Policy* (London: Belhaven).

Salter, John R. (1995) *European Environmental Law* (London: Kluwer Law International).

Schmidt, Alke (1992) 'Transboundary Movements of Waste Under EC Law: The Emerging Regulatory Framework', *Journal of Environmental Law*, vol. 4, no. 1, pp. 57–80.

Schnutenhaus, Jörn (1994) 'Integrated Pollution Prevention and Control: New German Initiatives in the European Environment Council', *European Environmental Law Review*, vol. 3, no. 11 (December), pp. 323–8.

Siedentopf, Heinrich and Jacques Ziller (1988) *Making European Policies Work: Comparative Synthesis* (London: Sage).

Skjaerseth, Jon Birger (1994) 'The Climate Policy of the EC: Too Hot to Handle?', *Journal of Common Market Studies*, vol. 32, no. 1 (March), pp. 25–45.

Smith, Michael (1997) 'The Commission and External Relations', in Geoffrey Edwards and David Spence (eds), *The European Commission*, 2nd edn (London: Cartermill).

Spence, David (1997) 'Structure, Functions and Procedures in the Commission', in Geoffrey Edwards and David Spence (eds), *The European Commission*, 2nd edn (London: Cartermill).

Stanners, David and Philippe Bourdeau (eds) (1995) *Europe's Environment: The Dobris Assessment* (Luxembourg: Office for Official Publications of the European Communities).

Stichting Natuur en Milieu (1995) *Greening the Treaty II: Sustainable Development in a Democratic Union* (Utrecht: Stichting Natuur en Milieu).

Sunkin, Maurice, David M. Ong and Robert Wight (1998) *Sourcebook on Environmental Law* (London: Cavendish Publishing).

Thatcher, Margaret (1993) *The Downing Street Years* (New York, N.Y.: HarperCollins).

UK Review Group on Acid Rain (1984) *Acid Deposition in the United Kingdom*, Warren Spring Laboratory.

United Nations Environment Programme (1993) *Environmental Data Report 1993–94* (Oxford: Blackwell).

—(1995) 'Environmental Effects of Ozone Depletion, 1994 Assessment', *Ambio*, vol. 3, pp. 138–96.

Vandermeersch, Dirk (1987) 'The Single European Act and the Environmental Policy of the European Economic Community', *European Law Review*, vol. 12, no. 5, pp. 407–29.

Verkerk, Pieter (1996) Address to the Joint Public Hearing 'Effective Environmental Protection – Challenges for the Implementation of EC Law', Brussels (30 May).

von Moltke, Konrad (1987) *The Vorsorgeprinzip in West German Environmental Policy* (London: Institute for European Environmental Policy).

Wagner, Jay P. (1997) 'The Climate Change Policy of the European Union', in Gunnar Fermann (ed.), *International Politics of Climate Change: Key Issues and Critical Actors* (Oslo: Scandinavian University Press).

Wallace, Helen and William Wallace (1996) *Policy-Making in the European Union* (Oxford: Oxford University Press).

Wells, Donald T. (1996) *Environmental Policy: A Global Perspective for the Twenty-First Century* (Upper Saddle River, N.J.: Prentice-Hall).

Westlake, Martin (1995) *The Council of the European Union* (London: Cartermill International).

—(1997) 'The Commission and the Parliament', in Geoffrey Edwards and David Spence (eds), *The European Commission*, 2nd edn (London: Cartermill).

Wetstone, Gregory S. and Armin Rosencranz (1983) *Acid Rain in Europe and North America: National Responses to an International Problem* (Washington, D.C.: Environmental Law Institute).

Wilkinson, David (1992) 'Maastricht and the Environment: The Implications for the EC's Environment Policy of the Treaty on European Union', *Journal of Environmental Law*, vol. 4, no. 2, pp. 221–39.

Williams, Rhiannon (1995) 'The European Commission and the Enforcement of Environmental Law: An Invidious Position', in A. Barav *et al.* (eds), *Yearbook of European Law* (Oxford: Clarendon Press).

Williams, Shirley (1991) 'Sovereignty and Accountability in the European Community', in Robert O. Keohane and Stanley Hoffmann (eds), *The New European Communty: Decisionmaking and International Change* (Boulder, CO: Westview Press).

World Bank (1997) *World Bank Atlas 1996* (Washington, D.C.: World Bank).

World Commission on Environment and Development (1987) *Our Common Future* (Oxford: Oxford University Press).

World Wide Fund for Nature *et al.* (1991) *Greening the Treaty* (Brussels: WWF European Policy Office).

Zito, Anthony (2000) *Creating Environmental Policy in the European Union* (Basingstoke: Macmillan).

ACEA Web page <http://www.acea.be/acea/index.html>
CEFIC Web page <http://www.cefic.org>
EDG/DGXI Web page
   <http://europa.eu.int/comm/dgs/environment/index_en.htm>
EMEP Web page <http://www.emep.int>
Environment Agency Web page <http://www.environment-agency.gov.uk/>
Environmental Protection Agency Web page <http://www.epa.gov/>
EUREAU Web page <http://users.skynet.be/eureau>
Europa Web page <http://europa.eu.int/>
European Environmental Bureau Web page <http://www.eeb.org/>
Greenpeace International Web page <http://www.greenpeace.org>

The Economist, various issues.
ENDS Report, various issues.
Environmental Liability Report, various issues.
European Voice, various issues.

Index